100 GREAT SNACKS

100 GREAT SNACKS
John Midgley

PAVILION

For Sue

First published in Great Britain in 1994 by
Pavilion Books Limited
26 Upper Ground, London SE1 9PD

Text and recipes copyright © John Midgley 1994
Illustration copyright © Hannah Firmin 1994

The moral right of the author has been asserted

Designed by Andrew Barron

A CIP catalogue record for this book is available from
the British Library

ISBN 1-85793-222-6

Printed and bound in Great Britain by Butler & Tanner Ltd.
Typeset in Berkeley Old Style and Futura
by Dorchester Typesetting Group Ltd.

2 4 6 8 10 9 7 5 3 1

This book may be ordered by post direct from the publisher.
Please contact the Marketing Department.
But try your bookshop first.

ACKNOWLEDGMENTS

The author would like to thank Sue Midgley for her help
with proof-reading, recipe checking and testing, but above all
for sharing a diet of snacks so cheerfully, for so long.
He also thanks Andrew Barron, James Murphy, and Hannah Firmin
for their professionalism in, respectively: design,
cover photography and illustration.

CONTENTS

FILLED SNACKS & SANDWICHES

INTRODUCTION

John Montagu, the fourth Earl of Sandwich (1718-1792) achieved a bizarre form of immortality, giving his name to a style of eating that we have all come to depend upon in our busy working lives. A notorious gambler, his addiction to the vice was so extreme that on one occasion, an entire day and night were devoted to its indulgence. When he ordered refreshment to be brought to him, thus avoiding having to retire to table, the meat sandwich was born. (Whether the filling was ham or beef is uncertain.)

Yet, if defined more loosely as a portable dough- or pastry-based food with one or more additional ingredients, sandwiches certainly predate the eighteenth century Earl by a very wide margin, having featured in many of the world's cuisines for centuries. The citizens of ancient Greece and Rome, the Egyptians and the Sumerians, the Aztecs of Mexico, and more recently, fishermen and sailors on the high seas and peasant labourers in the vineyards and olive groves have all shared a long tradition of convenient portable foods.

This is a broad collection of just over one hundred mouthwatering recipes for all kinds of hand-held foods. Following a mixture of classic and exotic bread and flatbread recipes comes a rich selection of their ideal accompaniments and fillings inspired by the cuisines of India, the Middle East, the Balkans and Mexico. Next a small assembly of buns, rolls and bagels includes recipes for truly great hamburgers, and sumptuous *brioches* filled with delicious wild mushrooms. Also on the menu are: a sequence of fashionable Italian toasts with many different toppings; an eclectic array of 'open' sandwiches ranging from Scandinavian *smörgås* to Spanish olive paste *tapas;* then some closed sandwiches, including a gargantuan triple-decker BLT, and properly delicate cucumber sandwiches with a special secret ingredient. Then come wonderful French and Italian savoury tarts and pizzas, followed by a selection of exotic pies, both big and small, and finishing with delicious fried snacks such as sesame prawn toast, *parathas* stuffed with spicy mashed potato, and *mozzarella in carrozza.*

As anyone can make a sandwich there are few, if any, obvious or pedestrian sandwich recipes, with the exception of a handful of classic ones which, I believe, are often botched up, and for which I can suggest genuinely helpful tips for improvement.

The degree of difficulty varies from nil to moderate, and wherever possible, I encourage shortcuts and cheats, but only when the end results are not compromised. Hence, both puff and shortcrust pastry (tart dough) are bought ready-made, and the same applies to vol au vent cases, filo pastry, spring roll wrappers and *wun tun* cases. (This does *not* apply to ready-made pizza bases, which are usually unsatisfactory.) Sometimes plain sliced sandwich bread achieves the desired result rather better than superior bread, especially for frying. For *bruschetta* and *crostini*, baguette-style bread and the increasingly popular *ciabatta* are ideal, but because these are widely available, of good quality, and rather difficult to re-create at home, I suggest they are bought. However, some flatbreads such as *chapatis, nan* and pitta are both easy and of superior quality when they are home-made. Preparation time varies as well. Many recipes can be put together in minutes, others take a little longer, and several take hours, but the bulk of this is 'free' time while a meat marinates or a dough proves. Many doughs in the book, not to mention some of the made-up snacks themselves, can be frozen or kept refrigerated for a few days.

Finally, as regards ingredients, nearly all are commonly stocked in good supermarkets and are therefore easy to obtain; of the hundreds in this book only three or four would require specialised shopping.

BREAD &
FLAT BREAD

Bread is both fashionable and varied. French-style baguettes have never been better; regional Italian breads such as *ciabatta* and *Pugliese,* authentic Middle Eastern pitta breads, the *nans* and *chapatis* of northern India and Pakistan, and Tex-Mex corn flatbreads can be found in supermarkets, delicatessens and specialist shops.

However, it would be a great pity to overlook the pleasures of home baking, which appeal to four of the five senses in a way that no other kitchen activity can match. The wonderful smell of baking bread is not unique. New-born babies secrete a very similar aroma, which is one of nature's ways of assisting maternal bonding. It is widely recognised that prospective house buyers react more favourably when inspecting a home permeated with the perfume of baking. Bread-making also appeals to the sense of touch. The agreeable sensation of kneading pliable dough can be deeply relaxing, and children delight in the way dough responds to the touch – so much so, that coloured doughs are sold commercially as a toy. Best of all are the irresistible sight and taste of really good, fresh bread, baked golden-brown and rising proud of the loaf tin. The added satisfaction that comes from taking pride in one's own achievement is a bonus.

Many experienced home bakers swear by fresh yeast. However, this has become decidedly rare unless you can get it from a professional baker. Even exacting restaurateurs use the much improved varieties of dried yeast now available. Most of the recipes in this chapter specify the easy-blend variety of dried yeast requiring no prior diluting in water that can be bought at any supermarket. However, any dried yeast can be used so long as the packet instructions are carefully followed. As regards flours, it is worth stating the obvious: do buy the best quality available, and try to find flours appropriate to the recipe for which they are intended. The *nan* and *chapati* recipes are best made with genuine *ata* flour, which is only stocked in Indo-Pakistani outlets; this is sometimes described on the label as '*chapati* flour', but please refer to the recipes for more detailed information about alternative flours.

The pleasures of touch notwithstanding, busy cooks will note that the recipes refer to machine-kneading as well as traditional hand-kneading. Many food processors have a dough hook attachment which makes light work of kneading. I use a hand-held machine with two dough hooks. Finally, it should be noted that different ovens perform with varying degrees of efficiency, and that room temperature and humidity introduce further random elements. When checking to see if your bread is ready please use eyes, nose, and even ears, since bread should sound hollow when tapped on the base.

NOTE ON FLOUR MEASURES

American cup measures have been included. Although many cookery books seem to agree that one US cup measure is equal to 110g/4oz of flour, in my experience, which comes of weighing out the flour in each recipe, then physically transferring it into a calibrated measuring cup (showing US cups), the true equivalent is nearer to 150g/5oz. When larger volumes are calculated many recipes appear to multiply the 110g/4oz/1 US cup formula, which creates increasingly inaccurate cup measures as the volume rises. The problem is further compounded by the tendency of flour to settle and become compact, thereby admitting more! In view of these uncertainties the user is well advised to weigh the flour and stick to weight measures throughout.

WHOLEMEAL BREAD

This recipe makes two small loaves, each weighing 450g/1lb.
The treacle gives a special richness, particularly to the crust.
This bread is perfect for all manner of excellent sandwiches, and
may be frozen.

575g/1¼lb/4 cups wholemeal (whole grain) flour
110g/4oz/1 scant cup strong white flour
1 tbsp salt
6g/¼oz sachet easy-blend dried yeast
1tbsp black treacle (molasses)
1tbsp sunflower oil
450ml/¾ pint/1½ cups warm water

In a warm bowl mix together the flours, salt, yeast, treacle and
oil, then gradually add the water. Knead either by hand or
machine until the dough is smooth and elastic. Cover the bowl
with a cloth and leave to rise in a warm place. After about an
hour or when the dough has risen appreciably, knead again
briefly, divide the dough in half and fit into greased 450g/1lb loaf
tins (pans). Leave to prove in a warm place for about 45 minutes
longer. Pre-heat the oven to 230°C/450°F/gas mark 8 and bake
for 30-40 minutes or until the loaves are well-browned and
sound hollow when tapped underneath.

GRANARY BREAD

To make delicious granary bread it is recommended to blend in some plain (all-purpose) white flour. As with the other bread recipes in this book, a light, unobtrusive oil is preferred to shortening, lard or butter. This recipe makes two small loaves, each weighing 450g/1lb.

450g/1lb/3¼ cups granary flour
225g/8oz/1¾ cups strong plain white flour
3 tsp salt
2 tbsp sunflower oil
6g/¼oz sachet easy-blend dried yeast
450ml/¾ pint/1½ cups warm water

Mix the flours and salt in a warm bowl, adding the oil and dried yeast. Make a well in the centre and pour in the water. Mix and knead by hand or machine until the dough is soft and elastic. Cover with a cloth and leave to rise in a warm place. Grease two 450g/1lb loaf tins (pans). When the dough has doubled in size (after about 45 minutes), knead it again briefly and divide in half. Fit the dough into the loaf tins. Leave to prove in a warm place for an hour or until the dough has risen to the top of the tins. Pre-heat the oven to 230°C/450°F/gas mark 8 and bake for 30-40 minutes or until the loaves are well-browned and sound hollow when tapped underneath.

Variation
WHITE BREAD

For a white loaf, replace the granary flour with strong plain white flour and proceed in exactly the same way.

ELIOTI

CYPRIOT OLIVE BREAD

This Cypriot olive bread is delicious sliced and eaten with slices of cheese or ham, and hunks of *elioti* make a wonderful snack in their own right. Unlike the yeastless Turkish version, this bread does rise quite considerably.

675g/1½lb/5 cups strong plain (all-purpose) flour
1 tsp salt
6g/¼oz sachet easy-blend dried yeast
2 tbsp extra virgin olive oil
450ml/¾ pint/1½ cups warm water
1 small red onion, peeled and finely chopped
24 black olives, stoned (pitted) and coarsely chopped
olive oil for greasing

Put the flour, salt, dried yeast, 1 tbsp of the oil and the water into a large bowl. Mix. Knead until the dough is smooth and elastic. (If kneaded by hand this will take about 15 minutes.) Shape the dough into a ball. Cover the bowl with a clean cloth and leave somewhere warm until the dough has doubled in size (45-60 minutes). Meanwhile, heat the remaining oil and sauté the onion until slightly brown. When risen, knock back the dough and mix in the onion and olives. Grease two 450g/1lb loaf tins (pans) with olive oil. Divide the dough in half and fit inside the loaf tins. Return the tins to a warm place and leave to rise a second time for approximately 1 hour or until the dough has risen almost to the top of the tins.

Pre-heat the oven to 190°C/375°F/ gas mark 5. Bake for 15 minutes, then reduce the heat to 180°C/350°F/ gas mark 4 and continue to bake for a further 20 minutes; by then the loaves should have browned and sound hollow when the bases are tapped. Cool on a wire rack.

TURKISH OLIVE BREAD

This moist, unleavened bread is more like a savoury batter pudding. Exceptionally quick and easy to make, it must be eaten hot, either straight out of the oven or re-heated. Accompany with tomatoes or cheese or eat as a snack on its own. This makes about six portions.

2 eggs
225ml/8fl oz/1 cup milk
small pinch of dried oregano, or some chopped fresh rosemary leaves
1 tsp salt
225g/8oz/1¾ cups plain (all-purpose) flour
175g/6oz roughly chopped green olives
110ml/4fl oz/½ cup extra virgin olive oil

Preheat the oven to 180°C/350°F/gas mark 4.

Beat the eggs and milk in a mixing bowl with a whisk until frothy. Add the herbs and salt and gradually mix in the flour. Beat thoroughly to a runny paste and mix in the chopped olives and the olive oil. Spoon the mixture into a large, shallow, oiled baking tin (pan) and bake for 25 minutes or until lightly browned.

WALNUT BREAD

Walnut bread is especially good with cheese, and makes wonderful cheese sandwiches. It is, however, a good substitute for ordinary wholemeal (whole grain) bread, and also freezes well. This recipe makes two loaves.

350g/12oz/2½ cups wholemeal (whole grain) flour
350g/12oz/2½ cups plain (all-purpose) flour
1tbsp salt
1tbsp sunflower oil
6g/¼oz sachet easy-blend dried yeast
450ml/¾ pint/1½ cups warm water
110g/4oz walnut kernels (meats), coarsely chopped

Mix the flours and salt in a warm bowl, adding the oil and dried yeast. Make a well in the centre and gradually pour in the water. Mix and knead by hand or machine until the dough is soft and elastic. Cover with a cloth and leave to rise in a warm place. Grease two 450g/1lb loaf tins (pans). When the dough has risen appreciably (after about 45 minutes), knead it again and add the walnuts, taking care to ensure that they are evenly distributed throughout the dough. Divide the dough in half, fit into the loaf tins, and leave to prove in a warm place for another hour. Pre-heat the oven to 230°C/450°F/gas mark 8 and bake for 30-40 minutes or until the loaves are well-browned and sound hollow when tapped underneath.

BANANA AND PISTACHIO BREAD

Pistachios give this delicious, slightly sweet bread an attractive green colour, and the cooked banana creates a dark flecked appearance and a wonderful aroma that is irresistible to adults and children alike. Those who appreciate the contrast of sweet and savoury will enjoy eating this with strong cheese. This makes two loaves, each one weighing about 450g/1lb and suitable for freezing.

3 ripe bananas
110g/4oz butter
225g/8oz/1 cup vanilla sugar
(or 225g/8oz/1 cup caster/superfine sugar and 1 tsp vanilla essence)
2 eggs
275g/10oz/2 cups plain (all-purpose) flour
1 tsp bicarbonate of soda (baking soda)
1 tsp salt
75g/3oz shelled pistachio nuts, chopped

Mash the bananas. Pre-heat the oven to 180°C/375°F/gas mark 5.
    Cream together the butter and sugar; when pale, beat in the eggs. Sift the flour into the mixture and add the bicarbonate of soda, salt, mashed bananas and chopped pistachio nuts. Mix thoroughly, spoon into two oiled loaf tins (pans) and bake for 45 minutes or until the loaves are golden brown. Cool on a wire rack.

SCOTTISH OATCAKES

These traditional oatcakes are best eaten with butter, cheese or jam. They are simple to make and, being dry and brittle, store very well. This recipe makes about 20 circular oatcakes.

575g/1¼lb/5 cups oatmeal
1½ tsp salt
25g/1oz butter, at room temperature
225ml/8fl oz/1 cup water

Pre-heat the oven to 200°C/400°F/gas mark 6.

Put about 450g/1lb/4 cups of oatmeal into a bowl. Add the salt and rub in the butter with your fingers. Add the water and mix well with a spoon. Apply more oatmeal to a clean work surface. Dust your hands with oatmeal and knead the dough for about 2 minutes. Keep shaking a little more oatmeal on to the surface of the dough to prevent it from sticking, then roll it out as thinly as possible. Stamp out about 20 rounds, each approximately 10cm/4 inches in diameter, with the rim of a coffee cup. Place the oatcakes on an oven tray and bake for 12 minutes. Turn them over and bake for 5 minutes longer. Cool on a rack and store in an airtight container.

Spread liberally with butter and jam. Alternatively, top with cheese and pickles. Oatcakes are also traditionally served with cured or pickled herrings.

PITTA BREAD

Although good ready-made pitta bread is widely available it is easy to bake at home, resulting in a fresher, softer texture. The dough must make direct contact with a very hot baking surface so the baking sheet must be pre-heated in the oven. Wrap the pittas in foil as soon as they are done; this stops them from going brittle and will keep them pleasantly warm. Pitta bread can be prised open to make a convenient pocket for all kinds of different fillings.

675g/1½lb/5 cups strong plain (all-purpose) flour, plus extra for
handling
1 tbsp salt
6g/¼oz sachet easy-blend dried yeast
2 tbsp olive oil plus a little extra for oiling a container
450ml/¾ pints/1½ cups warm water

Put the flour, salt, dried yeast, oil and water into a large bowl. Knead until the dough is smooth and elastic. (If kneading by hand this will take about 15 minutes; a machine fitted with dough hooks should do the job in half the time.) With floured hands lift the dough into an oiled container. Cover with a clean cloth and leave somewhere warm for about an hour or until it has doubled in size.

Knock back the dough, and divide it into about a dozen balls. Put them on a floured board and return them to a warm place to rise a second time; this may take another hour. Pre-heat the oven to its maximum setting with a clean baking sheet inside. When really hot, and the dough balls are ready, apply more flour to a work surface. Roll out the balls to make oval shapes then lay them in batches on to the hot baking sheet. Bake for 4 minutes on each side. When cooled slightly the walls should separate if the tops are sliced off and the pittas are gently prised apart.

CHAPATIS

INDIAN FLATBREAD

*C*hapatis are easy to make and taste delicious. However, they can be bought ready-made, not just in Asian shops but also in some supermarkets. This recipe makes about a dozen *chapatis*.

*275g/10oz/2 cups ata (chapati flour) plus a little extra for handling
(or 275g/10oz/2 cups in total of sieved wholemeal/whole grain flour
mixed equally with strong white flour)
1 tbsp oil
170ml/6fl oz/³⁄4 cup water*

Mix the flour with the oil and a little water. Kneading either by hand or machine, add the rest of the water. Knead until the dough is soft, smooth and elastic. With floured hands, lift out the dough and put it into a lightly oiled container, cover with a cloth and leave for 30 minutes.

With floured hands, divide the dough into 10-12 balls of equal size, adding a little extra flour to prevent it from sticking. Roll out each ball very thinly, turning the dough as you roll; you should end up with 10-12 discs, each one 15 cm/6 inches in diameter. Heat a dry, heavy cast-iron frying pan for several minutes. When very hot, place a *chapati* on the surface. After about 30 seconds, turn to cook the other side. The *chapati* should be puffy and speckled with dark brown spots. Remove and wrap in foil to keep warm (the cooked *chapatis* may also be buttered). Repeat until all the *chapatis* are cooked. They freeze well.

Nan

INDIAN LEAVENED BREAD

In Pakistan and northern India, *nans* are baked in the traditional clay *tandoor* oven. They are cooked with, and accompany, dry 'tandoori' meat or poultry, which is marinated in a reddish spice paste prior to cooking in the clay oven. *Nan* can be bought ready-made from many Asian shops and some supermarkets but home-made *nan* is even more delicious and very easy to make. Yoghurt gives it a characteristically sour taste. *Nans* are a delicious and essential accompaniment for chicken and *sheekh* kebabs.

110g/4oz/½ cup yoghurt
500g/1¼lb/4 cups ata flour plus extra for handling the dough
(or strong white flour mixed equally with sieved wholemeal/ whole grain flour)
6g/¼oz sachet easy-blend dried yeast
1 tsp salt
2 tsp sugar
170ml/6fl oz/¾ cup warm milk
2 tbsp sunflower or peanut oil
1 egg, beaten
1 tbsp poppy, onion or sesame seeds (optional)

Beat the yoghurt with a fork until creamy. Put everything except the seeds but including the beaten yoghurt into a mixing bowl. Mix then knead until the dough is smooth and elastic; it will be stickier than conventional bread dough. With floured hands lift the dough into an oiled container, cover with a clean cloth and leave somewhere warm until it has doubled in size. Flour your hands and knock back the dough. Divide into eight balls. On a floured surface, roll out the balls into elongated ovals, each about 23cm/9 inches long and 13cm/5 inches at their widest point. Pre-heat two large baking sheets in the oven set to its maximum temperature. If desired, scatter the seeds over the *nans*. Place the *nans* on the hot baking sheets and bake for 4 minutes on each side; they will swell and brown slightly. Eat warm.

FLATBREAD
SNACKS

Flatbreads are convenient and appropriate accompaniments to marinated meat and poultry, spicy kebabs, bean or vegetable salads and pureés, cooling yoghurt dips with a sly after-bite of chili, and hot Mexican snacks of re-fried beans, tomato or guacamole.

Of all the snacks and sandwiches in this book, these are among the most substantial, and most make a complete light meal for two or more people. They are equally suitable for supper parties, making authentically exotic but simple starters. For a rather more elaborate supper you could even combine recipes from this chapter with complementary snacks from other chapters; for example, Greek cheese and spinach pies from the penultimate chapter, the Indian potato patties called *aloo koftas*, or the stuffed *parathas* from the final chapter. With so much healthy carbohydrate, rice is superfluous. However, do add at least one other salad or vegetable dish, for balance.

With the possible exception of the Mexican ones, all the flatbreads referred to can be easily made at home or bought ready-made, so busy cooks have the option of devoting what little spare time they may have at their disposal to preparing the delicious fillings and toppings. Occasionally a long marinating time is required, but once the marinade is prepared there is little further work. Most of the snacks in this chapter are grilled (broiled), a healthy and currently fashionable technique. This can be done conventionally, under a radiated heat source, or by 'dry grilling' on a very hot iron surface such as a griddle or heavy frying pan, without additional oil. A popular Spanish technique, dry grilling produces a delicious smoky flavour that permeates the meat. (Gas is more effective than electricity when pre-heating a griddle.) In summer you can always barbecue instead.

MARINATED LAMB IN PITTA BREAD

This marinade imparts a wonderful flavour to the lamb, which should be cooked on a hot griddle or barbecued for optimum results. This type of substantial meaty snack is typical of the Balkans and the Middle East, and makes a complete meal for two people.

350g/12oz tender lamb from the leg (trimmed weight)
3 cloves of garlic, peeled and crushed
6 tbsp extra virgin olive oil
juice of 1 lemon
1 tsp ground cumin
1 bay leaf
pinch of oregano
freshly milled black pepper
salt
4 pitta breads, preferably home-made
shredded lettuce heart, sliced tomatoes, sliced peeled cucumber, diced
radishes, flat-leaf (Italian) parsley or mint, to garnish

Cut the well-trimmed lamb into even cubes, each about 2 cm/ ¾ inch square. Put them in a bowl and add the garlic, olive oil, lemon juice, cumin, herbs, and black pepper. Mix well, cover, and refrigerate for 2-24 hours (the longer the better).

Pre-heat a large, heavy frying pan or a cast-iron griddle. When very hot, thread the lamb on to lightly oiled metal skewers. Place on the dry cooking surface and sear for 3-4 minutes on each side; the lamb should be slightly charred but moist and pink inside; leave a little longer for well-done meat. Remove the lamb from the skewers and sprinkle with salt. Cut off the top of the pitta breads and carefully open them up to make pockets. Fit the lamb inside the pitta pockets together with the vegetable and herb garnishes.

YOGURTLU KEBABS

TURKISH KEBABS WITH YOGHURT

This delicious and popular snack from Turkey is almost a complete meal in itself, comprising tender marinated chunks of lamb, salad, and a cool yoghurt dressing stuffed into pitta bread envelopes. This makes enough for two or three people.

MARINADE
350g/12oz lean lamb cut from the leg (trimmed weight)
1 clove of garlic, peeled and crushed
3 tbsp extra virgin olive oil
1 tbsp red wine vinegar
freshly milled black pepper

PITTAS
4 pitta breads, preferably home-made
110g/4oz/¼ cup Greek yoghurt
salt
¼ tsp cayenne
2 tbsp olive oil
leaves from 3 sprigs of fresh mint, chopped
110g/4oz tomatoes, sliced
2 spring onions (scallions), thinly sliced

Trim the lamb of all remaining fat and cut into even cubes, each about 2cm/¾ inch square. Put them in a bowl and add the rest of the marinade ingredients. Mix well, cover and refrigerate for 4 hours or overnight.

Pre-heat a grill (broiler). Thread the lamb pieces on to two lightly oiled metal skewers and grill for about 4 minutes on each side or until browned but still slightly pink inside. (You could also barbecue the lamb over charcoal or dry grill it on a very hot griddle.) Sprinkle the lamb with salt and set aside. Slice off the tops of the pitta breads and carefully open them up. Beat the yoghurt in a bowl with about ½ tsp salt, the cayenne, olive oil and mint. Add the tomatoes and spring onions and mix. Stuff the lamb into the pitta pockets, and spoon in the salad and yoghurt mixture. Eat warm or cold.

BEAN SALAD IN PITTA BREAD

Cooked kidney beans flavoured with celery, shallots, chilies, extra virgin olive oil and fresh herbs make a delicious and nutritious filling for these pitta pockets. This makes enough for two people.

400g/14oz cooked red kidney beans (drained, canned ones are fine)
1 stick (rib) of celery, washed and very thinly sliced
2 shallots, peeled and finely chopped
2 chilies, washed, seeded and thinly sliced
4 tbsp extra virgin olive oil
2 tbsp garlic vinegar
salt and freshly milled black pepper
handful of fresh parsley, chopped
2 pitta breads

Combine all the ingredients except for the pitta bread, mix thoroughly and put to one side for at least 15 minutes to allow the flavours to develop. Warm the pitta breads in a moderate oven until pliable, slice off the tops and gently open them up. Fill the pitta envelopes with the bean salad and eat straight away.

HUMMUS WITH PITTA BREAD

Puréed seasoned chickpeas (garbanzos) make a wonderful Middle Eastern snack. Scoop up the hummus with strips of warmed pitta bread and add some trimmed, crisp vegetables for a nutritious light lunch or supper for two people.

400g/14oz cooked chickpeas (drained, canned ones are fine)
1 clove of garlic, peeled and very finely chopped
6 tbsp fresh lemon juice
2 tbsp water
110ml/4fl oz/¹⁄₂ cup extra virgin olive oil
2 tsp ground cumin
¹⁄₂ tsp cayenne

Put into a food processor the chickpeas, garlic, lemon juice, water, most of the extra virgin olive oil and the cumin. Blend to a smooth paste. Scoop into a bowl, dress with additional olive oil, to taste, and dust with cayenne.

Variation
For a milder version, first sauté the garlic in a little olive oil.

PITTA SALAD SANDWICH

This excellent vegetarian recipe puts to very good use freshly baked pitta bread and home-made mayonnaise, making four tasty sandwiches.

4 pitta breads, preferably home-baked
2 tomatoes, sliced
1 lettuce heart or a tight handful of Chinese leaf cabbage, shredded
6 red radishes, quartered
110g/4oz piece of cucumber, peeled and sliced
2 spring onions (scallions), sliced
salt and freshly milled black pepper
home-made mayonnaise, to taste (see the mayonnaise recipe on page 91)

Slice off the tops of the pitta breads and gently open them up. Fill with the salad ingredients, season, and add mayonnaise, to taste. Eat straight away.

SOUR, SPICY CHICKPEAS

To make this delicious snack you can use ready-made *chapatis*, which are available from Indo-Pakistani grocers and even some supermarkets, but they are very easy to make at home and are well worth the small extra effort; just follow the recipe on page 26. I find it more convenient to use canned beans as dried chickpeas (garbanzos) need to be soaked overnight, then boiled until tender. This makes enough filling for a dozen *chapatis*, which is ample for four people.

800g/1¾lb cooked chickpeas
4 tbsp tomato passata
3 cloves of garlic, peeled and finely chopped
1 bay leaf
small piece of cinnamon
4 cloves
1 tsp ground cumin
1 tsp ground coriander
1 tsp cayenne
1 tsp turmeric
salt and freshly milled black pepper
2 tbsp oil
2 tbsp rice vinegar
juice of ½ lemon or 1 lime
handful of fresh coriander (cilantro), chopped
mango chutney

Put into a saucepan all the ingredients except for the coriander and chutney. Bring to a simmer, cover and cook gently for 7-8 minutes. Remove the cover and simmer for 7-8 minutes longer or until the chickpeas are almost dry. (Add a little water if necessary.) Remove the bay leaf, cinnamon and cloves and mix in the coriander. Spoon a little of the mixture on to the centre of a *chapati*, add a dollop of chutney, and fold over the top and bottom edges of the *chapati* to envelop the chickpeas. Repeat as required and eat warm or cold.

MELITZANOSALATA

AUBERGINE PATÉ

This delicious aubergine (eggplant) paté is also known as aubergine caviar and aubergine salad. It is a standard item on Greek taverna menus, where it is served with bread. The local bread is deliciously moist when freshly baked but tends to harden quite quickly when cut and exposed to the air. I suggest that you scoop up the paté with strips of warmed pitta bread.

450g/1lb aubergines (2 medium-size ones)
2 cloves of garlic, peeled and finely chopped
2 tbsp Greek yoghurt
2 tbsp lemon juice
110ml/4fl oz/½ cup olive oil
1 tsp salt
chopped flesh of 6 black olives
pitta bread

Heat the oven to 220°C/425°F/gas mark 7. Place the aubergines on a sheet of aluminium foil and bake until soft.

When cool enough to handle, slice the aubergines in half, scoop out all the flesh and discard the skin. Put the flesh and all the other ingredients, except for the olives and the bread, in a food processor and blend briefly – a few small lumps may remain but a completely smooth paté is equally acceptable. Garnish with the olives.

SHEEKH KEBABS

SPICED MEAT SKEWERS

These *sheekh* kebabs are very spicy. The well-cooked meat contrasts pleasantly with the soft texture of *nan* bread and the creamy *raita* relish, with which the kebabs are usually served. This makes eight kebabs, which is enough for four people if served as a substantial starter or even as a complete light lunch or supper.

1 tsp cumin seeds
1 tsp coriander seeds
5 cloves
small piece of cinnamon
1 tsp black peppercorns
¼ tsp cardamon seeds
450g/1lb lean minced (ground) beef
1 small onion, peeled and very finely chopped
2cm/¾ inch piece of fresh ginger, peeled and finely chopped
3 cloves of garlic, peeled and finely chopped
salt
1 tsp cayenne
½ tsp turmeric
handful of finely chopped fresh mint
juice of half a lemon
3 tbsp oil plus extra for oiling
shredded lettuce, lemon wedges, and finely sliced mild onion rings, to
garnish

Grind the whole spices to a powder in a coffee grinder or pound with a pestle and mortar. In a bowl combine all the ingredients except for the garnishes. Knead the mixture until smooth and set aside for 30 minutes to 1 hour. Divide into eight balls and mould them into sausage shapes around large, oiled metal skewers. (Each kebab should be about 8cm/3½ inches long and 4cm/1¾ inches wide.) Cover a baking sheet with foil and oil it lightly. Carefully place the kebabs on the baking sheet; unless supported they may fall off the skewers. Pre-heat the grill (broiler).

Grill for about 15 minutes, turning once. The kebabs should be well-browned. Garnish and eat with *nan* and *raita*.

CHICKEN KEBABS

These delicately spiced, meltingly tender kebabs make a delicious and substantial snack for two people. Alternatively divide into four portions, garnish with fresh, crisp salad leaves and serve as a supper party starter.

2 large chicken breasts
3 cloves of garlic, peeled and crushed
2 tsp ground cumin
1 tsp ground coriander
½ tsp turmeric
½ tsp cayenne
salt and freshly milled black pepper
juice of 1 lemon
3 tbsp Greek yoghurt

Skin the chicken breasts and slice them into finger-size strips. Put them in a bowl and add the rest of the ingredients. Mix thoroughly, cover and leave for 1-6 hours (the longer the better).

Pre-heat the grill (broiler). Thread the chicken strips onto oiled metal skewers. Grill until golden-brown all over. You can also dry grill them with in hot cast-iron griddle or frying pan. Eat hot, accompanied by *nan* and *raita*.

RAITA

YOGHURT AND CUCUMBER RELISH

Excellent with *sheekh* or chicken kebabs, *raita* is cooling and silky in texture, but not without bite.

110g/4oz/¹/₂ cup Greek yoghurt
175g/6oz cucumber, peeled and very finely chopped
1 green chili, seeded and finely chopped
¹/₂ tsp salt
¹/₂ tsp ground cumin
¹/₂ tsp ground coriander
small handful of fresh mint, finely chopped

Beat the yoghurt with a fork until creamy. Mix in the remaining ingredients, cover and refrigerate until required but mix thoroughly before serving.

TACOS WITH RE-FRIED BEANS AND HOT SAUCE

This is a wonderful and substantial Mexican snack. You can buy the *taco* shells in any supermarket, so all you have to do is cook the hot sauce – which couldn't be easier – and make the re-fried beans. (Even that is a cinch if you use canned kidney beans). This serves two as a complete light meal, four as a snack or unusual supper starter.

HOT SAUCE
400g/14oz can of plum tomatoes, chopped
2 cloves of garlic, peeled and finely chopped
2 dried red chilies, crumbled
2 tsp red wine vinegar
3 tbsp olive oil
salt and freshly milled black pepper
handful of fresh coriander (cilantro), chopped

RE-FRIED BEANS
450g/1lb cooked red kidney beans, drained if canned
1 large onion, peeled
6 tbsp olive oil
2 fresh green chilies, seeded and coarsely chopped
salt and freshly milled black pepper

TACOS
5 taco shells
50g/2oz Cheddar cheese, grated
1 lettuce heart, finely shredded
2 tomatoes, diced
1 fresh chili pepper, seeded and finely chopped (optional)

Put all the sauce ingredients except for the coriander into a saucepan. Mix thoroughly and bring to the boil. Stirring occasionally, simmer without a lid until the sauce is thick – about 20 minutes.

Put into a pan the beans and barely enough water to cover them. Bring to a boil and cook for about 10 minutes. Meanwhile, cut the onion in half from top to bottom. Slice each hemisphere thinly. Drain the beans, then mash them. Heat the oil in a non-stick frying pan. Soften the onion and chilies and add the bean paste. Season, mix well and fry until the mixture forms a dry 'cake', turning a few times. Both sides should develop a brown crust, but take care not to burn the bean paste. Cut into wedges to fit inside the *taco* shells.

Arrange the *taco* shells on an oiled baking tray. Stuff them with the re-fried bean wedges, spoon the hot sauce over the bean mixture and cover with grated cheese. Bake at 200°C/400°F/gas mark 6 until the cheese has melted and the *tacos* are heated through – about 10 minutes. Transfer to plates and garnish with the shredded lettuce, diced tomatoes and finely chopped chili pepper (if desired).

CORN TORTILLAS WITH GUACAMOLE AND SOUR CREAM

Here is another tasty and substantial Mexican snack, to which the guacamole imparts a deceptively cool, creamy taste that packs a fiery after-bite. Ready-made corn *tortillas* and *taco* shells are widely available in delicatessens and supermarkets.

4 corn tortillas *or taco shells*
2 tomatoes, peeled and chopped
¼ mild onion, peeled
2 fresh chilies, seeded
½ green pepper, seeded and de-pithed
juice of a lime or ½ lemon
1 large ripe avocado
salt
4 tbsp sour cream
6 black olives, chopped
1 'little gem' lettuce heart, shredded
8 cherry tomatoes, quartered

Heat the *tortillas* or *taco* shells for 10 minutes in the oven set at 200°C/400°F/gas mark 6.

Meanwhile, make the guacamole. In a food processor, blend the tomatoes, onion, chilies, green pepper and lime or lemon juice until smooth. Put the mixture in a bowl. Peel and stone (pit) the avocados, then mash the flesh to a pulp with a fork. Add to the blended mixture, season with salt, and mix thoroughly.

Remove the *tortillas*, spread the guacamole over them (or fill the *taco* shells with guacamole), then dribble over the sour cream. Garnish with the olives, shredded lettuce and tomatoes.

SPECIAL NACHOS

This very quick and tasty snack also makes an excellent canapé to hand round with drinks.

oil
6 corn tortillas or taco shells
tomato passata
110g/4oz Cheddar cheese, grated
2 fresh green chili peppers, seeded and finely chopped
some fresh coriander (cilantro) leaves

Pre-heat the oven to 180°C/350°F/gas mark 4.

Cover a large baking sheet with foil or greaseproof (waxed) paper and wipe with oil. Break the *tortillas* or *taco* shells into quarters to make 24 triangles. Arrange them on the baking sheet, spaced apart. Spread a dessertspoonful of tomato passata over each one. Cover with grated cheese and dot with the chopped chilies. Bake until the cheese has melted – about 10 minutes – then garnish with coriander leaves and eat very hot.

BUNS, ROLLS &
BAGELS

This short chapter eschews the many different filled rolls and baps which anyone can buy in a sandwich bar, concentrating instead on a small selection of well-known classic snacks and a couple of more unusual recipes.

The great American hamburger is often a miserable travesty outside the United States. I am amazed by the extraordinary complacency of customers who patronise restaurants serving hamburgers and evidently enjoy the tough, gristly bullets that pass for hamburgers. The awful flavour of low-grade, fatty beef is masked by the garish relishes and ketchups that these establishments serve in those irritating rotating steel bowls that take up so much space on the table.

The well-made hamburger prepared from top quality beef is altogether different. Contrary to popular belief, hamburgers need few, if any, added ingredients to bind them together, although I do recommend a little olive oil. The essential ingredient is good quality, medium-ground beef. (Finely-ground beef does not make a good 'burger.) Many butchers respond very defensively if asked to put a tender cut of steak through the mincer, or simply gape at you in astonishment. I am fortunate to have an excellent butcher whose standard mince is perfectly suitable, but this is unlikely in most cases. For flavour, I add a few drops of Worcester sauce, but popular additives such as herbs, garlic or chopped onions are alien to the true hamburger. What is appropriate is a selection of garnishes including dill cucumbers or gherkins, sliced tomatoes, lettuce, ketchup and mustard – and, of course, the sesame seed bun.

Very good bagels are stocked in supermarkets so another American classic – bagels and smoked salmon with cream cheese – can also be enjoyed at home. Ordinary smoked salmon is very good, but *lox* (unsmoked salted salmon) is a more popular deli speciality in America. The weight-conscious can use low-fat cream cheese, but the richer taste and texture of full-fat cheese complement the salmon beautifully.

Quince cheese is not a cheese at all, but a sweet fruit preserve. Some specialist Italian delicatessens sell quince preserve, and *dulce de membrillo*, the delicious Spanish variety, can be ordered direct from an organization called Brindisa, at Winchester Square, Winchester Walk, London SE1 9AG (telephone 071 403 0282). They carry a varied stock of traditional, high quality Spanish foods, including the authentic *Manchego* cheese that goes so well with quince preserve. However, there is a minimum order limit (£60 at the time of writing).

Brioches are more easily obtained, and my creamy mushroom *ragoût* makes a wonderful filling, delicious for a quick but impressive light lunch or supper.

BUFFALO MOZZARELLA, BASIL AND TOMATO ROLLS

Buffalo milk mozzarella is much softer and creamier than the cheaper, mass-produced cow's milk version. Until recently *mozzarella di bufala* was very hard to find but, as with so many other ingredients, the leading supermarkets have made it more widely available. It is a superb ingredient for making fast gourmet sandwiches.

1 buffalo mozzarella cheese weighing about 200g/7oz
4 large ciabatta rolls
2 tomatoes
4-6 fresh basil leaves, torn up
fine crystal sea salt and freshly milled black pepper
extra virgin olive oil, to taste

Cut the mozzarella into four thick slabs. Slice open the rolls and divide the mozzarella between them. Slice the tomatoes and put two slices on top of each slab of cheese. Top with basil, season and dribble over a little oil. Eat straight away or leave for a while to allow the delicious juices to mingle.

GREAT HAMBURGERS

Hamburgers can be great or awful, depending on the quality of the minced (ground) beef used. Minced steak is best; never use supermarket mince! It is also important to handle the beef mixture briefly and gently to keep the 'burgers tender. This makes two great hamburgers.

3 tbsp olive oil
2 tsp Worcester sauce
freshly milled black pepper
350g/12oz minced steak
salt
2 soft sesame hamburger buns, halved horizontally and very lightly toasted

GARNISHES
Add any or all of the following:
thinly sliced mild onion
grated Cheddar or Emmental cheese
shredded lettuce
thinly sliced tomatoes
dill pickles or gherkins
mayonnaise
corn relish
American or German mustard
tomato ketchup

Add about 1 tbsp of oil, the Worcester sauce, and a generous sprinkling of black pepper to the mince. With clean hands, quickly combine the mixture to form two even balls and shape them into fairly thick hamburgers. Coat with the rest of the oil and allow to stand while you pre-heat a grill (broiler), griddle or heavy cast iron frying pan. (A barbecue is best of all.)

Grill or dry grill until both sides are well-browned and the centres are done to your liking. If barbecuing, cook over the hottest spot to sear, then move to a cooler place to complete the cooking. When done, sprinkle with salt and place the hamburgers between the buns, adding the desired garnishes. French fries make this a complete meal.

CHEESE AND QUINCE CHEESE ROLLS

Quince 'cheese' is a delicious sweet preserve that is very popular in Spain and Italy. It can be a little difficult to obtain but you should find it in good delicatessens. This is a very popular Spanish snack, and is especially good when made with aged *Manchego* cheese.

2 ciabatta *rolls*
Manchego, *mature Gouda or Cheddar cheese*
quince cheese or preserve

Slice open the rolls, which can be slightly warmed, if preferred. Cut some cheese to fit into the bread, and spread with a thick layer of quince cheese.

Variation
Replace the cheese with Parma ham or salami.

BAGELS AND SMOKED SALMON

Good quality bagels are readily available in supermarkets so this delicious snack can be whipped together at home in a jiffy. *Lox*, which is unsmoked, salted salmon is also a popular filling.

4 onion bagels (or plain bagels)
cream cheese, to taste
110g/4oz smoked salmon
freshly milled black pepper
1 lemon quarter

Slice open the bagels horizontally. (I like to warm them slightly in the oven first.) Spread both sides as generously as you like with cream cheese, top with the smoked salmon, season generously with black pepper and squeeze over a few drops of lemon juice. Eat straight away.

BRIOCHES WITH WILD MUSHROOMS

Brioches of reasonably good quality can now be found in most leading supermarkets. This creamy mushroom filling complements the soft texture of the *brioches* perfectly, and makes a light and elegant lunch or supper dish for two people; a green salad is the perfect accompaniment.

2 brioches
12g/¹⁄₂oz dried ceps or morels
225g/8oz mixed fresh mushrooms such as chestnut caps, oyster, and shiitake
25g/1oz butter
1 clove of garlic, peeled and finely chopped
small handful of fresh parsley, washed and chopped
salt and freshly milled black pepper
110ml/4fl oz/¹⁄₂ cup single (light) cream

Slice the *brioches* open horizontally. Remove some of the soft centre to make shallow hollows. Soak the dried mushrooms for 20-30 minutes in a teacup of hot water. Strain and reserve their soaking liquid. Rinse and chop the reconstituted mushrooms. Clean and slice the fresh mushrooms.

Melt the butter in a pan and add all the mushrooms. Stirring often, sauté until tender (6-8 minutes), adding the garlic and the parsley halfway through the cooking. Season and add the strained soaking liquid. Raise the heat and cook until the liquid has evaporated, stirring a few times. Add the cream, mix well, and heat through. Turn off the heat and keep warm; meanwhile toast the cut sides of the *brioches* until golden. Re-heat the mushroom mixture briefly and fill the *brioches*. Eat straight away.

BRUSCHETTA & CROSTINI

Bruschetta and *crostini* are currently in vogue, but like many other rustic snacks, they originated as portable peasants' or labourers' meals that could be assembled in the groves, fields or at the place of work. The difference between the two is simple: *bruschetta* is bread, toasted over a naked flame or on a hot griddle, then rubbed with garlic and liberally lubricated with fruity olive oil. Other ingredients are sometimes added. *Crostini* and *crostoni* (depending on whether the bread slices are little or large) are Italian toast with some sort of topping, often of finely ground or pounded ingredients such as mushrooms, pork products and liver paté. They can be grilled (broiled) like *bruschetta* or baked in a hot oven.

They make excellent, quick and filling lunchtime snacks but are also suitable to serve as a starter. The recipes vary from the traditional Italian garlic bread to relatively simple combinations of olive oil, nuts, herbs, cheese, vegetables and mushrooms.

The best loaves for *bruschetta* and *crostini* are baguettes and regional Italian breads such as *ciabatta* and *Pugliese*. The bread should not be sliced too thickly, nor should it be very thin; 1½ – 3cm (¾ – 1¼ inches) is about right.

BRUSCHETTA

ITALIAN GARLIC BREAD

Originally peasants' or labourers' fare, *bruschetta* could not be simpler to prepare and, when toasted on a griddle and dressed with the best olive oil and fresh, juicy new season's garlic, tastes absolutely wonderful. Use a good baguette loaf or *ciabatta* bread: both make excellent *bruschetta*. This recipe provides enough for four or six people.

1 crusty loaf
2 cloves of garlic, peeled and lightly crushed
110ml/4fl oz/½ cup best extra virgin olive oil
fine crystal sea salt

Slice the loaf at a slightly oblique angle into 2cm/¾ inch sections. Toast each side on a pre-heated, dry cast-iron griddle, or lightly toast under the grill (broiler). Rub one side with garlic, and pour the oil over the rubbed side; it should just soak through to the base of the toast. Season, and eat as warm as possible.

TOMATO AND BASIL BRUSCHETTA

Squash two very ripe, juicy tomatoes over the toasted bread before adding the oil, and top with four freshly torn basil leaves.

BRUSCHETTA WITH CHILI OIL

Proceed as in the original recipe but dress with less oil and add chili-flavoured olive oil, to taste. (You can buy chili oil or make your own by steeping 1 tbsp of crumbled, extra hot dried chilies or chili flakes in a bottle of olive oil for several weeks.)

BRUSCHETTA WITH GARLIC OIL

Toast the bread as before but do not rub with garlic. Replace some of the extra virgin olive oil with garlic-flavoured oil, which you can either buy or make at home by steeping the cloves of a whole head of garlic in a large bottle of olive oil for several weeks.

BRUSCHETTA WITH ROCKET AND SHAVED PARMESAN

This makes a delicious, peppery-tasting starter or snack. The Parmesan should be shaved thin but you could also slice it with a very sharp knife if it is of the relatively soft, pale, immature variety stocked in supermarkets.

½ baguette loaf
1 clove of garlic, peeled and slightly crushed
6 tbsp extra virgin olive oil
fine crystal sea salt and freshly milled black pepper
6 rocket leaves, chopped
25g/1oz piece of Parmesan cheese

Cut the loaf obliquely into six slices. Toast the bread on a very hot, dry cast-iron griddle or frying pan. (Or grill/broil conventionally.) Rub one side with garlic, and pour equal measures of extra virgin olive oil over the rubbed sides. Season with sea salt and freshly milled black pepper. Scatter some chopped rocket leaves over the *bruschetta*. Shave the Parmesan through the coarsest blade on your grater and cover the rocket with the shavings. Eat straight away.

ROASTED PEPPER TAPAS

This simple but highly effective combination of fruity roasted red peppers, anchovies and olive oil makes an excellent starter for four or six people if you are serving some other *tapas* as well.

1 thin baguette loaf
2 red peppers
small can of anchovy fillets in oil (about 12 fillets)
1 tsp capers, rinsed and drained
freshly milled black pepper
extra virgin olive oil

Slice the bread into rounds about 2cm/1 inch thick and toast both sides lightly. Roast the peppers over a high flame or under the grill (broiler) until the skins blister and blacken. Leave them to steam in a covered bowl until cool enough to touch.

Remove and discard the skins; scrape away the seeds. Slice off the white membranes and slice the peppers into strips the width of your little finger. Curl two strips of roasted pepper and an anchovy fillet over each slice of bread, dot with capers, season with a little black pepper and dribble over a thread of oil.

SWEET PEPPER BRUSCHETTA

Toast the bread as before, then rub with two crushed cloves of garlic. Cover with the same amount of skinned red pepper strips as in the preceding recipe, adding some flat-leaf (Italian) parsley and half a dozen chopped Kalamata olives. Season with fine crystal sea salt and freshly milled black pepper, and drizzle with extra virgin olive oil, to taste. Eat straight away.

MUSHROOM CROSTINI

This is wonderful with wild mushrooms, but you can use a combination of dried, reconstituted ceps and cultivated mushrooms. If using dried ceps, soak 25g/1oz in warm water for 20 minutes, strain the liquid through kitchen paper (paper towel) and reserve it, adding the mushrooms and their liquid at the same time as the wine.

4 tbsp extra virgin olive oil
450g/1lb mushrooms, trimmed and sliced
3 slices of smoked bacon, trimmed and finely diced
2 cloves of garlic, peeled and chopped
salt and freshly milled black pepper
2 tbsp tomato passata
110ml/4fl oz/½ cup white wine
handful of fresh parsley, chopped
1 ciabatta loaf, sliced
extra virgin olive oil, to dress the crostini

Heat the olive oil in a heavy pan and add the mushrooms and bacon. Sear them over a high heat, stirring around for 2 minutes, then add the garlic, reduce the heat and sauté for 5 minutes longer. Season, mix well and add the tomato and the wine. Reduce until the liquid has all but evaporated, then add the parsley. Mix, and remove from the heat.

Pre-heat a grill (broiler); meanwhile, mince the mushroom mixture as finely as possible with two sharp knives. Cut each slice of bread in half. Lightly toast the bread on one side, then spread the mushroom mixture thickly on the untoasted side. Pour over a trickle of extra virgin olive oil and heat under the grill for 3-4 minutes. Eat hot or cold.

GOAT'S CHEESE AND WALNUT CROSTONI

The essential difference between *crostini* and *crostoni* is size; in Italian the *-ini* suffix is diminutive, whereas *-oni* implies a greater size. These *crostoni* make a substantial snack or they can provide a wonderful supper party starter, accompanied by a salad.

1 ciabatta loaf
2 fresh goat's cheeses, rinds removed
4 sun-dried tomatoes, from a jar
4 walnuts, shelled
2 tbsp extra virgin olive oil

Cut at an oblique angle four large ovals from the *ciabatta* loaf, each about 4cm/1½ inches thick. Toast lightly but without browning. Cut the cheeses in half and put one half on each slice of bread. Cut the sun-dried tomatoes into thin strips, chop the walnuts finely and scatter both ingredients over the *crostoni*. Sprinkle with oil and bake at 190°C/375°F/gas mark 5 for about 10 minutes; the cheese should be only slighty melted. Eat hot.

CROSTINI WITH SUN-DRIED TOMATO PESTO

These delicious *crostini* have a touch of heat and make a
wonderful snack or supper-party starter. The sun-dried
tomato pesto keeps well in the fridge and is quite versatile. You
can use it to fill vol au vent cases, put it in filo pastry pies, or
just stir a few tablespoons into freshly boiled pasta. Jars of sun-
dried tomatoes in oil are widely available in supermarkets and
delicatessens. Dried tomatoes, which are sold loose, must be
soaked in water until soft. This makes enough for four people.

10 sun-dried tomatoes
1 chili pepper (fresh or dried)
1 clove of garlic, peeled
handful of fresh parsley or basil (or a little of each)
4 shelled walnuts or 2 tbsp pine nuts or blanched almonds
110ml/4fl oz/½ cup extra virgin olive oil
salt
1 baguette loaf

Put all the ingredients except for the bread into a food processor
and blend until you have a smooth paste. Slice the bread into
2cm/¾ inch sections. Lightly toast both sides. Spread the pesto
on one side of the bread and eat hot.

CROSTINI WITH WALNUT PESTO

Walnut pesto is a delicious accompaniment to char-grilled lamb or chicken. I had some left over and happened to spread the pesto on toasted bread, thereby discovering a very good *crostini* recipe.

1 baguette loaf
12 walnuts
1 clove of garlic, peeled
salt
generous handful of flat-leaf (Italian) parsley
tender leaves from 3-4 sprigs of basil
140ml/5fl oz/⅔ cup extra virgin olive oil
freshly milled black pepper

Slice the bread into 2cm/¾ inch sections. Toast lightly on one side only.

Shell the walnuts and put them into a food processor. Crush the garlic with a little salt and add to the walnuts. Add the herbs and process, adding in a steady stream all but 2-3 tbsp of the oil, until you have a fairly smooth, aromatic green paste. Spread the pesto on the untoasted side of the bread slices, drizzle with the remaining oil and grill (broil) for 2-3 minutes longer. Eat hot.

OPEN SNACKS &
SANDWICHES

This is a large and very diverse group of international recipes. Some, such as the Catalan snack *Pa'amb tomaquet*, and the green olive paste *tapas*, are almost like the *bruschetta* and *crostini* of the preceding chapter; others – *Pinchos morunos* and *Montaditos de lomo* spring to mind – are closer to the flatbread snacks of the second chapter, but are eaten on more familiar European bread; others are very traditional British savouries; others still, especially the five *smörgås* recipes and the *gravadlax,* are very nordic both in character and origin. The recommended bread base for these open sandwiches varies from crusty baguette-style bread and conventional toasted sandwich bread to less conventional rye and crispbreads.

Here too are other popular Spanish *tapas* that make delicious lunch or suppertime snacks; Provençal marinated goat's cheese, deliciously soft and easy to spread on walnut bread; a very delicate smoked salmon paté; a Victorian egg and anchovy spread for toast or crispbread; Polish and Russian favourites such as *matjes* herrings with sour cream; and aubergine (eggplant) 'caviar'.

Montaditos de Lomo

MARINATED LOIN OR FILLET OF PORK

The marinade gives this ubiquitous *tapa* its special flavour and a melting tenderness. The meat is quickly cooked on a *plancha* or cast-iron griddle and eaten on chunks of bread. If you don't have a griddle use a heavy cast-iron frying pan instead. This recipe makes a very hearty snack for two people but if served as a starter will stretch comfortably to serve four.

350g/12oz pork fillet or loin, trimmed
3 cloves of garlic, peeled and crushed
½ onion, peeled and chopped
2 bay leaves
2 tsp paprika
1 tsp fennel seeds
4 tbsp extra virgin olive oil
4 tbsp dry white wine
1 ripe tomato, finely chopped
freshly milled black pepper
salt
1 baguette loaf

Cut the pork into 2cm/¾ inch cubes and put them in a bowl. Add the other ingredients, except for the salt and bread, mix thoroughly, and cover. Marinate for 1-24 hours; the longer the better.

Heat a cast-iron griddle or grill (broiler). Meanwhile slice the bread. Remove the pork from the marinade, thread on to oiled skewers and put the skewers on the very hot cooking surface or under the grill. When one side has browned turn to cook the other side; the meat should be perfectly done after about 8 minutes. Sprinkle with salt, remove from the skewers and eat with the bread.

PINCHOS MORUNOS

SPICY PORK KEBABS

Pinchos are small *tapas* that are widely available in bars
throughout Spain. Any morsels of food speared with
toothpicks to chunks of bread qualify as *pinchos*. These 'Moorish
thorns' are pork (occasionally lamb or veal), marinated with
herbs and spices and barbecued over charcoal or wood embers.
They are especially popular in the south where the Moorish
legacy is strongest. This makes enough for four.

675g/1½lb lean (preferably loin) pork, lamb or veal, trimmed
2 tsp ground cumin
2-3 sprigs of thyme
sprig of rosemary
2 cloves of garlic, peeled and crushed
freshly milled black pepper
1 tbsp hot paprika
(or 1 tbsp sweet paprika and 1 tsp cayenne)
6 tbsp olive oil
1 tbsp sherry vinegar or red wine vinegar
salt
1 baguette loaf, sliced

Cut the meat into even, bite-size cubes and combine in a bowl
with the other ingredients (down to the vinegar). Cover and
marinate for 12-24 hours, turning the meat a few times.

Thread the meat on to oiled metal skewers. Basting each
side once with the marinade, barbecue the *pinchos* over white-
hot charcoal, or grill (broil) them conventionally under a pre-
heated grill until just browned. Season with salt, remove the
kebabs from the skewers, divide into equal serving portions and
eat on slices of bread, or use toothpicks to spear two or three
morsels to each chunk of bread.

MATJES HERRING AND SOUR CREAM OPEN SANDWICHES

*M*atjes herrings are much appreciated by Polish people, and will be found in Polish and continental delicatessens, usually vacuum packed in oil. They are relatively mild and less fatty than larger, more mature herrings. This recipe converts a traditional Polish hors d'oeuvre into a quick and delicious open sandwich.

4 matjes herring fillets in oil
4 large slices of rye bread
butter
freshly milled black pepper
4 tbsp sour cream
2 spring onions (scallions), thinly sliced

Drain the herrings and cut each fillet in half. Arrange the herrings on the buttered bread and season with black pepper. Cover with a dollop of sour cream and scatter over some spring onion slices. Eat straight away.

SMOKED SALMON PATÉ

The best smoked salmon comes from wild fish, and is dry and very tender in texture, with none of the nasty slipperiness that you sometimes find in packets of sliced farmed salmon. The best is so good that buttered wholemeal (whole grain) bread, a few drops of lemon juice and a grinding of freshly milled black pepper are the only accompaniments necessary. However, farmed smoked salmon makes a very tasty paté.

175g/6oz smoked salmon, in small pieces
50g/2oz butter, at room temperature
4 tbsp double cream
3 tbsp cream cheese
salt and freshly milled black pepper
1 tsp mustard
juice of half a lemon

Put all the ingredients into a food processor and process until smooth. Put into a bowl, cover with foil and chill to firm. Spread on buttered toast, wholemeal bread or rye crispbread.

GRAVADLAX WITH MUSTARD MAYONNAISE

A Scandinavian speciality consisting of raw marinated salmon, *gravadlax* makes a delicious gourmet snack as well as an elegant starter for entertaining. This recipe makes a large quantity and is suitable for a sizeable gathering.

2 plump salmon fillets weighing 1kg/2¼ lb in total, with the skin on
4 tbsp sea salt
freshly milled white or black pepper
4 tbsp sugar
bunch of fresh dill

Wash the salmon fillets, drain, then blot them dry with kitchen paper (paper towel). Sprinkle about 1 tbsp of the salt over the bottom of a dish large enough to accommodate the salmon. Place one salmon fillet on top of the salt, the skin facing down. Sprinkle the flesh with 2 tbsp salt, a generous grinding of pepper and half the sugar. Cover with half the dill. Place the other fillet on top, the skin facing up. Sprinkle the rest of the salt, pepper, and sugar over the fish, and cover with another layer of dill.

Cover the dish with aluminium foil, top with a plate slightly smaller than the dish and weigh down with a heavy object. Refrigerate for 24-48 hours. Before serving, pour off the liquid that will have collected on the dish, and scrape off the dill and seasoning. With a sharp knife, slice the fillets thinly. Arrange the *gravadlax* on thin, buttered slices of rye or wholemeal (whole grain) bread, and spread over some mustard mayonnaise, or pass it round in a bowl.

MUSTARD MAYONNAISE
1 tbsp mild German mustard
1 tbsp sugar
1 tbsp white wine vinegar
salt
1 egg yolk, at room temperature
5 tbsp sunflower oil
1 tbsp sour cream
sprig of fresh dill, finely chopped

In a food processor, blend the mustard, sugar, vinegar, salt, and egg yolk, adding the oil in a thin stream with the motor running. Stop as soon as the mayonnaise is thick and glossy. Stir in the sour cream and dill.

Note

This sweet version of mustard mayonnaise complements the flavour of *gravadlax* better than the more pungent version that appears on page 89.

MARINATED GOAT'S CHEESES

These opulent marinated goat's cheeses – fresh immature varieties work best – are wonderfully aromatic, soft, rich, and superbly flavoured. However, you will need about 1 litre/1¾ pints of olive oil, making this something of an investment! Eat with crusty bread; it is also excellent with walnut bread (see the recipe in the first chapter).

4-6 small, soft fresh goat's cheeses
1 tsp black peppercorns
2 sprigs of rosemary
2 sprigs of thyme
2 sprigs of sage
2 bay leaves
3 large, dried red chili peppers
olive oil to fill a large preserving jar

Cut the goat's cheeses in half and put them together with the peppercorns, the herbs and chili peppers into a large, sterile preserving jar. Add enough olive oil to cover all the cheese and marinate for at least 10 days. Use up within a month.

Ensaladilla

SPANISH 'RUSSIAN' SALAD

This is probably the most popular *tapa* in Spain, and will be found in any bar. I suggest that you make the *ensaladilla* the day before you intend to eat it because the flavours need a little time to develop. This makes at least six portions.

4 medium carrots, peeled
900g/2lb salad potatoes, peeled
150g/5oz peas (thawed, if frozen)
4 tbsp olive oil
2 tbsp white wine vinegar
a little fresh parsley, washed and finely chopped
2 tsp salt
freshly milled black pepper
½ tsp paprika
225ml/8fl oz/1 cup home-made mayonnaise
(see the recipe on page 91)
2 tbsp flaked tuna (optional)

Cut the carrots into 2cm/1inch chunks. Bring a pan of water to the boil and put in the carrots and the potatoes. Cover and boil until the vegetables are just soft, adding the peas to cook for the last few minutes. Drain, plunge into cold water, and drain again. Dice the potatoes and the carrots finely.

Mix together the oil, vinegar, parsley, salt, pepper and paprika. Put the vegetables, the mayonnaise, and the tuna (if using) into a bowl, add the oil and vinegar mixture and combine everything thoroughly. Transfer the salad to a shallow serving dish and level with a knife or the back of a spoon. When ready to eat scoop up the *ensaladilla* with chunks of crusty bread.

AUBERGINE 'CAVIAR' SANDWICHES

This is similar to the Greek aubergine (eggplant) salad known as *Melitzanosalata* (see the recipe on page 37). However, it is made without yoghurt, and is much sharper-tasting. This makes about 350g/12oz/1½ cups, enough to spread on a whole sliced loaf of rye or wholemeal (whole grain) bread. It is worth making the full quantity because the 'caviar' will keep for a few days if refrigerated in a covered bowl.

2 large aubergines
2 spring onions (scallions), finely chopped
1 clove of garlic, peeled and finely chopped
3 fresh ripe tomatoes, finely chopped
handful of parsley, finely chopped
salt and freshly milled black pepper
¼ tsp cayenne
3 tbsp olive oil
1 tbsp wine vinegar

Pre-heat the oven to 220°C/425°F/gas mark 7. Bake the aubergines for about 25 minutes or until soft. When they have cooled a little scoop out the flesh, discarding any liquid. Chop very finely with a cleaver or heavy knife and squeeze out as much liquid as possible. Put the pulp into a large bowl. Add all the other ingredients and beat until everything is thoroughly amalgamated. Spread on buttered slices of rye or wholemeal bread.

SMÖRGÅS

SCANDINAVIAN OPEN SANDWICHES

These Scandinavian-style open sandwiches, of which the following are but a small selection, are part of the *smörgåsbord* or buffet table, and are eaten together with other delicacies such as meat balls, sausage, hams, salads, omelettes, and marinated or pickled fish. Liver paté, scrambled eggs, salami, and cold goose or turkey breast are just some of the many popular *smörgås* toppings. Rye bread or dark rye crispbread are the usual base but wholemeal (whole grain) bread could be susbtituted. Drink beer, chilled aquavit or vodka.

SMOKED SALMON AND LEMON BUTTER

50g/2oz butter, at room temperature
2 tbsp lemon juice
1 tbsp capers, rinsed, drained and chopped
½ tsp lemon pepper
(or ½ tsp white pepper mixed with 2 tsp grated lemon rind)
4 sprigs of fresh dill, finely chopped
8 thin slices of rye bread or dark rye crispbread
225g/8oz thinly sliced smoked salmon
1 lemon, quartered

Mash together the butter, lemon juice, chopped capers, lemon pepper or white pepper and grated lemon rind, and dill.

Spread all the bread slices with the spiced butter. Place the smoked salmon on top and squeeze over a few drops of lemon juice just before eating.

HERRING AND CHEESE

4 matjes herring fillets in oil, drained
110g/4oz Jarlsberg, Vasterbotten or mature Gouda cheese
8 thin slices of rye bread or dark rye crispbread, buttered
6 small pickled gherkins, thinly sliced

Cut the herrings in half crossways. Thinly slice the cheese and arrange neatly on the bread or crispbread. Place the herrings on top and decorate with the sliced gherkins.

HAM, BOILED POTATO AND SOUR CREAM

4 thick slices of best ham, cut in half
8 thin slices of rye bread or dark rye crispbread, buttered
4 small new potatoes, boiled until tender in their skins
freshly milled black pepper
6 tbsp sour cream
small bunch of fresh chives or the green parts of 3-4 spring onions
(scallions), finely chopped

Put the ham on the buttered bread or crispbread. Thickly slice the boiled potatoes and arrange them on top of the ham. Season with pepper. Put a spoonful of sour cream on each open sandwich and sprinkle with chives or green spring onions.

HAM AND PICKLED BEETROOT

4 thick slices of best ham, cut in half
8 thin slices of rye bread or dark rye crispbread, buttered
mustard, to taste
8 slices of pickled beetroot (beet)

Place the ham on the buttered sides of bread or crispbread, spread with mustard and arrange the beetroot on top.

EGG AND ANCHOVY

4 hard-boiled (hard-cooked) eggs, peeled
8 thin slices of rye bread or dark rye crispbread, buttered
8 anchovy fillets, rinsed and drained if salted
mayonnaise, to taste
½ tsp cayenne

Slice the hard-boiled eggs and arrange them neatly on the bread or crispbread. Put an anchovy fillet on top, add a dollop of mayonnaise and dust lightly with cayenne.

GREEN OLIVE PASTE TAPAS

Wherever olives are grown they are pounded with aromatic ingredients into delicious pastes which can be spread on bread. Spain grows a huge range of indigenous olive varieties, from the rare *Arbequina* to the ubiquitous *Manzanilla* and *Hojiblanca*, and is a leading exporter of olives. This delicious green olive paste can be kept refrigerated and used repeatedly whenever temptation or hunger draw you.

225g/8oz stoned (pitted) green olives
50g/2oz blanched almonds
2 tsp capers, rinsed and drained
1 tbsp brandy
6 tbsp extra virgin olive oil
1 clove of garlic, peeled
handful of fresh parsley, washed
salt and freshly milled black pepper, to taste
1 baguette loaf

In a food processor blend to a smooth paste all the ingredients except for the bread, which should be warmed in the oven and sliced. Alternatively, slice the bread and lightly toast it or leave untoasted. Spread the olive paste thickly over each slice.

PA' AMB TOMAQUET

CATALAN BREAD AND TOMATO SNACKS

This snack comes from the Catalan region of Spain. *Pa' amb tomaquet* translates as 'bread and tomato', and the local tomatoes are so fragrant and tasty that the only way to re-create the true flavour is to use home-grown tomatoes freshly picked during a particularly good summer! Since the Catalans, like all other Spaniards rarely drink without nibbling something on the side, *Pa'amb tomaquet* is a very popular *tapa*, but also makes a tasty light lunch, accompanied by a salad.

1 baguette or ciabatta *loaf*
2 cloves of garlic, peeled and crushed
2 excellent, juicy tomatoes
extra virgin olive oil
fine crystal sea salt and freshly milled black pepper

Slice the loaf obliquely into eight rounds, each about 3½ cm/ 1½ inches thick. Very lightly toast these on both sides or leave untoasted.

Rub one side with the garlic. Cut the tomatoes in half and gently both squeeze and rub them on to the rubbed sides of the bread. Dribble about 1 tbsp of oil over each slice and season. Eat straight away.

PAMB' OLI

MALLORCAN OPEN SANDWICH

A popular snack from the Balearic islands, *pamb'oli* literally means 'oily bread'. It is served in many cafés and *merenderos* (picnic bars), and is very similar to Catalan *Pa'amb tomaquet*. Authentic *serrano* ham is very pungent, and virtually unobtainable outside Spain, but Parma or Bayonne ham may be substituted. The same applies to the local variety of strong-tasting bread; Italian bread is a fine substitute.

> Pugliese *or* ciabatta *loaf*
> *2 ripe, juicy tomatoes*
> *extra virgin olive oil*
> *4 slices of* serrano *or another aged raw ham*
> *about 6 chopped, stoned (pitted) black olives (optional)*

Cut four large slices from the loaf, each about 3cm/1¼ inches thick. (If you are using *ciabatta* bread slice at an oblique angle to increase the surface area.) Very lightly toast both sides or leave untoasted. Cut the tomatoes in half and squeeze and rub them on to one side of the bread. Dribble over at least 1 tbsp of oil per slice, then place a slice of ham on top. Scatter over some olive pieces (if desired) and eat straight away.

Note

The ham may be omitted altogether; if so please add a little coarse salt.

EGG AND ANCHOVY TOAST

This egg and anchovy paste is based on a Victorian sandwich spread recipe, but tastes even better on toast. Eggs and anchovies are combined in many sandwich recipes, particularly open Scandinavian *smörgås*. The flavour of the paste improves if made a few hours in advance. This makes six toasts.

2 eggs
5 anchovy fillets, coarsely chopped
3 tbsp grated Cheddar cheese
¼tsp curry powder
¼tsp cayenne
1 tbsp butter, at room temperature
6 slices of brown bread

Boil the eggs until the whites are solid but the yolks retain moist centres; if unrefrigerated eggs are brought to the boil in a pan of cold water, this should take exactly 4 minutes from when the water reaches a rolling boil. Allow the eggs to cool, then peel them; remove and discard the whites.

Pound the anchovy fillets with the egg yolks, cheese, curry powder, cayenne, and butter: this is best done with a pestle and mortar. When the mixture is smooth and sticky, toast and butter the bread. Spread the egg and anchovy paste generously on the toast and eat straight away.

WELSH RAREBIT

The next four recipes are adapted from Victorian originals. They make excellent light snacks when speed and simplicity are essential.

150g/5oz Cheddar or Cheshire cheese
butter
2 tbsp ale or lager
1 tsp English mustard powder
2 tsp Worcester sauce
freshly milled black pepper
6-8 slices of bread
1 fresh chili, seeded and finely chopped (optional)

Cut or crumble the cheese into little pieces and put them into a saucepan with all the remaining ingredients except for the bread and chili, then stir over a low heat until smooth and creamy. Set aside. Toast and butter the bread, re-heat the mixture, stirring thoroughly, and spread neatly over the toast. Grill (broil) until golden-brown. If liked, sprinkle with a finely chopped chili pepper.

YORKSHIRE RAREBIT

Exactly as above, but top with neatly trimmed poached eggs, allowing one per person.

IRISH RAREBIT

As the first recipe, but substitute milk for the ale, and finish with a
topping of thinly sliced pickled gherkins.

SCOTCH WOODCOCK

6-8 slices of bread
butter
Patum Peperium *('Gentlemen's Relish' – an anchovy relish)*
110ml/4 fl oz/¹⁄₂ cup single (light) cream
2 egg yolks
¹⁄₂ tsp cayenne

Toast and butter the bread. Spread thinly with anchovy relish.
Warm the cream over a low heat. Meanwhile beat the egg yolks
with the cayenne, then add to the cream, stirring thoroughly
until the mixture thickens. Remove from the heat before the eggs
become scrambled and carefully pour over the toast. Eat as hot
as possible.

FILLED SNACKS & SANDWICHES

Meat lovers will enjoy the Spanish *Pepito* and the French hunter's sandwiches, each with a tender, juicy steak filling. Hungry vegetarians should opt instead for *Pan bagnat*, a hefty salad sandwich from Nice, and I can also recommend to non-meat eaters one of my own favourites, *Bocadillos de tortilla*, a potato omelette dressed with pungent *aïolli* and sandwiched between slabs of crusty bread – not for the faint-hearted! Far more delicate but equally delicious are the excellent cucumber sandwiches, salted to purge them of excess moisture and gently flavoured with vinegar which, although barely detectable on the palate, really perks up the flavour. Egg mayonnaise sandwiches are another British favourite, and the recipe comes with a fool-proof method for making your own mayonnaise. Just as eggy and wonderfully flavourful are the Provençal *tapenade* and hard-boiled (hard-cooked) egg sandwiches. The cheese in the triple-decker BLT sandwiches adds an unusual dimension and extra flavour to a popular and substantial American snack.

BLT SANDWICHES

Bacon, lettuce and tomato sandwiches are an American classic. I find that a little cheese gives a more interesting flavour. Ordinary tomatoes are normally tasteless, and I prefer to use cherry tomatoes, of which well-flavoured large varieties are commonly available. This makes two triple-decker BLT sandwiches, substantial enough for a light lunch or supper for two.

175g/6oz large cherry tomatoes
175g/6oz iceberg or 'little gem' lettuce
salt and freshly milled black pepper
3 tbsp mayonnaise (on page 91)
225g/8oz back bacon
6 thick slices of wholemeal (whole grain) sandwich bread
butter
50g/2oz coarsely grated or thinly sliced Cheddar cheese (optional)
potato crisps (chips) and sprigs of watercress, to garnish

Wash the tomatoes and lettuce, drain well and blot dry. Slice the cherry tomatoes and put them in a salad or mixing bowl. Shred the lettuce with a sharp knife and combine with the tomatoes. Season generously. Add the mayonnaise and combine thoroughly so that all the pieces are coated. Set aside.

Grill (broil) the bacon until lightly browned. Lightly toast the bread. Spread one side of each slice with a little butter. Spoon over a layer of the mayonnaise mixture. Cover with some bacon and cheese (if using). Repeat, then cover with a third slice of toast, the buttered side facing down. Repeat for the second sandwich, garnish and eat immediately while still warm.

CUCUMBER SANDWICHES

Perfectly made cucumber sandwiches are an unbeatable tea-time snack. The trick is to salt very thinly sliced cucumber to draw out water, and a little vinegar perks up the flavour without being obtrusive. This makes 8-12 dainty sandwiches.

½ large cucumber, washed
salt
freshly milled black pepper
1 tsp white wine vinegar
soft butter
4-6 thin slices of wholemeal (whole grain) sandwich bread
4 sprigs of watercress

Peel the cucumber or leave the skin on, as preferred. Slice the cucumber as thinly as possible or grate through the coarsest blade of a grater. Sprinkle with salt and leave to drain in a wire strainer for about 1 hour. Rinse thoroughly and blot dry with kitchen paper (paper towel). Put into a bowl, sprinkle with pepper and the vinegar and mix. Butter all the bread slices. Divide the cucumber between half the slices of bread, cover with the other slices and press together firmly. Trim off the crusts and slice each sandwich into four little triangles. Serve on a plate, on a clean folded napkin, and garnish with sprigs of watercress.

SMOKED HAM SANDWICHES WITH
MUSTARD MAYONNAISE

Make your own mustard mayonnaise (see the recipe opposite), or, if in a hurry, cheat by simply stirring mustard or mustard powder, to taste, into some Hellman's. This makes two fairly substantial sandwiches.

50g/2oz iceberg or 'little gem' lettuce heart
50g/2oz cucumber, peeled
3 tbsp mustard mayonnaise
freshly milled black pepper
50g/2oz wafer thin, sliced smoked ham
25g/1oz mature Cheddar cheese, grated
4 thick slices of wholemeal (whole grain) sandwich bread, buttered

Wash the lettuce, blot dry with kitchen paper and shred finely. Slice the cucumber as thinly as possible. Combine the lettuce with the mustard mayonnaise and season with pepper. Arrange the cucumber slices on two buttered slices of bread. Add the lettuce and mustard mayonnaise mixture, dividing equally between the two sandwiches. Add the ham, top with grated cheese, then cover with the two other slices of bread. Slice the sandwiches in half diagonally.

MUSTARD MAYONNAISE
1 tbsp prepared English mustard or mustard powder
1 tbsp white wine vinegar
salt
1 egg yolk, at room temperature
6 tbsp sunflower oil

In a food processor, blend the mustard, vinegar, salt, egg yolk, and about 1 tbsp of the oil. Add the rest of the oil in a thin stream with the motor running. Stop as soon as the mayonnaise is thick and glossy.

Note
If the egg is too cold the mayonnaise will not emulsify so don't use eggs that have come straight out of the 'fridge. This is a more pungent version than the previous recipe.

EGG MAYONNAISE SANDWICHES

Very quick and easy to make, egg mayonnaise is a favourite English sandwich filling, but tastes so much better when the mayonnaise is home-made. This recipe makes four sandwiches.

2 hard-boiled (hard-cooked) eggs
freshly milled black pepper
1 tsp paprika
4 tbsp mayonnaise (see the next recipe)
3 tsp water
2 heaped tbsp mustard and cress
8 slices of wholemeal (whole grain) sandwich bread, lightly buttered

Shell and chop the eggs. Put them in a bowl and season with pepper and paprika. Thin the mayonnaise with the water, then add the mustard and cress and mix in the chopped, seasoned eggs. Combine quite thoroughly. Spread the mixture generously over half the slices of bread and cover with the remaining slices. Alternatively, fill soft baps or mini baguette loaves with the egg mayonnaise mixture.

MAYONNAISE

Perfect mayonnaise can be made very easily in a food processor, and if three golden rules are obeyed, it should never fail. First, to emulsify properly, your eggs must not be too cold; if refrigerated, they must be taken out of the 'fridge and allowed to reach room temperature. Secondly, the oil must be added little by little: only a few drops at first, then, once the mixture has begun to emulsify, in a slow, steady stream. Finally, the motor must be switched off as soon as the mayonnaise is thick and glossy; over-beating can destroy the emulsion, turning the mixture thin and runny. Use a refined olive oil as the fruity flavour of extra virgin oil is too obtrusive. Alternatively, a mixture of olive and sunflower oils may be substituted. Mayonnaise (Mahon-*esa*) was invented in the Menorcan port of Mahon.

2 egg yolks
1 tsp salt
2 tsp wine vinegar or lemon juice
1 tsp mustard
200ml/7fl oz/³⁄₄ cup pure olive oil

Put the egg yolks, salt, vinegar or lemon juice, and mustard into the bowl of a food processor. With the engine running, add the oil in a very thin, steady stream; stop the engine as soon as all the oil has been used up and the mayonnaise is thick and glossy. Use immediately or keep refrigerated in a sealed jar until required. This makes about 225ml/8fl oz/1 cup.

Note
Should the mayonnaise fail, add a fresh egg yolk and some mustard to the mixture and switch on again, adding just enough oil in a very thin trickle to rescue the emulsion.

TAPENADE AND HARD BOILED EGG SANDWICHES

When making this delicious and substantial Provençal snack do bear in mind that eggs over a week old are much better for hard-boiling than very fresh ones, which are notoriously fiddly to peel. The best olives for *tapenade* are the local *Niçois* variety, which are small, shrivelled and very pungent. I prefer to omit tuna, even though it is a popular ingredient of *tapenade*. This is an excellent picnic snack.

8 hard-boiled (hard-cooked) eggs
1 baguette loaf
175g/6oz black olives
4 anchovy fillets (soaked and drained, if salted)
1 clove of garlic, peeled
3 tbsp capers (soaked and drained, if salted)
1 tbsp pine nuts
pinch of dried thyme
2 tsp brandy
1 tbsp lemon juice
freshly milled black pepper
6 tbsp extra virgin olive oil

Peel the eggs and chop them coarsely. Cut the loaf into two equal lengths and halve them horizontally.

Stone (pit) the olives, discarding the stones and retaining as much of the flesh as possible. Put the olives into a food processor together with the remaining ingredients except the eggs, and process until you have a fairly smooth paste. Spread the *tapenade* thickly over the opened bread, cover with the chopped eggs, and close up the sandwiches. Eat there and then or keep for a few hours until required.

PEPITOS

SPANISH STEAK SANDWICHES

Although Spaniards usually use veal for *pepitos*, juicy beef steak, beaten thin, seasoned with pepper, and dipped in flour and olive oil makes an equally satisfying filling. This is nourishing fast food at its very best, making two substantial sandwiches.

225g/8oz (trimmed weight) lean rump, sirloin or fillet steak, in a piece
freshly milled black pepper
2 sections of baguette loaf, each 15cm/6 inches long
flour and olive oil (for coating)
fine crystal sea salt
mustard (optional)
sliced pickled gherkins (optional)

Remove any remaining fat and cut the steak into pieces of similar size. Place the steaks between two sheets of plastic or greaseproof (waxed) paper. Beat with a mallet or rolling pin; they should be very thin but intact. Season both sides generously with black pepper.

Slice the bread open horizontally and warm briefly in a moderate oven. Heat a cast-iron griddle or heavy frying pan until very hot. Meanwhile shake a little flour on to a plate and pour a little olive oil into another, less shallow container. Coat the steaks in the flour, then dip both sides in olive oil. Lay the steaks on the hot cooking surface and sear for 30-45 seconds, then turn to sear the other side. Sprinkle with salt, then place a steak between each section of bread and, if desired, add some mustard and sliced gherkins. Eat straight away.

BOCADILLOS DE TORTILLA

SPANISH OMELETTE SANDWICHES

Small chunks of potato omelette on hunks of bread are a popular *tapa* in Spanish bars. A *bocadillo de tortilla* is a potato omelette sandwich. Although I was educated in England I spent the school holidays in Spain, and whenever we went on picnics and excursions into the mountains or date palm forests near Alicante, where my parents lived, my Spanish mother would make a supply of *bocadillos de tortilla* of truly heroic proportions. This recipe makes two similarly substantial *bocadillos*, which are especially tasty dressed with *aïolli* (garlic mayonnaise), and washed down with well-chilled Spanish beer.

1 medium onion, peeled and halved from top to bottom
4 tbsp olive oil
350g/12oz potatoes, peeled and sliced
5 large free-range eggs
salt to taste
1 large baguette loaf

Slice both onion halves thinly. Heat the oil in a medium non-stick frying pan. Put in the potatoes and the onion. Stir-fry over a high heat for 2-3 minutes. Reduce the heat, cover and cook gently for about 7 minutes or until the potatoes are soft, mixing several times to prevent the onion from burning. (The onion should be sweet and golden-brown.)

Meanwhile, pre-heat the grill (broiler). Beat the eggs with a generous pinch of salt and pour them into the pan. When the underside is golden-brown (lift up a corner of the omelette to verify this), remove the pan and put it under the grill. The top side will bubble up and foam a little. It is done when the surface is golden. Drain off any surplus oil and allow the omelette to cool.

Divide the loaf into two equal lengths and slice each one open from end to end. Cut the omelette into sections to fit into the bread, spread a generous layer of garlic mayonnaise on top and close the sandwiches.

AÏOLLI

GARLIC MAYONNAISE

If your eggs are at room temperature and not straight from the 'fridge this garlic mayonnaise should work perfectly every time. If it fails to emulsify and turns runny add a fresh, unrefrigerated egg yolk and turn the machine on once more. The mixture should then emulsify. For a more conventional mayonnaise with a less obtrusive garlic flavour you could replace the garlic cloves and wine vinegar with garlic vinegar or omit the garlic and use unflavoured wine vinegar and garlic-flavoured olive oil.

3 cloves of garlic, peeled
1 tsp salt
2 egg yolks
2 tbsp wine vinegar
200ml/7fl oz/¹⁄₃ cup olive oil

Crush the garlic to a paste with the salt. Put the crushed garlic, egg yolks, vinegar and 1 tbsp of oil into a food processor. With the motor running, add the rest of the oil in a very thin stream; stop when the mixture is thick and glossy.

FRENCH HUNTER'S SANDWICH

This is similar to the *pepitos* recipe but with a more substantial filling. It is based on a French recipe which I saw Michael Barry prepare on television. Other than size, the chief difference is that the sandwich is meant to be eaten cold, having become well flavoured with the meat juices.

Fry a small sirloin steak about 15cm/6 inches long and 1½cm/¾inch thick in a little olive oil until done to the desired degree of pinkness. Season with salt and freshly milled black pepper and set aside to extract some juices. Slice open a section of baguette loaf as long as the steak. Remove the bready middle, leaving a hollow. (If necessary, cut the steak in half lengthways to fit into the sandwich hollow, stacking one strip above the other.) Pour over the meat juices, then spread liberally with grain mustard and add a topping of sliced pickled gherkins. Close up the sandwich, wrap in foil and weigh down with a heavy object for about 1 hour. This is the perfect moveable feast, making one very hefty sandwich.

PAN BAGNAT

PROVENÇAL SALAD SANDWICH

This delicious salad sandwich from Nice is ideal for picnics. You can try it with other summer vegetables, but avoid lettuce, which goes unpleasantly limp and slimy. This is for two very hungry people.

1 large baguette loaf
1 clove of garlic, lightly crushed
4 tbsp extra virgin olive oil
1 tbsp wine vinegar
fine crystal sea salt and freshly milled black pepper
¼ red onion, peeled and very thinly sliced
½ green pepper, seeded and thinly sliced
½ red pepper, seeded and thinly sliced
3-4 ripe tomatoes, thinly sliced
12 black olives, stoned (pitted) and chopped
6 fresh basil leaves, torn up
2 hard-boiled (hard-cooked) eggs, sliced

Slice the loaf in half horizontally. Remove and discard some of the soft middle part. Place the two crusts under the grill (broiler), the concave sides facing up. Grill very lightly; this makes rubbing with garlic easier. Now rub the lightly toasted sides with the garlic, then drizzle with 3 tbsp of olive oil and sprinkle with vinegar. Season. Fill the cavities with the vegetables, olives and basil. Season again and dribble the remaining oil over the filling. Close up the sandwich, ensuring a tight, neat fit. Wrap up with foil and weigh down with a heavy object. Leave for about an hour, then open and add the hard-boiled egg. Slice the bread into two sections of equal length.

TARTS, PIZZA & FOCACCIA

Home-made savoury tarts and pizzas are rather special, and are far superior to the often debased versions retailed by the fast food industry. They are greatly appreciated by my fussy young children, and are a popular way of sharing a family meal without compromising adult tastes and quality of ingredients.

The beauty of the two tart recipes is that you don't have to bother making the pastry base. Unlike ready-made pizza bases, which I do not like as much as my own version, popular brands of commercial shortcrust pastry (tart dough) are usually very good, producing results that are virtually indistinguishable from authentic home-made pastry. They leave you free to concentrate on making a good savoury custard filling, and I salute that!

I like a thin, crisp pizza base, similar to the kind you are served in Italy. I would not deny that absolutely spot-on Neapolitan pizza is hard to re-create in a domestic oven, but the six recipes that I have provided come quite close. One of the advantages of home-made pizza is that you can experiment with almost limitless toppings. However, I prefer not to overload the pizza base, which can sometimes become soggy. Now that pizza has truly circumnavigated the globe, and appears with a bewildering variety of multiethnic toppings – often far from successfully – this seems a good moment to re-create some classic and authentic recipes such as *Quatro stagioni* and *Margherita*.

Finally, fabulous *focaccia*. This fashionable bread is the perfect healthy snack. It must have plenty of fruity olive oil, sea salt, and either herbs or savoury toppings such as *pancetta* or sausage. My favourite version has a colourful topping of scorched summer vegetables, red onions, and fresh herbs, as shown on the cover of the book. Delicious straight out of the oven, but even better eaten cold the following day, by which time the wonderful flavours will have intensified, this *focaccia* recipe is hard to resist.

ONION TART

This classic Alsatian tart is made with a simple but delicious onion custard topped with crisp bacon.

flour (for handling and rolling the pastry)
225g/8oz shortcrust pastry (tart dough), thawed if frozen
baking beans
3 medium or 2 large onions, peeled
2 tbsp olive oil
40g/1½oz butter
75g/3oz unsmoked bacon, diced
3 eggs
110ml/4fl oz/½ cup single (light) cream
50g/2oz grated Gruyère cheese
salt and freshly milled black pepper

Roll out the dough and bake blind as in the previous recipe.

Slice the onions from top to bottom, then slice each hemisphere into thin strips. Heat the oil and butter and fry the bacon until pale golden but not crisp; it will crisp up in the oven. Remove with a slotted spoon and drain on kitchen paper (paper towel). Sauté the onions until soft and golden-brown, remove with a slotted spoon and drain on kitchen paper.

In a mixing bowl beat the eggs with the cream, the cheese, salt and pepper. Add the onions, mix well and cover the pastry base, spreading evenly over the surface. Scatter over the bacon and bake as before. Slice and eat hot or cold.

WILD MUSHROOM TART

This tart is also based on authentic Alsatian recipes, but I add Parmesan cheese to the custard for a better flavour, as well as some dried wild mushrooms. (You could substitute fresh wild mushrooms.) This makes a 23cm/9 inch *tarte*, which is ample for four hearty snacks.

soft butter for wiping
flour for handling and rolling the pastry
225g/8oz ready-made shortcrust pastry (tart dough), thawed if frozen
baking beans
2 tbsp olive oil
40g/1½oz butter
4 shallots, peeled and chopped
1 clove of garlic, peeled and finely chopped
225g/8oz oyster and chestnut mushrooms, sliced fairly thin
12g/½oz dried ceps or morels, soaked in a teacup of hot water, plus their soaking liquid, strained through kitchen paper (paper towel)
salt and freshly milled black pepper
handful of fresh parsley, washed and chopped
3 eggs, beaten
110ml/4fl oz/½ cup single (light) cream
40g/1½oz Parmesan cheese, freshly grated
½tsp salt
leaves from 3 sprigs of fresh tarragon, chopped

Pre-heat the oven to 220°C/425°F/gas mark 7. Butter a 23cm/9 inch flan dish (pie plate).

Apply a little flour to a clean work surface and roll out the pastry to make a disc large enough to just overlap the flan dish. Line it with the pastry and trim off any jagged edges. Prick the pastry base repeatedly with a fork. Line the pastry with a sheet of greaseproof (waxed) paper, and weigh down with baking beans.

Bake blind for 10 minutes. Remove the paper and the baking beans. Ensure that the base is almost dry and lightly coloured; if still soggy, return it to the oven and bake until dry.

Heat the olive oil and butter in a pan. Add the shallots and fry them gently for a few minutes, add the garlic, mix well, then add the mushrooms. Stir-fry over a high heat for 2 minutes, then reduce the heat and sauté for 2-3 minutes longer. Pour in the ceps' or morels' soaking liquid and boil until it has almost evaporated. Season, add the parsley, and mix well. Cover the base of the pastry with the mushroom mixture, which should make a thin layer.

Beat the eggs with the cream and Parmesan, and season with salt. Pour the mixture over the mushrooms, ensuring that it does not spill over the sides. Scatter over the tarragon and bake at 180°C/350°F/gas mark 4 for 35-40 minutes, by which time the surface will have set and browned a little. Divide into large slabs and eat hot or cold.

PISSALADIÈRE

PROVENÇAL SWEET ONION TART

This traditional tart from Nice is closely related to pizza but the similarity in names is coincidental. Make with the full quantity of the standard pizza dough (see opposite).

ONION TOPPING

1¼kg/3½lb onions, peeled
110ml/4fl oz/½ cup olive oil
4 cloves of garlic, peeled and thickly sliced
salt and freshly milled black pepper
2 tsp fresh chopped thyme or 1 tsp dried thyme, crumbled
1 tsp oregano
pizza dough
about 20 anchovy fillets
handful of stoned (pitted) black olives
olive oil

Halve the onions from top to bottom. Slice each hemisphere very thinly. Heat the olive oil in a large pan. Add the onions and garlic and cook very gently for 45-60 minutes, stirring from time to time. They should become sweet and brown. Remove with a slotted spoon and put them into a bowl. Season, mix in the herbs and set aside.

Pre-heat the oven to 220°C/425°F/gas mark 7.

Make the dough exactly as directed in the basic pizza recipe but do not divide the dough up into balls once kneaded. Roll out the dough to a thickness of 6mm/¼ inch (thicker than for pizza). Place the dough sheet on an oiled rectangular baking pan or a circular tart pan. Pinch up the edges with thumb and forefinger to create a raised rim. Bake for about 20 minutes or until the crust is golden-brown.

Pile the onion mixture over the dough base, spreading it out evenly to reach the rims. Arrange a diamond-shaped latticework of anchovy fillets on top, and place an olive in the centre of each diamond. Drizzle with olive oil and bake for 15 minutes. Cut into wedges and eat hot.

PIZZA DOUGH

Pizza is among Naples' greatest contributions if not to gastronomy, then to everyday eating, having become the most popular fast food in the Western world, while spreading rapidly eastwards too! Yet, with few exceptions, the pizza that is retailed commercially and served in fast food franchises bears very little resemblance to the real thing. It is often overloaded with ingredients and consequently soggy, as well as being far too thick and bready. The dough base, which is critical, should be relatively thin, crisp and firm, and the toppings rather austere. Here are a few traditional pizzas, but you might like to experiment with your own toppings. Each recipe makes two 25cm/10 inch pizzas.

400g/14oz/3 cups plain (all-purpose) flour, plus extra for handling
1 tsp salt
1½ tsp easy-blend dried yeast (about ½ a 6g/⅛oz sachet)
1 tbsp olive oil
225ml/8fl oz/1 cup warm water

Put the flour, salt, yeast and olive oil into a bowl and add a little water. While kneading either by hand or machine add the rest of the water. When the dough is smooth and elastic (after about 15 minutes if kneading by hand or after 5 minutes' machine-kneading) transfer it to an oiled container, cover with a clean cloth and leave in a warm place for an hour or until the dough has almost doubled in size.

Dust your hands, a work surface and a rolling pin with flour. Knock back the dough and divide it into two balls of equal size. (They may now refrigerated for a few days or frozen; store in oiled plastic food bags.) Roll out the dough balls quite thinly, sprinkling with flour and turning as you roll so that the shapes are circular. Pinch up the edges to make a shallow rim. They are now ready for the topping. Pre-heat the oven to 220°C/425°F/ gas mark 7.

PIZZA MARGHERITA

175ml/6fl oz/³⁄₄ cup tomato passata
225g/8oz Italian mozzarella cheese, diced
salt and freshly milled black pepper
olive oil
16 basil leaves, torn up

Place the pizza bases on two oiled baking sheets. Spread the tomato over them, dot evenly with mozzarella, season, and drizzle with a little olive oil. Bake for 15-20 minutes, swapping the trays if one pizza cooks more quickly; check that the edges and base are firm and golden-brown. Decorate with the basil fragments and eat immediately.

MUSHROOM PIZZA

3 tbsp olive oil
225g/8oz chestnut mushrooms, thickly sliced
110ml/4fl oz/¹⁄₂ cup tomato passata
110g/4oz Italian mozzarella cheese, diced
salt and freshly milled black pepper
olive oil

Heat the olive oil in a small pan. Sauté the mushrooms for 2-3 minutes. Remove from the heat and set aside. Place the pizza bases on two oiled baking sheets. Spread the tomato over each pizza and dot evenly with mozzarella. Cover with the mushrooms, season, and drizzle over a little olive oil. Bake for 15-20 minutes or until firm and golden-brown.

SMOKED HAM AND MUSHROOM PIZZA

Reduce the quantity of mushrooms to just 110g/4oz, sliced thinly. Do not fry them. Assemble the pizza as in the preceding recipe, scattering the raw mushrooms over the tomato and mozzarella cheese base, then cover with 8-10 paper thin slices of smoked ham, and a few black olives or capers. Season, drizzle with oil and bake for 15-20 minutes or until firm and golden-brown.

PEPERONE SAUSAGE AND CHILI PIZZA

olive oil
400g/14oz canned tomatoes, chopped
2 cloves of garlic, peeled and finely chopped
salt and freshly milled black pepper
8 large basil leaves
50g/2oz thinly sliced peperone *sausage*
4 fresh or preserved green chilies, roughly chopped

Heat 2 tbsp of olive oil with the tomatoes, garlic and seasoning. Simmer without a lid until the sauce is thick (15-20 minutes). Mix in the basil and remove from the heat. Place the pizza bases on two oiled baking sheets. Spread the tomato sauce over the pizzas, and dot evenly with the *peperone* sausage slices and chili pieces. Season, drizzle with a little olive oil and bake for 15-20 minutes or until firm and golden-brown.

PIZZA QUATRO STAGIONI

The 'four seasons' in this famous topping are represented by anchovies, capers, Parma ham and mushrooms, arranged in quarters over a base of tomato and mozzarella.

175ml/6fl oz/²⁄³ cup tomato passata
110g/4oz Italian mozzarella cheese, diced
6 anchovy fillets, roughly chopped
1 tbsp capers, rinsed and drained
2 thin slices of Parma ham, cut into scraps
50g/2oz button mushrooms, very thinly sliced
salt and freshly milled black pepper
1 tsp dried oregano
12 stoned (pitted) black olives
olive oil

Place the pizza bases on two oiled baking sheets. Spread with the tomato and dot evenly with mozzarella. Arrange the anchovy scraps on one quarter of each pizza. Place the capers opposite to make another quarter, then do the same with the ham and the mushrooms. Season with salt, pepper and oregano, decorate with olives, drizzle with olive oil and bake for 15-20 minutes or until firm and golden-brown.

FOCACCIA

ITALIAN FLATBREAD

ocaccia is a delicious flatbread from Italy made with olive oil
and seasoned with sea salt and fresh herbs. The *focaccia* is
sliced into wedges for a simple hot snack or it can be
accompanied by Parma ham, sun-dried tomatoes, cheeses and
pickles. The dough can also provide a base for other ingredients
such as chopped, fried *pancetta* or bacon, sausage meat,
mozzarella and Parmesan cheeses, and grilled (broiled)
vegetables. This will feed four people.

> *450g/1lb/3¼ cups strong plain (all-purpose) flour, plus extra for*
> *handling*
> *3 tsp fine crystal sea salt*
> *1½ tsp easy-blend dried yeast (about ½ a 6g/¼ oz sachet)*
> *110ml/4fl oz/½ cup extra virgin olive oil*
> *225ml/8fl oz/1 cup warm water*
> *leaves from 2-3 sprigs of sage, finely chopped*
> *leaves from 2-3 sprigs of rosemary, finely chopped*

Mix the flour, 1 tsp salt, yeast and 2 tbsp of oil in a bowl. Add
the water gradually, kneading all the while by hand or with a
machine fitted with dough hooks. When the dough is smooth
(after 15 minutes, if kneading by hand or 5 minutes' machine-
kneading), lift it out with floured hands and transfer to an oiled
container. Cover with a clean cloth and leave to rest somewhere
warm for about an hour or until it has doubled in size.

Dust your hands, a work surface and a rolling pin with
flour. Pre-heat the oven to 220°C/425°F/gas mark 7. Knock back
the risen dough and knead by hand for 1 minute. Oil a shallow,
34cm/13 inch, circular oven-proof container. (Alternatively, use
two smaller, square or circular oven trays.)

Roll out the dough – not too thinly – and fit it into the container, stretching so that the dough touches all the edges. Make regular indentations on the surface with the ball of your thumb. Pour over the remaining oil and spread it over the entire surface. Sprinkle with the remaining salt, scatter over the herbs and bake for 15-20 minutes or until golden. Cut into generous wedges. This delicious plain version is best enjoyed hot.

PANCETTA FOCACCIA

Make the dough as before. When ready to bake, briefly fry 110g/4oz *pancetta* or bacon, cut into julienne strips, and scatter the half-cooked *pancetta* or bacon over the dough base. Bake as before. This excellent version should be enjoyed hot.

FOCACCIA WITH GRILLED VEGETABLES

Make up the original dough recipe but omit the herbs. Bake as previously directed. Meanwhile, prepare the vegetables.

4 sweet peppers (orange, yellow or red – preferably mixed)
1 aubergine (eggplant), quartered
6 ripe tomatoes
3 red onions, peeled and thickly sliced crossways
4 tbsp extra virgin olive oil
1 clove of garlic, peeled and finely chopped
salt and freshly milled black pepper
about 12 fresh basil leaves
small handful of flat-leaf (Italian) parsley
12 black olives

Grill the peppers, aubergine and tomatoes in batches until charred. Meanwhile, scorch the onion slices with 1 tbsp of the oil in a heavy frying pan. When both sides are brown, reduce the heat and, turning a few times, cook until the onions are slightly limp. Remove from the heat.

Put the peppers in a bowl, cover and leave for 10 minutes. Remove the skins, pith and seeds, then slice the flesh into finger-size strips. Slice the aubergine pieces into wide strips. Skin, seed and chop the tomatoes. Put all the vegetables including the garlic into a clean bowl. Add the remaining oil, season, and mix. Spread the vegetables over the cooked dough base. Decorate with the herbs and olives and serve warm or cold. This version actually improves overnight.

PIES & BAKES

This chapter is something of a miscellany, featuring a variety of pies made with filo, puff and shortcrust pastry (tart dough), as well as a pizza pie, some savoury vol au vents, and delicious baked polenta snacks.

Filo pastry is notoriously difficult to make; just about everybody buys it ready-made – even in Greece, where the cheese and spinach pie recipes come from. Filo is very fragile, and each thin sheet must be brushed with melted butter or oil. However, it makes excellent flaky pies, and all kinds of different fillings can be used.

The Russian *pierogi* come with two fillings – meat and mushrooms. Once again, I suggest ready-made puff pastry for convenience. Mushrooms also feature in the Spanish *empanadas,* in which they are combined with red peppers and paprika to make a very tasty and robust vegetarian filling, and also in the puff pastry dish called *setas en hojaldre*, only this time I have added some dried wild mushrooms for extra flavour.

Anyone who has eaten *calzone* in Italy should enjoy making his or her own version at home. These pizza turnovers usually have a filling of ricotta and mozzarella cheese with some finely chopped ham or salami mixed in, but yet again, others will work equally well – perhaps you might like to try stuffing them with the pizza toppings from the previous chapter?

Baked polenta is another Italian inspiration. I much prefer cooked polenta that has cooled and set into a 'cake'. Solidified wedges of this rather bland yellow porridge taste superb fried in hot olive oil until they have acquired a crisp golden-brown crust, but they are also very good baked with tomato or cheese toppings. So I often cook up a batch of polenta, spread it out on a board to soldify, then slice it up and freeze the wedges in batches or refrigerate them for a few days; that way, delicious polenta snacks are always close at hand.

TIROPITTAKIA

GREEK CHEESE PIES

Greek cheese pies can be bought locally from street vendors and bakers, and sometimes appear on taverna menus. The best ones I can remember came from an old-fashioned *ouzeri* in Chania, the rather elegantly decaying former capital of Crete. Although I have also enjoyed eating them in the narrow, swallow-infested streets of Corfu town *tiropittakia* are even more delicious when freshly made at home, and make an unusual supper party starter. This makes 12 little cheese pies.

75g/3oz feta cheese, crumbled
50g/2oz Parmesan cheese, grated
3 tbsp ricotta cheese
1 egg, beaten
freshly milled black pepper
leaves of 3 sprigs of fresh mint, finely chopped
4 sheets of filo pastry, thawed if frozen
olive oil, for brushing the pastry and the baking sheet

Put the cheeses, egg, pepper and mint into a small bowl and mix until creamy. Set aside.

Pre-heat the oven to 200°C/400°F/gas mark 6. Brush the filo pastry sheets with oil, taking care not to break them. Stack the sheets neatly and cut through the stack making three long strips of equal width. Carefully separate the strips. Place a little of the cheese mixture on one end of each strip. Fold over two or three times, then continue folding to make alternating triangles, completely enveloping the filling. This gives the pies their characteristically flaky texture. Brush the pastry surfaces with more oil. Place the cheese pies on an oiled baking sheet and bake for about 10 minutes or until golden brown. Eat hot.

PIEROGI

RUSSIAN SAVOURY PIES

Each recipe makes about a dozen little pies. The first is for a traditional mushroom filling; the second has a delicious but far from authentic meat filling. (A true Russian meat filling would be much more austere.) These *pierogi* make an excellent starter; serve each person two or three pies.

PIEROGI
*500g/18oz packet of puff pastry, thawed if frozen
a little flour for handling
milk or beaten egg*

Pre-heat the oven to 200°C/400°F/ gas mark 6.

Shape the pastry into a ball. On a floured work surface roll out the pastry into a thin sheet. With the rim of a coffee cup stamp out about a dozen circles, each approximately 10cm/4 inches in diameter. Place the pastry discs on an oiled baking sheet. Spoon a little of the filling on to the centres of the discs, leaving a good margin of pastry. Moisten the rims and fold the top halves over to form semi-circular shapes. Squeeze the edges together to seal, and brush the surfaces with milk or beaten egg. Bake for 15-20 minutes or until golden.

MUSHROOM FILLING
*12g/¹⁄₂oz dried ceps
25g/1oz butter
1 tbsp olive oil
1 small onion, peeled and finely chopped
225g/8oz mushrooms, chopped
salt and freshly milled black pepper
2 fresh dill fronds, chopped
3 tbsp sour cream*

Soak the dried ceps in hot water for about 20 minutes. Strain the soaking liquid and reserve it. Rinse and chop the ceps.

Heat the butter and oil in a frying pan. Add the onion and the fresh and dried mushrooms, raise the heat and stir-fry for 2 minutes. Reduce the heat and cook very gently for 8 minutes longer, stirring occasionally. Raise the heat to maximum, add the ceps' soaking liquid, and allow it to boil away. Season, and mix in the dill. Add the sour cream and cook for a minute to allow the mixture to thicken, then remove from the heat and allow to cool.

MEAT FILLING
110g/4oz salad potatoes, peeled
2 tbsp oil
½ onion, peeled and finely chopped
1 clove of garlic, peeled and finely chopped
250g/8oz minced (ground) beef
salt and freshly milled black pepper
225ml/8fl oz/1 cup dry white wine or cider
2 tsp tomato purée (paste)
2-3 sprigs of parsley, chopped
2 tbsp sour cream

Boil the potatoes until tender, then chop them finely. Heat the oil in a frying pan and sauté the onion and garlic until soft. Add the meat and potatoes, season, and cook until the meat has lost all trace of rawness. Add the wine or cider, tomato and parsley and simmer until all the liquid has evaporated and the meat is tender. Stir in the sour cream and leave to cool a little before filling the *pierogi* as described in the main recipe.

S<small>ETAS</small> <small>EN</small> H<small>OJALDRE</small>

WILD MUSHROOMS IN PUFF PASTRY

When in season, wild mushrooms are avidly collected in the less arid parts of northern Spain, especially in Catalonia and the Basque country. Mixed cultivated mushrooms such as shiitake, oyster, and chestnut mushrooms are almost as good as wild fungi. This recipe makes enough for four people and is equally good hot or cold.

450g/1lb mixed mushrooms, wild or cultivated
4 tbsp olive oil
1 medium onion, peeled and chopped
4 tbsp tomato passata
handful of fresh parsley, washed and chopped
salt and freshly milled black pepper
flour
450g/1lb ready-made puff pastry, thawed if frozen
a little flour, for handling
milk, for brushing the pastry

Wipe the mushrooms clean. Trim off and discard any tough parts of the stalks, then slice the mushrooms thinly.

Heat the olive oil. Soften the onion, add the mushrooms and stir-fry over a high heat for about 3 minutes. Reduce the heat and sauté for 5 minutes longer. Add the tomato passata and the parsley and cook for 3 minutes longer, stirring a few times. Season, then remove from the heat while you prepare the pastry. Pre-heat the oven to 200°C/400°F/gas mark 6.

Apply a little flour to a clean work surface and to the pastry. Roll out the pastry to a thin sheet and cut it in half. Lightly oil the base of a wide, shallow oven-proof container; a 25cm/

10 inch flan dish (pie plate) is ideal. Fit one sheet of pastry on to the base and trim off any surplus. Cover the base with the mushroom mixture. Moisten the pastry edges, fit the other sheet on top then press the edges together to seal. Pierce the surface repeatedly with a fork. Decorate the surface with pastry scraps – mushroom shapes are appropriate. Brush with milk and bake until risen and evenly golden-brown (25-30 minutes).

SPANAKOPITTES

GREEK SPINACH PIES

These are as easy to make as the cheese pies.

175g/6oz fresh or frozen spinach
40g/1½oz feta cheese, crumbled
25g/1oz Parmesan cheese, freshly grated
2 tbsp ricotta cheese
1 small egg, beaten
½ tsp salt
freshly milled black pepper
4 sheets of filo pastry, thawed if frozen
olive oil, for brushing the pastry and the baking sheet

Wash the spinach and put it straight into a pan. Cook until wilted and chop finely. When cooled, mix thoroughly with the cheeses, egg and seasoning. Continue as for the cheese pies (page 115).

EMPANADAS

SPANISH PASTIES

These pasties from the north-western corner of Spain have become very popular in many Spanish-speaking countries. Like the smaller *empanadillas*, which are usually fried, they come with a variety of vegetable, meat and fish fillings. Spanish grocers sell the *masa* (dough) but ready-made shortcrust pastry (tart dough) may be substituted with excellent results. These rustic vegetable *empanadas* are very good, but chunks of tuna sautéed with onion, garlic, red peppers and tomatoes are also a popular filling in Galicia.

675g/1½ lb red potatoes
6 tbsp olive oil
2 bay leaves
1 onion, peeled and chopped
2 cloves of garlic, peeled and chopped
175g/6oz mushrooms, thickly sliced
175g/6oz shelled fresh (or frozen) peas
1 red pepper, seeded, de-pithed and diced
salt and freshly milled black pepper
2 tsp hot paprika
(or 2 tsp sweet paprika and a pinch of cayenne)
4 ripe, peeled tomatoes (or canned tomatoes), chopped
glass of white wine
handful of fresh parsley, washed and chopped
flour for handling and rolling the pastry
500g/18oz packet shortcrust pastry (tart dough), thawed if frozen
1 beaten egg or milk

Peel the potatoes and cut them into small, dice-size cubes. Heat the olive oil in a large pan. Add the potatoes and bay leaves and stir-fry them for about 5 minutes or until golden. Add the onion and garlic, mix well and soften over a medium heat. Add the mushrooms, peas and red pepper and stir-fry for 5 more minutes. Season, add the paprika, and the cayenne if using, and mix well. Add the tomatoes, the wine and the parsley, mix again and simmer until the mixture is dry, stirring a few times. Remove the bay leaves.

Pre-heat the oven to 220°C/425°F/ gas mark 7. Roll the pastry out on a floured work surface. Cut out two square, oblong or circular sheets, whatever shape will fit your oven-proof container, which should be large and shallow. Oil the base of the container, lay one pastry sheet over the base and spread the filling over it. Moisten the edges of both sheets of pastry. Cover with the other pastry sheet, fold over the edges and press them together with the prongs of a fork, to seal. Pierce the top, brush with beaten egg or milk and bake until the surface is golden. Cut into squares or wedges and eat hot or cold.

Note

Alternatively, make several individual pies in little earthenware ramekins.

EGG AND ANCHOVY VOL AU VENTS

Refer to the egg and anchovy recipe on page 81 but prepare double the quantity. Put 16 vol au vent cases on an oiled baking sheet. Brush them with milk and bake at 220°C/425°F/gas mark 7 for 10 minutes or until risen and golden. Fill the centres with the egg and anchovy mixture and eat warm or cold.

CALZONE

STUFFED PIZZA TURNOVERS

Imagine pizza pies with a filling rather than a topping. These fragrant turnovers are a good example of fast food *alla Napoletana*. The best *calzone* I have ever tasted came from a little shop just off the main square of the enchanting village of Ravello on the Amalfi coast. The following is my favourite filling, but you can experiment with other ingredients such as mushrooms or vegetables. First refer to the pizza dough recipe on page 105. This makes four *calzone*.

½ the quantity of basic pizza dough
a little flour, for handling
175g/6oz mozzarella cheese, diced small
110g/4oz ricotta cheese
50g/2oz Parmesan cheese, freshly grated
50g/2oz salami, cut into small strips
2 ripe fresh, or canned, tomatoes, finely chopped
salt and freshly milled black pepper
pinch of grated nutmeg
¼ tsp cayenne
milk

Knead the dough. While the dough rises combine the cheeses, salami, tomato, salt, pepper, nutmeg and cayenne in a bowl. Knock back the dough when it has doubled in size and, working with floured hands, divide it into four balls.

On a floured surface roll out the dough balls to make thin circular sheets. Place them on a large, oiled baking sheet. Pre-heat the oven to 220°C/425°F/gas mark 7. Divide the filling into four portions, and spread a portion on to the bottom half of each of the dough sheets but take care to leave a rim of virgin pastry. Moisten the entire rim with milk. Turn over the top half of each sheet and join up the rim, making a half moon shape. Pinch the rims together to seal in the filling. Brush with milk and bake for 15-20 minutes or until puffed and golden-brown. Eat immediately.

POLENTA WEDGES

Providing you use Italian 'instant' polenta (which is sometimes labelled *5 minuti*), this recipe makes a perfect solidified polenta 'cake', which can then be sliced into wedges. I always keep a batch of cooked polenta wedges in my freezer because they are delicious baked, grilled, or fried in olive oil. If you decide to do the same just double the quantities to make a worthwhile amount.

750ml/1½ pints/3¾ cups water
200g/7oz/1 generous cup 'instant' polenta
2 tbsp olive oil
25g/1oz freshly grated Parmesan cheese
freshly milled black pepper

Bring the water to a boil in a capacious pot, adding about 2 tsp salt. Add a steady stream of polenta with one hand while you stir continuously with the other. Keep stirring while the polenta thickens and sputters like molten lava; it will come cleanly away from the sides of the pot after 5-8 minutes. Stir in the remaining ingredients while still piping hot and mix thoroughly.

Pour the polenta onto a clean wooden chopping board. Level with the back of a wooden spoon to make an even layer about 2cm/¾ inch thick, then allow to cool and solidify. Slice into oblongs or squares ready for cooking. (They may be stored in the 'fridge for a few days wrapped in foil or in a plastic food bag.)

BAKED POLENTA WITH TOMATO AND CHEESE

This is a very simple way to use up cooked polenta – see the preceding recipe. A crisp green salad is a very good accompaniment.

3 tbsp olive oil
50g/2oz Parma ham, finely chopped
1 clove of garlic, peeled and finely chopped
200g/7oz canned tomatoes, chopped
salt and freshly milled black pepper
pinch of cayenne
some fresh basil leaves, washed and torn up
polenta wedges from the preceding recipe
50g/2oz fontina or mozzarella cheese, sliced
25g/1oz Parmesan cheese, freshly grated
extra virgin olive oil

Heat the olive oil in a pan. Add the pieces of ham, fry for a minute, then add the garlic. Reduce the heat, mix and sauté for 30 seconds longer, then add the tomatoes. Season, add the cayenne and cook down to a fairly thick sauce. Mix in the basil.

Pre-heat the oven to 200°C/400°F/gas mark 6. Put the polenta wedges on an oiled oven dish. Spread the tomato sauce over them, cover first with fontina or mozzarella, then with grated Parmesan. Bake until the cheese has melted and turned golden – about 25 minutes. Eat hot.

POLENTA AND GORGONZOLA SNACKS

Here is another excellent way to use up leftover polenta wedges, making two serving portions.

6 cold polenta wedges
3 thin slices of Parma ham, cut in half
110g/4oz gorgonzola cheese, cubed

Pre-heat the oven to 200°C/400°F/gas mark 6 and heat a grill (broiler). Put the polenta on an oiled baking sheet and bake until heated through. Put the scraps of ham on the polenta slabs, top with cheese and grill until the cheese has melted. Eat straight away.

FRIED SNACKS

Last but far from least come these valedictory snacks from China, India, Thailand, France and Italy. Some do require a little more preparation time than many of the preceding recipes, but the results certainly justify the small extra effort.

First come some Chinese, Thai and Indian delicacies: spring rolls with dipping sauces; curried vegetable parcels; and scrumptious *wun tun* wrappers filled with spiced chicken meat cooked in coconut milk; and sesame prawn toast – this is the best recipe in the book, in my wife's opinion. The spring roll wrappers and *wun tun* cases are too fiddly to make at home so a trip to a Chinese supermarket will be necessary. The *croûtes, Croques monsieur* and *Mozzarella in carrozza* recipes are essentially variations on the theme of cheese, but each has a different character and texture. If you don't want to fry the *croques* you can just as well toast them in a sandwich maker or even under the grill (broiler). Spiced mashed potatoes feature in the last three recipes, which I have to count among *my* favourites. (They can all be frozen prior to frying so I usually make up the full quantity.)

Having completed this short culinary odyssey, I hope that the humble snack and sandwich will never seem pedestrian again!

SPRING ROLLS

The filling for Chinese spring rolls can be made at home with
only a modicum of time and effort, mostly in the preparation
stage. The wrappers are very thin pastry sheets which quickly
become brittle. For this reason they should be kept in their
packaging until the very last moment. Since they can only be
found in Chinese supermarkets and usually come frozen it is
worth buying several packs and storing them in the freezer.
Spring rolls make a substantial exotic snack or they can be
served as a starter followed by two or three Oriental dishes and
plain boiled rice. This makes eight spring rolls.

2 tbsp plain (all-purpose) flour
3 tbsp water
225ml/8fl oz/1 cup peanut oil
75g/3oz Parma ham, finely chopped
½ red pepper, seeded, de-pithed and finely chopped
1 fresh chili pepper, seeded and finely chopped
1 carrot, peeled and finely chopped
1 lettuce heart, finely shredded
75g/3oz beansprouts
2 spring onions (scallions), very finely sliced
splash of Shaohsing wine
salt
1 tsp sugar
2 tsp soy sauce
1 tsp sesame oil
8 spring roll wrappers, thawed if frozen

DIPPING SAUCES
Put into little individual bowls:

1. 3 tbsp Chinese chili sauce
2. 2 tbsp Hoisin sauce, diluted with 1 tbsp rice vinegar
3. 1 tbsp sesame oil beaten with 2 tbsp soy sauce, 1 tsp sugar, ½ tsp
cayenne, 2 finely sliced spring onions, 1 finely chopped clove of garlic

Mix thoroughly the flour and water. This will seal the spring rolls.

Heat 2 tbsp peanut oil in a wok. When smoking, add the ham and stir-fry for 30 seconds. Add all the vegetables and stir-fry for 2 minutes. Splash in the *Shaohsing* wine and let it boil away – this will take a few seconds. Add the salt, sugar, soy sauce and sesame oil, mix well and stir-fry for another minute or until the vegetables are reasonably dry. Remove from the heat and let the mixture cool.

Peel off eight spring roll wrappers and lay them out on a work surface. Divide the filling into eight equal portions. Spoon the filling on to the top left or right hand corner of each wrapper, leaving a broad rim. Fold the corner flap over the filling, then fold the other three corners into the centre. Roll up the spring rolls to make cigar shapes. Seal the folds with the batter, smoothing any seams with your finger.

Heat the remaining oil in a wok or large, non-stick frying pan. When smoking, fry the spring rolls in batches until golden-brown. Drain them on kitchen paper (paper towel), and eat hot, with the dipping sauces.

VEGETARIAN SPRING ROLLS

Replace the ham with 50g/2oz finely chopped fresh mushrooms and a handful of dried Chinese shiitake mushrooms. The dried mushrooms must be reconstituted for 30 minutes in a cup of hot water, then drained. Remove the stems and thinly slice the caps. Stir-fry all the mushrooms for 30 seconds, then add the other vegetables and proceed as before.

CURRIED VEGETABLE 'PARCELS'

Faced with some unused spring roll pastry wrappers, and curious as to how they would taste when fried with a curried vegetable filling, I created these rather successful snacks, which are not unlike *samosas*. Incidentally, the dry curried vegetables are equally good accompanied just with boiled rice, *nans* or *chapatis,* and a relish or chutney. This makes eight 'parcels', which is ample for four people if served as a supper party starter.

1cm/¹⁄₂ inch piece of cinnamon
3 cloves
1 tsp cumin seeds
1 tsp coriander seeds
225g/8oz salad potatoes, peeled and boiled until tender
3 tbsp sunflower or peanut oil plus 225ml/8fl oz/1 cup (for deep frying)
1 small onion, peeled and finely chopped
1 carrot, peeled and finely chopped
3 cloves of garlic, peeled and finely chopped
1cm/¹⁄₂ inch piece of fresh ginger, peeled and finely chopped
2 fresh chilies, seeded and chopped
1 tsp turmeric
¹⁄₂ tsp cayenne
salt and freshly milled black pepper
110g/4oz peas, thawed if frozen
2 chopped, canned tomatoes, including a little juice
4 tbsp water
generous handful of fresh coriander (cilantro), finely chopped
8 spring roll wrappers

Grind the whole spices in a clean coffee grinder or pound to a
coarse powder with a pestle and mortar. Dice the potatoes.

Heat the oil in a pan and sauté the onion and carrot. When
soft, add the garlic, ginger and chilies. Stir-fry for about 2
minutes, then add the ground spices, turmeric and cayenne.
Season, add the cooked potatoes and the peas and stir-fry for a
minute longer. Add the tomatoes and water and cook,
uncovered, until the mixture is fairly dry – about 5 more
minutes. Stir in the coriander and put on one side until cool.

Peel off eight spring roll wrappers and lay them out on a
work surface. Working quickly before the spring roll wrappers
dry out, spoon about 2 heaped tbsp of the vegetable mixture on
to the centre of each wrapper. Fold the four corners into the
centre, making a squarish parcel. Moisten the open flaps with
water and squeeze together to seal.

Heat the rest of the oil in a wok or a large, non-stick frying
pan. When smoking, carefully put in two of the parcels. Fry
until golden-brown on both sides, turning carefully. Repeat with
the remaining parcels.

SPICY THAI 'BUNDLES'

To make these deliciously spicy little pastry 'bundles' you will need to buy *wun tun* wrappers, which are stocked by most Chinese supermarkets. Do not be put off by the preparation; the superb results more than justify it. Serve as a starter or with drinks, as a exotic canapé.

a skinned chicken breast weighing about 225g/8oz
225ml/8fl oz/1 cup canned, unsweetened coconut milk
peanut oil
3 cloves of garlic, peeled and finely chopped
4 spring onions (scallions), finely chopped
2cm/³⁄₄ inch piece of fresh ginger, peeled and finely chopped
1 carrot, peeled and finely chopped
3 fresh chilies, seeded and finely chopped
2 tsp good quality Thai or Malaysian curry paste
½ tsp turmeric
freshly milled black pepper
1 tbsp soy sauce
2 tsp Thai, Vietnamese or Filipino fish sauce
2 tsp rice vinegar
2 tbsp roasted peanuts, crushed
handful of fresh coriander (cilantro), finely chopped
20 wun tun *wrappers, thawed if frozen*

Put the chicken breast and coconut milk into a pan and simmer for 15-20 minutes. Remove the chicken breast, allow to cool a little, then chop as finely as possible. Save the coconut milk.

Heat 2 tbsp peanut oil in a wok or non-stick frying pan. Add the chopped chicken, the garlic, spring onions, ginger, carrot and chilies, as well as the curry paste, turmeric and a generous grinding of black pepper. Stir-fry for a minute, then add the soy and fish sauces, vinegar, crushed peanuts, and the reserved coconut milk. Stirring constantly, boil down to a thick, dryish mixture or until the oil has separated. Transfer to a large bowl, mix in the coriander and allow the filling to cool.

Lay out the *wun tun* wrappers on a work surface. Put a heaped teaspoonful of filling on to the middle of each sheet. Draw together the four corners, twisting them together just above the bulge to make a tight little bundle. Repeat until everything has been used up.

Heat a deep layer of peanut oil to smoking point in a clean wok or non-stick frying pan. Fry the bundles in batches until evenly golden-brown; this only takes a few seconds for each side. Remove with a strainer or slotted spoon, drain on kitchen paper (paper towel), and eat the bundles hot, dipped into any of the spring roll dipping sauces on page 128.

SESAME PRAWN 'TOAST'

This delicious speciality from southern China is a very popular starter in Chinese restaurants. 'Toast' is a misnomer because the bread is actually fried. Ginger, spring onion and sesame oil give a lovely fragrance and savour, complementing the nutty sesame seeds. This makes 32 little 'toasts' – ample for four people.

8 thin slices of white sandwich bread
350g/12oz cooked, peeled prawns (shrimps), thawed if frozen
4 spring onions (scallions)
1½ cm/½ inch peeled piece of fresh ginger
½ tsp sugar
1 tsp salt
freshly milled black pepper
1 egg, beaten
3 tsp Shaohsing wine or dry sherry
1 tbsp light soy sauce
1 tbsp sesame oil
2 tbsp sesame seeds
peanut oil for frying

Unless the bread is very stale bake for just a few minutes in a warm oven (350°C/180°F/gas mark 4). This will harden it slightly.

Chop the prawns coarsely, then mince them as finely as you can with two Chinese cleavers or heavy knives, chopping with a fast drumming motion. Put the prawn paste into a bowl.

Finely chop the spring onions and ginger and add to the bowl. Mix in the remaining ingredients except for the sesame seeds and peanut oil. Mix thoroughly until the paste is quite smooth and marinate for at least 30 minutes. Mix again and spread the paste generously but evenly over the bread, right up to the crusts. Sprinkle with the sesame seeds. Trim off the crusts then divide each slice diagonally, making four triangles.

Heat a generous layer of oil in a wok. When just smoking fry the prawn 'toasts' in batches with the spread sides facing down. When golden brown turn and fry the other sides. Remove with a slotted spoon and drain on kitchen paper (paper towel). Eat hot.

CROÛTES AU FROMAGE

FRIED CHEESE CRUSTS

This makes about eight *croûtes*, which is ample for four people.

½ baguette loaf
25g/1oz butter, at room temperature
1 tbsp plain (all-purpose) flour
110ml/4fl oz/½ cup milk
salt and freshly milled black pepper
40g/1½oz Gruyère or Emmenthal cheese, grated
2 eggs, beaten
olive oil for frying

Cut the bread into slices each about 2cm/³⁄₄ inch thick.

Melt the butter and stir in the flour, milk, salt and pepper. Keep stirring until thick and creamy. Allow to cool a little, then mix in the cheese and half of the beaten egg mixture. Beat until thoroughly amalgamated. Refrigerate for about 20 minutes to thicken the mixture.

Spread one side of the bread with a thick layer of the cheese mixture. Heat a shallow layer of oil until it just threatens to smoke. Meanwhile dip the bread in the remaining beaten egg. Fry until both sides are lightly browned (this is best done in two batches). Drain on kitchen paper (paper towel), and eat hot.

CROQUES MONSIEUR

FRIED CHEESE AND HAM SANDWICHES

This classic sandwich is usually fried but it can also be made in a toasted sandwich maker, or even grilled (broiled) conventionally. The fried version, however, has a better texture. *Croques monsieur* are very good with sliced gherkins.

butter, at room temperature
4 slices of white sandwich bread
2 slices of ham
Dijon mustard, to taste
75g/3oz Emmenthal or Gruyère cheese, thinly sliced
sunflower oil, for frying

Butter two slices of bread on one side only. Lay the ham on the buttered slices and trim off any overhang. Spread with mustard, then put the cheese on top and cover with the other bread slices. Press the sandwiches together.

Heat a shallow layer of oil in a non-stick frying pan until just smoking. Put in one *croque monsieur* and fry until the bottom side is golden-brown. Carefully turn – this is best done with two implements to keep the top side from sliding off – and fry the other side until golden-brown, then remove and drain on kitchen paper (paper towel). Repeat for the second sandwich. Eat hot.

MOZZARELLA IN CARROZZA

FRIED MOZZARELLA SANDWICHES

The name of this very popular snack from Naples translates as 'mozzarella in a carriage'. The 'carriage' is bread and a coating of breadcrumbs, which encase the mozzarella. This makes two delicious 'carriages', the perfect snack or light lunch, accompanied by a crisp green salad.

4 slices of white sandwich bread
milk
175g/6oz Italian mozzarella cheese, cut into 4 thick slabs
salt and freshly milled black pepper
1 egg, beaten
home-made breadcrumbs for coating
olive oil for frying

Trim off the bread crusts. Moisten one side of two slices of bread with milk, then put two slabs of mozzarella side by side on to *each* of the moistened sides. Season generously with salt and pepper. Moisten the two other slices of bread on one side and press them, the moist sides facing down, on to the mozzarella. Press the sandwiches together. Dip the sandwiches, first in beaten egg, then in breadcrumbs. Heat a shallow layer of oil in a non-stick frying pan. When just smoking, put in the sandwiches. Fry them gently on one side until golden brown, then carefully turn and fry until the other side is also golden brown and the mozzarella has started to melt and ooze from the sides. Drain on paper towel (kitchen paper), and eat while still very hot.

Variations
The classic version is deliciously milky and mild. For a perkier version, add to the filling 2 sun-dried tomato halves from a jar, 6 chopped black olives, and 1 tsp of rinsed, drained capers.

ALOO KOFTA

SPICY POTATO PATTIES

These delicious Indian potato patties make a fine vegetarian snack or starter. The texture is wonderfully light and fluffy and the flavour authentically spicy. This makes about a dozen *koftas*.

675g/1½ lb baking potatoes, peeled
3 tbsp sunflower oil
pinch of ground cinnamon
½ tsp curry powder
¼ tsp cayenne
½ tsp turmeric
salt and freshly milled black pepper
2 eggs
2 spring onions (scallions), thinly sliced
2 green chilies, seeded and finely chopped
small handful of fresh coriander (cilantro), chopped
175g/6oz/generous cup plain (all-purpose) flour
sunflower oil for frying

Boil the potatoes until tender. Drain and mash them with 3 tbsp oil and the ground spices. Season generously.

Beat the eggs with the spring onions, chilies and coriander. Add the mixture to the mashed potatoes and combine thoroughly. Add half of the flour and continue to mix until well-blended. Allow the mixture to cool until comfortable to handle. Sprinkle the remaining flour on to a work surface and, with amply floured hands, make twelve balls of roughly equal size, rolling them in plenty of flour. Form a rather flat sausage shape with each ball and coat liberally with flour; although the *koftas* may seem very soft and fragile, they will firm up in the hot oil.

Heat a layer of oil just to smoking point in a large non-stick frying pan. Carefully add the *koftas* in batches without crowding the pan. Fry on both sides until light brown and drain on kitchen paper (paper towel). Eat hot with an Indian relish or chutney. Any leftover *koftas* are delicious re-heated in the oven.

STUFFED PARATHAS

STUFFED INDIAN BREAD

The *paratha* dough is identical to the *chapati* dough on page 26, and can be made very easily at home. Frying the bread with a delicious potato stuffing makes a substantial and warming meal in its own right. This makes enough for six stuffed *parathas*.

675g/1½ lb floury potatoes, peeled
2 tbsp sunflower oil
1 tbsp black mustard seeds
salt and freshly milled black pepper
½ tsp turmeric
¼ tsp cayenne
2 tbsp good quality Indian curry paste
handful of fresh coriander (cilantro)
the full amount of chapati *dough, divided into*
12 balls of equal size
extra flour for dusting
oil for frying

Boil the potatoes until nearly soft, then drain and mash them – not too thoroughly as a few lumps give a pleasant texture to the filling. Heat the oil to smoking point in a small pan. Add the mustard seeds and remove the pan from the heat as soon as they start to pop. Pour the pan contents over the mashed potatoes, season with salt, pepper, turmeric and cayenne, and add the curry paste and coriander. Mash thoroughly and divide into six equal portions.

On a floured work surface, roll out each dough ball to a disc about 15cm/6 inches in diameter (you should also dust your rolling surface with flour). Spoon the potato mixture over half of the discs, cover with the remaining discs, fold over the edges and squeeze them together, if necessary sealing with a little water. Press the *parathas* with the palm of your hand to flatten them.

Heat a layer of oil in a non-stick frying pan. When hot, fry each *paratha* for 2 minutes on each side or until a dark golden-brown. Drain on kitchen paper (paper towel), and eat hot, with chutney.

PARATHA TURNOVERS

For a less filling snack, make half the dough. Roll it out into 15cm/6 inch circles. Spoon the filling into the centre, then fold over to make half moons, pressing the edges together. Fry as above.

INDEX

AUTHOR BIOGRAPHY

John Midgley was born in Singapore of English and Spanish parents and has lived in Asia, the Caribbean, Spain and England, where he was educated. An enthusiastic self-taught cook, he works as a food writer, consultant cookery editor and cookery book packager. He makes daily creative use of fresh seasonal ingredients to feed family and friends, was a finalist in the 1991 Observer Mouton Cadet cookery competition, and is the author of several cookery books including, for Pavilion, *The Goodness of . . .* series on healthy ingredients.

Word 2000

for Busy People

Make Word Work the Way You Want

**Click Tools | Options (ALT+T+O)
to mess with Word's basic
settings.** (pages 21-26)

**Change a toolbar
by clicking the little
arrow on its right
side, clicking the
Add or Remove
Buttons button, and
then choosing the
buttons you want
to add or remove.**
(pages 21–23)

**Make sure Word will
back up your work
automatically.**
(page 25)

**Reduce interruptions to your
train of thought by turning off
background proofreading and
spell checking.** (pages 23–24)

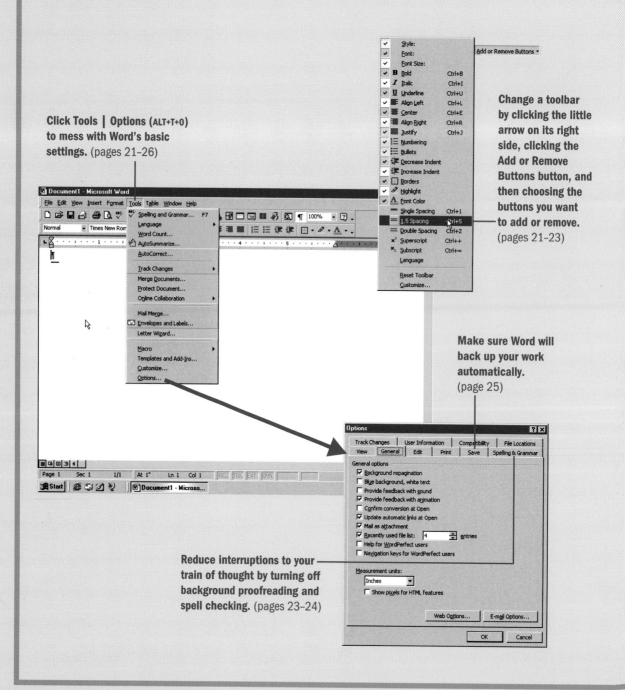

Clarify Information with a Table

Format selected lines (borders). (page 131)

Choose or change a fill color for selected cells. (page 133)

Save time and energy by letting Word help you format your tables. (pages 214–215)

Add or remove border lines. (page 132)

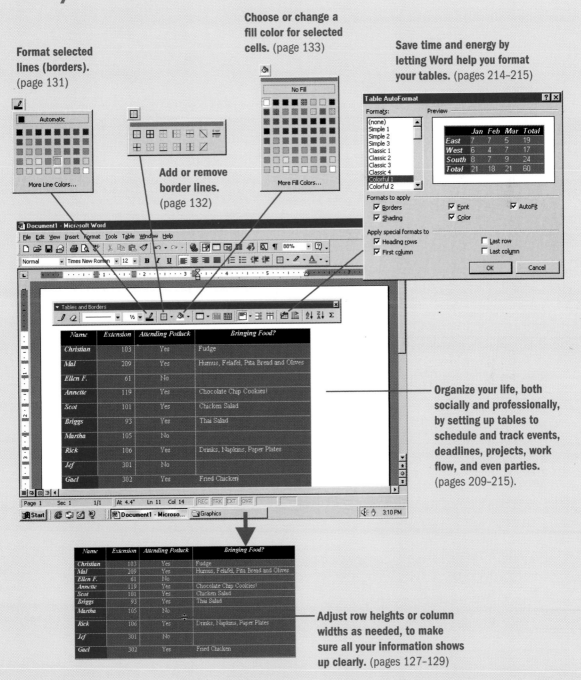

Organize your life, both socially and professionally, by setting up tables to schedule and track events, deadlines, projects, work flow, and even parties. (pages 209–215).

Adjust row heights or column widths as needed, to make sure all your information shows up clearly. (pages 127–129)

Enhance Your Document with Dynamic Charts

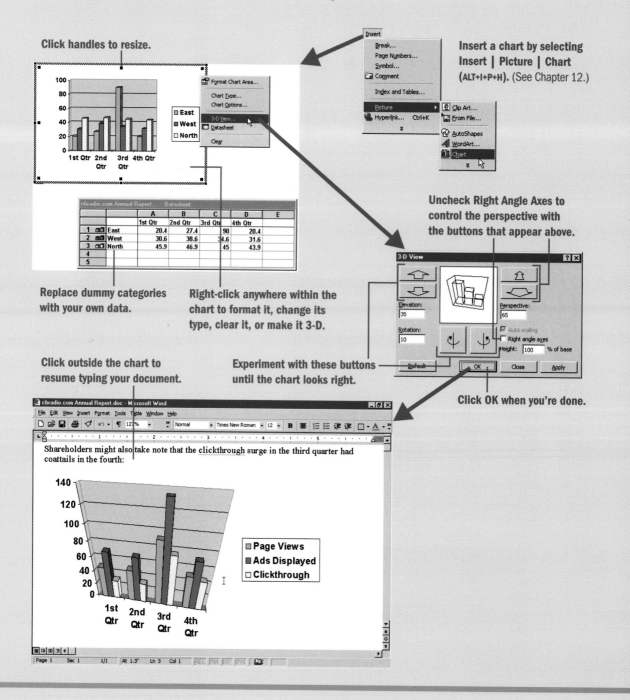

Click handles to resize.

Insert a chart by selecting **Insert | Picture | Chart** (ALT+I+P+H). (See Chapter 12.)

Replace dummy categories with your own data.

Right-click anywhere within the chart to format it, change its type, clear it, or make it 3-D.

Uncheck Right Angle Axes to control the perspective with the buttons that appear above.

Click outside the chart to resume typing your document.

Experiment with these buttons until the chart looks right.

Click OK when you're done.

Shareholders might also take note that the clickthrough surge in the third quarter had coattails in the fourth:

Select Tools | AutoCorrect (ALT+T+A). (page 26)

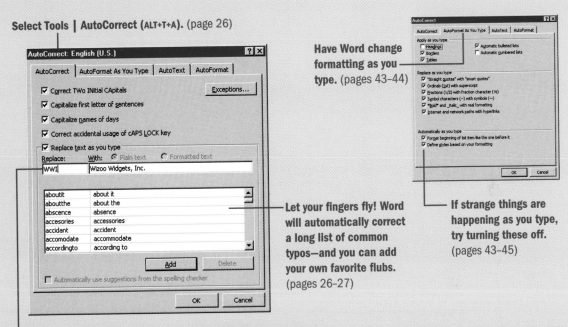

Have Word change formatting as you type. (pages 43–44)

Let your fingers fly! Word will automatically correct a long list of common typos—and you can add your own favorite flubs. (pages 26–27)

If strange things are happening as you type, try turning these off. (pages 43–45)

Preserve your sanity with the Replacement feature, which enables you to type abbreviations for common words and phrases, letting Word spell them out for you each time, as you type. (pages 26–27)

If you select formatted text before going to the AutoText tab of the AutoCorrect dialog box, your AutoText entry will automatically get the same formatting. (pages 58–60)

If you don't want Word mucking with your text while you type, AutoFormat can fix things on command. (page 43)

Have Word complete common names and phrases for you.

Put in your own entries (names and initials come from installation).

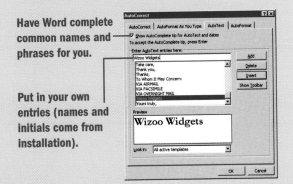

Communicate on a Grand Scale with Form Letters

Select Tools | Mail Merge (ALT+T+R) to start the Mail Merge Helper. (pages 146–147)

Choose Create | Form Letters.

Add form fields to your form letter.

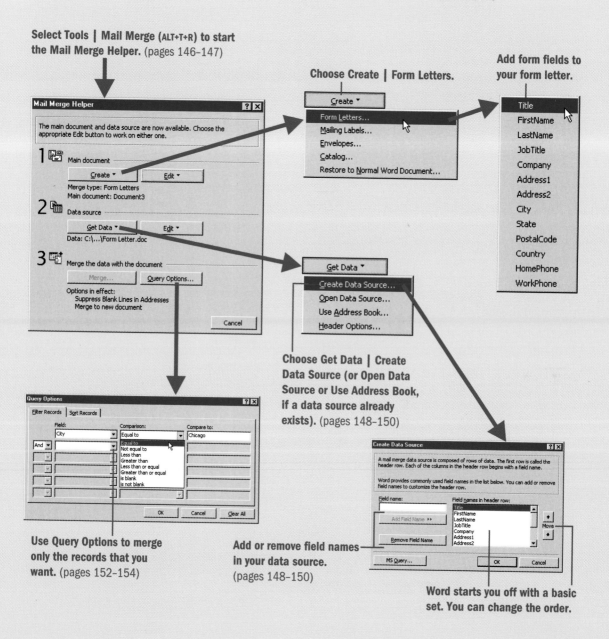

Choose Get Data | Create Data Source (or Open Data Source or Use Address Book, if a data source already exists). (pages 148–150)

Use Query Options to merge only the records that you want. (pages 152–154)

Add or remove field names in your data source. (pages 148–150)

Word starts you off with a basic set. You can change the order.

Design Your Own Business Templates

Create special templates. (pages 63–65)

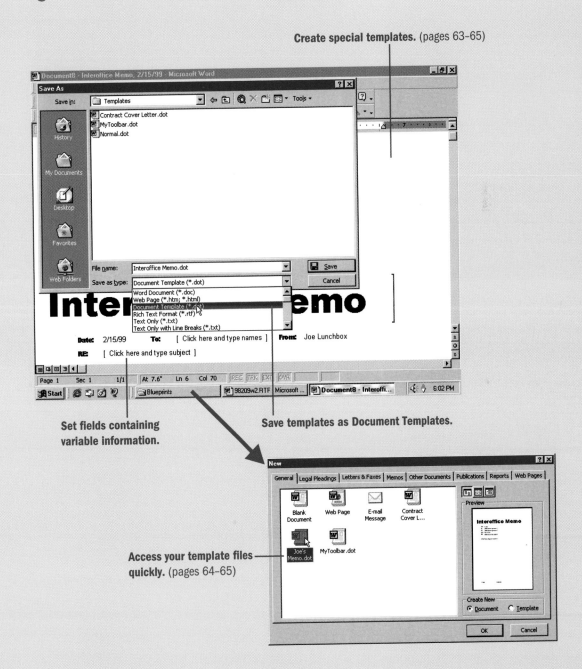

Set fields containing variable information.

Save templates as Document Templates.

Access your template files quickly. (pages 64–65)

Show Off Your Work on the Web

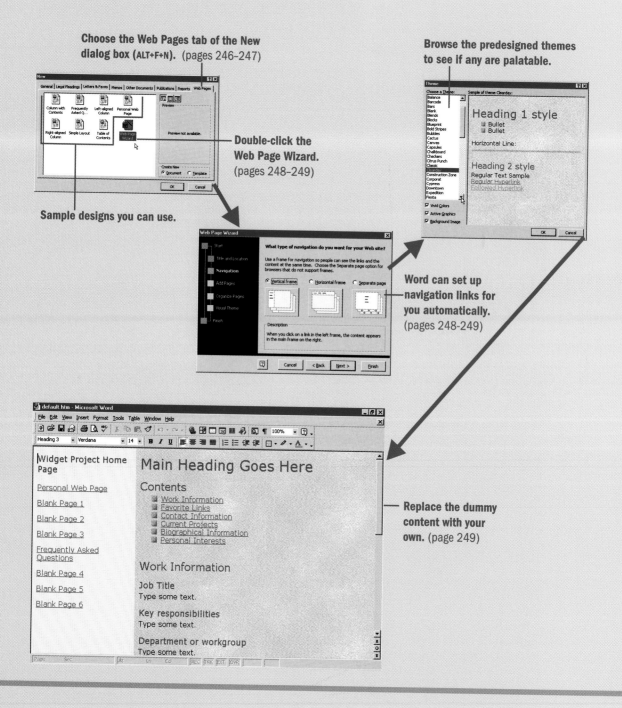

Choose the Web Pages tab of the New dialog box (ALT+F+N). (pages 246–247)

Double-click the Web Page Wizard. (pages 248–249)

Sample designs you can use.

Browse the predesigned themes to see if any are palatable.

Word can set up navigation links for you automatically. (pages 248-249)

Replace the dummy content with your own. (page 249)

Extra! Extra! Design Your Own Newsletter

(For help with Newsletters, visit our Web site at **www.osborne.com/busypeople/word**.)

Insert section breaks to separate headlines from columns of text.

Choose Format | Drop Cap to add fancy initial letters.

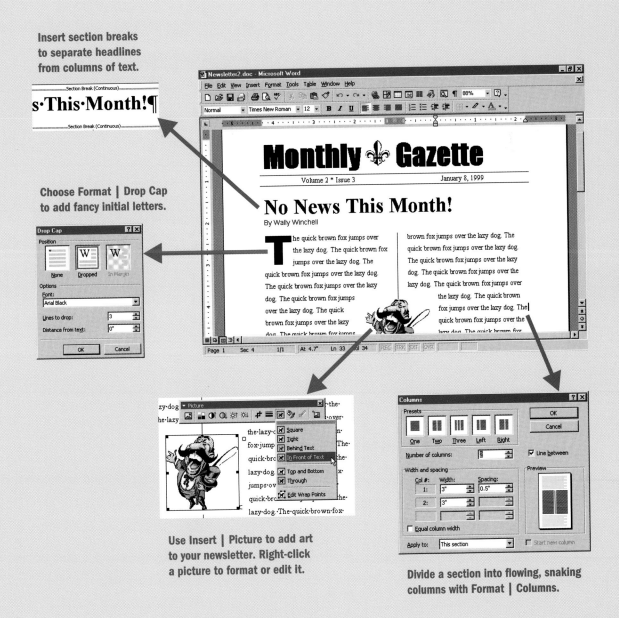

Use Insert | Picture to add art to your newsletter. Right-click a picture to format or edit it.

Divide a section into flowing, snaking columns with Format | Columns.

Online Forms for the Paperless Office (See Chapter 8.)

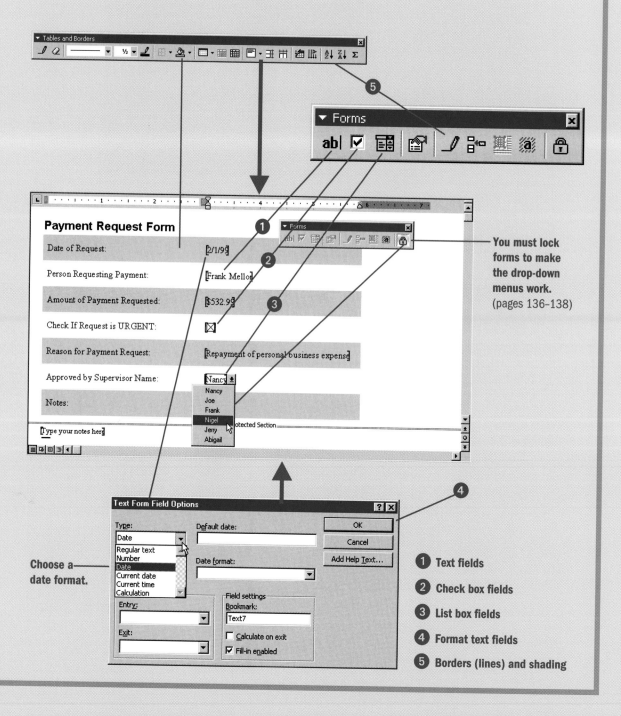

You must lock forms to make the drop-down menus work. (pages 136–138)

Choose a date format.

1 Text fields

2 Check box fields

3 List box fields

4 Format text fields

5 Borders (lines) and shading

Word 2000

for Busy People

The Book to Use When There's No Time to Lose!

Christian Crumlish

OSBORNE

Osborne/**McGraw-Hill**

Berkeley / New York / St. Louis / San Francisco / Auckland / Bogotá
Hamburg / London / Madrid / Mexico City / Milan / Montreal / New Delhi
Panama City / Paris / São Paulo / Singapore / Sydney / Tokyo / Toronto

A Division of The **McGraw·Hill** *Companies*

Osborne/**McGraw-Hill**
2600 Tenth Street
Berkeley, California 94710
U.S.A.

For information on translations or book distributors outside the U.S.A., or to arrange bulk
purchase discounts for sales promotions, premiums, or fund-raisers, please contact
Osborne/**McGraw-Hill** at the above address.

Word 2000 for Busy People

1234567890 DOC DOC 90198765432109

ISBN 0-07-211982-9

Publisher   Brandon A. Nordin
Associate Publisher and Editor-in-Chief   Scott Rogers
Acquisitions Editor   Joanne Cuthbertson
Project Editor   Betsy Manini
Editorial Assistant   Stephane Thomas
Technical Editor   Ellen Finkelstein
Copy Editor   Andy Carroll
Proofreader   Karen Mead, Patty Mon
Indexer   David Heiret
Graphic Artists   Robert Hansen, Brian Wells, Beth Young
Computer Designers   Michelle Galicia, Gary Corrigan, Roberta Steele
Adaptation of Series Design   Peter F. Hancik
Series Designer   Jil Weil
Cover Designer   Damore Johann Design, Inc.
Cover Illustrator/Chapter Opener Illustrator   Robert deMichiell

This book was composed with Corel VENTURA.

To bnisbet

CONTENTS

Acknowledgments

This book would not have been possible without the timely help of Gordon Hurd. Briggs Nisbet helped me work out the original outline of this book and develop the specific approach I take to explaining Word.

I've never met a nicer group of taskmasters than the gang at Osborne. Betsy Manini pulled the whole project together, calmly juggling a thousand conflicting priorities. Andy Carroll's copyedit was exacting without undermining my writing style. Ellen Finkelstein's technical edit clarified nuances that threatened to escape me. Karen Mead did an amazingly thorough job of smoothing the rough spots during her quality check of type and page proofs. Another calm, reassuring presence at Osborne is Stephane Thomas, who sometimes had to deal with reams of manuscript pages flooding in over the e-mail wires. Thanks to all those who got their hands dirty on this project.

I'd never have gotten the opportunity to write this or other Busy People books if it weren't for Joanne Cuthbertson. I'd also especially like to thank the sales, marketing, and publicity people at Osborne, who've really pulled out all the stops with these books and who deserve a lot of credit for the success of the series so far.

As anyone who's ever been around a publishing house can tell you, it's one thing to plan (or re-plan) a beautiful design but quite another thing to implement such a design and make it look as good as—or better than—the sample pages. The art and production team, headed by Jean Butterfield, and including Michelle Galicia, Gary Corrigan, Roberta Steele, Robert Hansen, Brian Wells, and Beth Young, has raised my personal standards for design, layout, and typesetting.

Thanks to the little elves at Microsoft for writing software that needs some explaining. Thanks to Briggs and my friends who cheered me through yet another nearly impossible ordeal. Thanks to my family for their love and patience.

Christian Crumlish

Introduction

How busy have you become lately? Has your job mushroomed with sprawling layers of responsibility? Do you feel like you have almost no time for anything? How often do you hear people say things like "Fax me that draft," "E-mail me those statistics," "Our product release deadline's been moved up due to competitive pressure," and "It took longer than we thought—can you make up the time on your end?"

This book is for people with only a night or a few lunch hours to learn the latest version of Word. (In the words of radio station 1010 WINS in New York City, "Give us 22 minutes; we'll give you the world.") The digital revolution has given with one hand, creating all kinds of efficiencies and organizational wizardry, and taken away with the other, accelerating everyone's expectations and constantly moving the goalposts. The eruption of the Internet, the Web, and in-house intranets has, if anything, picked up the pace.

I Know You're in a Hurry, So . . .

If you're sitting there with an as yet uninstalled copy of Word, start off by flipping to the Appendix where you'll be taken effortlessly through the installation process. If someone has mercifully set up Word for you already, you need not know the Appendix is there.

Let's agree right now to dispense with the traditional computer book preliminaries. You've probably used a mouse, held down two keys at once, and know (or choose not to know) the history of Microsoft. So, we'll cut to the chase. After reading the first few chapters, you'll be able to:

- Create a simple document in Word
- Format your document

- Reuse your work whenever possible
- Produce a simple report

Later chapters will show you how to convert other people's documents, find missing files, create forms, share work on-line, send out mass mailings, create your own web page, and more. As long as you've picked up the basics of Word (and you can pick them up in the first few chapters if you need to), you shouldn't have to work your way through the book chapter by chapter. You'll also be able to skim through it, reading only the parts you need, when you need them. Remember: just because you can do something with Word doesn't mean that you should. Simple is often best, particularly when you are busy. I'll try to remind you of that from time to time.

How Word 2000 Differs from Earlier Versions

A lot of the changes in the new version of Word are refinement, improving the functionality of existing tools, making some more visible, hiding some away. The toolbars have been updated, and I'll admit they're getting better. Both the toolbars and the menus now voluntarily hide away the features you haven't been using (without rendering them inaccessibly), resulting in a slightly more streamlined look as you go along.

Many of the other changes to the program are piecemeal refinements, or part of Microsoft's ongoing Net strategy (such as the establishment of Web Folders to make publishing to intranets or the Web much easier).

Things You Might Want to Know About this Book

You can read this book more or less in any order. I suggest cruising Chapter 1 and reading Chapter 2 first, but you'll be fine no matter how you go. Use the book as a reference. When you're stuck, not sure how to do something, and you know there must be an answer, just pick up the book, zero in on the solution to your problem and put the book down again. Besides the clear, coherent explanations of this all-over-the-map software product, the book includes some special elements to help you get the most out of Word. Here's a quick rundown:

Blueprints

The *Blueprints* at the front of the book depict and demonstrate key task and goals you can accomplish with Word. They will provide you with instant help at a glance, and will point you to the chapter that covers the topic in more depth.

Fast Forward

Every chapter begins with a section called *Fast Forward*. Each of these sections is, in effect, a book within a book—a built-in quick reference guide, summarizing the key tasks explained in the chapter that follows. If you're a fast learner, or somewhat experienced, the Fast Forwards may be the only material you need for some tasks. Written step-by-step, point-by-point, they even include page references to guide you to the more complete information later in the chapter.

Expert Advice

Timesaving tips, techniques, and worthwhile additional ideas are all reported under the rubric of *Expert Advice*. (Look for the lecturing professor-in-a-box.)

EXPERT ADVICE

Force yourself to develop some good habits now, while it's still possible! These notes also give you the big picture and help you plan ahead. From time to time, for example, I'll suggest that you save your document before performing some magical automatic transformation that you might live to regret.

Margin Notes

Look for these in the margins.

Throughout the book, minor asides and cross references appear in *margin notes*.

Shortcuts

These are designed for the busy person—when there's a way to do something that may not be as full-featured as the material in the text, but is faster, *Shortcut* tips will show up in the margin, in a green sidebar.

Cautions

Sometimes it's too easy to plunge ahead and fall down a rabbit hole, resulting in hours of extra work just to get you back to where you were before you went astray. This red sidebar in the margin will warn you before you commit time-consuming mistakes.

Definitions

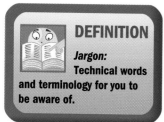

Usually, I'll explain computer- or word-processing jargon in the text, wherever the techno-babble first occurs. But if you encounter words you don't recognize, look for this purple sidebar in the margin. *Definitions* point out important terms you reasonably might not understand. When necessary, they're strict and a little technical, but most of the time they're informal and conversational.

Upgrade Notes

If you've used earlier versions of Word for Windows, such as 2.0, 6.0, or Word 95 (7.0), then be on the look-out for *Upgrade Notes* in the margins. They will tell you when something has changed.

Let's Do It!

Ready? Let's dig into Word 2000 before 2001 arrives!

Incidentally, I'm always happy to hear your reactions to this or any of my other books. You can reach me through Osborne, or on the Net at:

w2k@syx.com

Christian Crumlish

CHAPTER 1

What Every Word User Needs to Know

INCLUDES

- Starting Word and learning the parts of the screen
- Saving time and work when typing
- Background proofreading
- Undoing mistakes
- Saving your work
- Printing
- Exiting Word

Start Word ➡ pp. 4–5

1. Click the Start button.
2. Point to the Programs submenu.
3. Click on Microsoft Word.

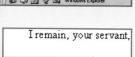

Save Time Typing ➡ pp. 7–8

- Let Word handle the line breaks.
- Press ENTER only when you get to the end of a paragraph.
- Allow Word to finish common words for you, such as days of the week and your own company or name, and fix capitalization problems as you go.
- Let AutoCorrect fix a long list of typical typos and correct additional errors with the background spell checker.

Deal with Proofreading Suggestions ➡ pp. 9–10

1. Right-click on any word marked with a red, wavy line (a green line indicates a grammatical suggestion).
2. Make one of four choices:
    - If the word is correct as is, click Add on the shortcut menu.
    - If the word is spelled incorrectly and the shortcut menu offers the correct spelling as one of the choices, choose the correct spelling. To always replace this misspelling with one of the suggested words, choose a word from the AutoCorrect list on the shortcut menu.
    - For unusual words that are spelled correctly but that you don't want to add to your dictionary, simply choose Ignore All. That word will not be queried for the rest of your Word session.
    - If Word doesn't suggest the correct spelling but you know what it is, just retype the word yourself.

Erase a Character ➡ p. 10

- To the left of the insertion point, press BACKSPACE.
- To the right of the insertion point, press DELETE.

Erase a Word ➡ p. 10

- To the left of the insertion point, press CTRL+BACKSPACE.
- To the right of the insertion point, press CTRL+DELETE.

Undo a Mistake ➡ p. 11

Click the Undo button on the Standard toolbar.

Save Your Work ➡ pp. 11–12

Click the Save button on the Standard toolbar. If this is the first time you're saving this document:

1. Choose where to save the document.
2. Type the filename in the Save As dialog box that appears.
3. Click Save.

Print a Document ➡ p. 13

1. Open the document if it's not already open.
2. Click the Print button on the Standard toolbar.

Exit Word ➡ p. 13

1. Click the Close box in the upper-right corner of the Word window.
2. Click Yes to save any unsaved work, if necessary.

If Word 2000 is not yet installed on your computer, jump now to the Appendix for basic installation instructions. Then come back here once everything's set. If you are new to Windows, look for Mansfield and Weverka's *Windows 98 for Busy People* (Osborne/ McGraw-Hill, 1998). Or, try Christian Crumlish's *Windows 2000 for Busy People* (Osborne/McGraw-Hill, 1999).

As a busy person, you don't have a lot of time to study the niceties of whatever computer programs you have to use. You've got to be able to get the gist of them quickly and start getting work done right away. This chapter covers the things you'll do every time you use Word. If all you need to do for now is fire up Word, type a document, save it, print it, and quit, this chapter will show you how. If you already know the basics for these tasks, feel free to skip ahead to whatever chapter discusses your specific goals for today. You can always come back here if you need a refresher.

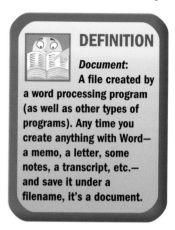

DEFINITION

Document: A file created by a word processing program (as well as other types of programs). Any time you create anything with Word— a memo, a letter, some notes, a transcript, etc.— and save it under a filename, it's a document.

Getting Busy with Word

There are a few routines that you'll follow every time you sit down at your computer to work on a writing project. As soon as you have a comfortable way of performing these steps, they will take up much less of your time, so the sooner we buzz through these basic routines, the better.

By the way, Word 2000 is Y2K compliant, which means it won't contribute to the general breakdown of modern civilization by choking on buggy year-2000 mathematical nonsense. Still, I think the folk at Microsoft may have named it that way this time to give themselves plenty of slack time in their development cycle.

Starting Word

Starting Word is easy. Just follow these steps:

1. Click the Start button.
2. Point to the Programs submenu.
3. Click on Microsoft Word.

If you don't have a Microsoft Word option on your Programs menu, read down the menu for a Microsoft Office submenu or another option that might lead to Word. If you still can't find it, go get the person who installed Word for you and make him show you where it is! You also can make a *shortcut* (an icon on your desktop) for Word or add Word to the main Start menu. For more on these two options, see Chapter 2.

When Word starts, it comes up with a blank document. If the Word window does not fill up the whole screen, click the Maximize button.

You can also start Word or open Word documents with the Office Shortcut bar, which may appear on the screen when you turn the computer on. Ignore it for now. We will discuss it in Chapter 2.

EXPERT ADVICE

To reopen a Word document you've worked on recently from within Windows, select **Start | Documents** and choose the document from the menu that pops up. Similarly, from within Word you can select the File menu and then choose to open one of the most recent files from the bottom of the menu.

Taking a Look Around

Let's take a look at the basic Word screen (see Figure 1.1). You can see the normal elements typical of every program that runs under Windows on the screen, such as the taskbar at the bottom of the screen and the title bar and menu bar at the top. In addition, you see many specific Word elements, which are there either to give you information or to make certain procedures automatic.

UPGRADE NOTE The Standard and Formatting toolbars now show up squeezed together into one row, so not all the buttons are shown onscreen. However, it's easy to get at the buttons that aren't showing with the More Buttons button at the right end of each toolbar. To learn more about Word's toolbars see "Changing Your Toolbars" in Chapter 2.

- The Standard and Formatting toolbars help you create, edit, and format your documents.
- The Ruler helps you set margins and indents.
- The typing area is where you do (and see) all your work. The more room you have there, the better.
- The insertion point shows you where the next character you type will appear.
- The end-of-document marker marks (surprise!) the end of the document. It moves down as you type.

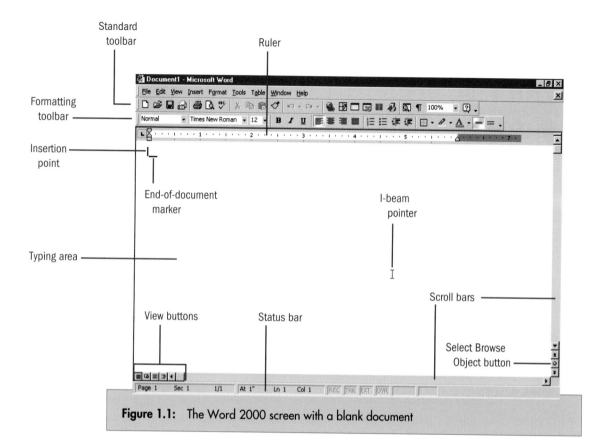

Standard toolbar

Ruler

Formatting toolbar

Insertion point

End-of-document marker

I-beam pointer

Typing area

Scroll bars

View buttons

Status bar

Select Browse Object button

Figure 1.1:   The Word 2000 screen with a blank document

- The I-beam pointer can be used to move the insertion point and make selections.
- The scroll bars, as in all Windows programs, enable you to get to parts of the document that are temporarily off the screen.
- The View buttons allow you to see your documents in a variety of ways.
- The Select Browse Object button provides an easy way to move quickly to a certain page or object in your document.
- The status bar tells you useful information about your document, such as what page you're on and whether you're in Insert or Overtype mode (more on this in Chapter 2).

The Crux of the Matter: Typing

The whole purpose of having a program such as Word on your computer is to make it possible and, ideally, easy for you to type and print documents. You have probably typed before, so there most likely won't be any surprises here for you. Every new version of Word comes out with additional "IntelliSense" features that attempt to correct errors, help you format your documents, and even anticipate your intentions and complete tasks for you. Some of these features are still in a fairly crude (if not intrusive) stage.

Some of the shortcuts and automatic features that can help streamline your typing jobs are

- AutoCorrect, which can correct typing errors and change abbreviations into full text
- AutoText, which you can use to store boilerplate text or anything else you want to insert into your document after typing just a few characters
- AutoFormat, which can make systematic changes or improvements to your document's layout
- Automatic proofreading, which can help you notice errors and fix them yourself

As with any other word processor, there are also a few basic rules you have to follow, just as in typing up any document. For example, don't press ENTER when you get near the end of a line (as you would with a typewriter). Let Word handle the line breaks for you. That way, when you make changes, you won't have to redo the line breaks yourself. Similarly, don't line up columns of text by inserting spaces. Instead, use tabs, tables, or columns, depending on the text involved. Some people go so far as to eschew typing a tab at the beginning of each paragraph; they use the indent markers on the Ruler to create first-line indents, but that's probably a little hard-core computery for most people. Oh, one other difference from old typewriter-based touch-typing is that you don't add two spaces after the end of a sentence.

One of the most important rules of thumb in word processing is that you shouldn't do anything that the computer can do for you. This is not simply to make life easier, but also because the computer can often do a better job of keeping things consistent.

EXPERT ADVICE

Pressing ENTER starts a new paragraph. Pressing ENTER twice is a quick-and-dirty way to space the paragraphs out. In longer documents, it's more efficient to use Format | Paragraph to control paragraph spacing.

If you're in the mood for a brief, painless exercise, you can type up the beginning of a short set of meeting notes. To follow along, use the blank document that came up when you started Word:

1. In your blank document, type the following text:

    Ms. Hoople opened the meeting by reminding us all that we are entering the busiest time of year. She then reviewed the minutes of the previous meeting.

2. Press ENTER twice after the second sentence to start a new paragraph spaced out from the first. Compare your document to what you see in Figure 1.2.

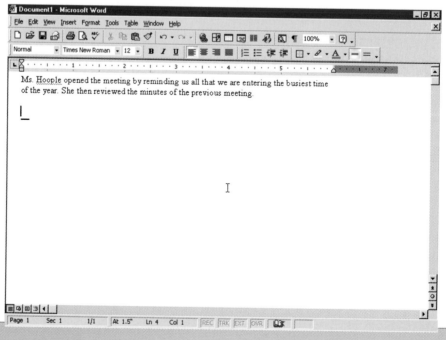

Figure 1.2: The beginning of some meeting notes

Background Spell Checking

What's that red wavy line under the name "Hoople?" you might be wondering. It indicates a word that Word's automatic background spell checking does not recognize.

You may regard background spell checking as a godsend or as a royal pain. When you're in a hurry and you don't have time for a conventional spell checking session, the automatic checker finds your typos and allows you to correct them on the fly. For more involved documents, however, you may find the constant queries distracting and you might prefer to do all your spell checking at once, when you've completed an entire draft. While I would normally recommend that you do your writing in one session and your editing and proofreading in another, the decision here is a matter of personal preference.

For now, I'll show you how to respond to a spelling query from the background spell checker. When you notice that Word has used its squiggly underline to call your attention to a suspect word, either edit (or retype) it yourself manually or right-click on the word. If you right-click on it, a shortcut menu pops up, offering suggested spellings along with the options to ignore the unusually spelled word or add it to the dictionary.

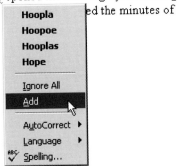

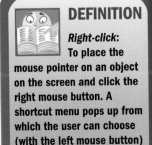

DEFINITION

Right-click:
To place the mouse pointer on an object on the screen and click the right mouse button. A shortcut menu pops up from which the user can choose (with the left mouse button) a command.

In Chapter 2, I'll show you how to turn off background spell and grammar checking when you don't want to deal with it.

- For a proper name such as Hoople (or other unusual word that's in fact correct), choose Add so that you won't have to explain the word to Word again.
- If the word is spelled incorrectly and the shortcut menu offers the correct spelling as one of the choices, choose the correct spelling. To always replace this misspelling with one of the

suggested words, choose a word from the AutoCorrect list on the shortcut menu.

- For unusual words that are spelled correctly but that you don't want to add to your dictionary, simply choose Ignore All. That word will not be queried for the rest of your Word session.

- If Word doesn't suggest the correct spelling but you know what it is, just retype the word yourself.

Creating a Paragraph

Now let's continue our exercise by adding more text to the meeting notes. Follow these steps:

1. In a new paragraph, type this text:

   Following this, she invited the department heads to report on their progress.

2. Press ENTER twice to start a new paragraph (remember, you press ENTER only when you get to the end of the paragraph). Then type this:

   Mr. Stencil, the head of the supply department, reported that the company will run out of legal pads by next Tuesday if we don't order more soon.

3. Notice that Word finishes the word Tuesday for you (if you let it) using the new AutoComplete feature. To accept Word's suggestion, press ENTER when the word Tuesday appears. Press ENTER twice when you get to the end of the third paragraph. Your document should look similar to Figure 1.3.

Correcting Little Mistakes

For more complicated text changes and corrections, see Chapter 3.

Gone are the days when a single typo meant having to retype an entire document. With BACKSPACE and DELETE, you can click right next to your error and erase it quickly (or even rub out entire words at once):

To Erase	Press
A character to the left of the insertion point	BACKSPACE
A character to the right of the insertion point	DELETE
A word (or portion of a word) to the left of the insertion point	CTRL+BACKSPACE
A word (or portion of a word) to the right of the insertion point	CTRL+DELETE

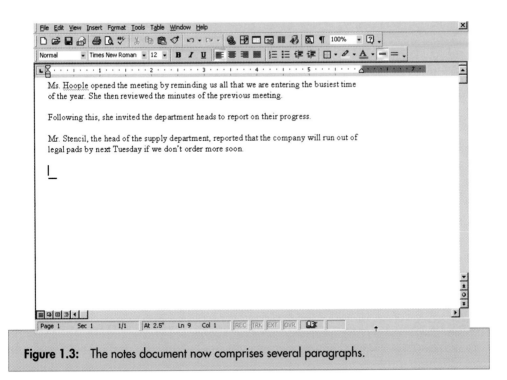

Figure 1.3: The notes document now comprises several paragraphs.

Undoing Big Mistakes

Another benefit you derive from creating documents with a computer is that you can go back and undo big mistakes. Word keeps track of the state of your document as you work on it and can restore your work to a previous state (most of the time). If you realize you've done something you really want to undo, just click the Undo button on the Standard toolbar.

Saving Documents

When a document is completed, you need to save it. In fact, to be safe, you should save your work regularly, even before it's done. You can save your document at any point by clicking the Save button on the Standard toolbar.

The first time you save a document, Word suggests saving it in the My Documents folder, which may or may not be the best place for it. Select a different folder by clicking the drop-down Save In list, or by selecting one of the folders to the left of the dialog box.

For more on how to use the Undo feature and how to undo several steps at once, see Chapter 3.

SHORTCUT
You can always press CTRL+Z to undo your last action without having to take your hands away from the keyboard.

Pressing ENTER in a dialog box (such as the Save As dialog box) has the same effect as clicking the highlighted button (in this case, the Save button).

You need to name your new document (unless you want to use the suggested filename, which is based on the first sentence in it). Word allows long, descriptive filenames, so type something like **Meeting (June 3)** and press ENTER. (Yes, you can include spaces in filenames.)

When you click the Save button (see Figure 1.4) to save a document the second time and thereafter, Word simply updates the saved document without asking you for a filename.

> **CAUTION**
>
> Even though Word's AutoRestore feature automatically saves a backup of your document every ten minutes, it is no substitute for using the Save command. (This may be why they changed the name from AutoSave with the release of Word 97). The AutoRestore backup will survive if your computer crashes, but if you quit Word the normal way, it will be deleted.

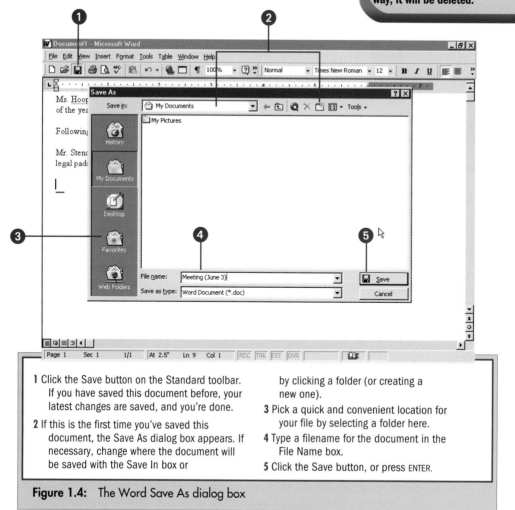

1 Click the Save button on the Standard toolbar. If you have saved this document before, your latest changes are saved, and you're done.

2 If this is the first time you've saved this document, the Save As dialog box appears. If necessary, change where the document will be saved with the Save In box or by clicking a folder (or creating a new one).

3 Pick a quick and convenient location for your file by selecting a folder here.

4 Type a filename for the document in the File Name box.

5 Click the Save button, or press ENTER.

Figure 1.4: The Word Save As dialog box

Printing Your Work

Although some documents nowadays are made and passed around from computer to computer and are never committed to paper (hard copy, in computer-geek lingo), most of us still use computers as typewriters, and most documents still get printed out.

This may seem obvious, but from within Word you have to open a document before you can print it. After that, printing a document is a simple matter of clicking the Print button.

By the way, I purposely presented the information on saving before I discussed printing, because you should get into the habit of always saving your work before printing it. You never know when something will go wrong during the printing process, and you don't want to risk losing your work because you forgot to save it.

See Chapter 10 for more on sharing documents and Chapter 11 for other alternatives to printing.

SHORTCUT

Press **CTRL+P** and then press **ENTER** to print your document without lifting your fingers from the keys.

Exiting Word

Once you've typed something up, saved it, and printed it out (and sure, maybe made some changes, saved it again, printed it out again, made some more changes, and so on), it's time to quit Word. To do so, pull down the File menu and select Exit.

If you try to exit Word after making unsaved changes to a document, Word first asks if you want to save your changes before exiting. Generally, you will want to save the changes, and you should click Yes. If you're not sure about saving changes, it's usually safer to click Cancel and review things instead of clicking No and possibly losing important work. No matter how busy you are, rushing and accidentally losing your work will ruin your day. Unsaved work is harder to recover than deleted work.

UPGRADE NOTE In Word 2000, each open document gets its own separate window (Mac style), so the Close box in the upper-right corner of each window now just closes the current document and exits Word only if the window is the last document open.

EXPERT ADVICE

You can also right-click any document icon in Windows and choose Print from the menu that pops up. Windows automatically launches Word (if it's not running already), opens the document, and prints it.

There's More . . .

There! In one relatively short chapter you've picked up all the main points of Word. There's lots more that you'll learn, but your word processing sessions will always revolve around the lines of these basic steps: start a new document, type it, save it, print it, close it, and similar variations. So, where to go from here?

Chapter 2 explains some simple things you can do (and you'll only have to do them this one time) to make Word easier and more comfortable to use. If you're so busy that you can't even spare a little tinkering time, you can skip ahead. Chapter 3 elaborates on how you can use Word right out of the box to edit and format a document.

Stuff to Do Once to Make Your Life Easier

INCLUDES

- Choosing your default font
- Word's new self-customizing toolbars
- Establishing your preferences
- Controlling the proofreading feature
- Specifying the default folder where Word should save your work
- Adding a Word icon to your Windows desktop
- Listing Word on your Start menu
- Hiding the Office Assistant

Change the Default Font ➡ pp. 20–21

1. Select Format | Font.
2. On the Font tab, choose the font and size you want.
3. Click the Default button to make your choice the default font.
4. Click Yes.

Customize a Toolbar ➡ pp. 21–23

1. Click the More Buttons button at the right edge of the toolbar you wish to customize.
2. Click the Add Or Remove Buttons button.
3. Select a button you want to add or remove from the toolbar.
4. Repeat steps 2 and 3 until the toolbar looks the way you want.

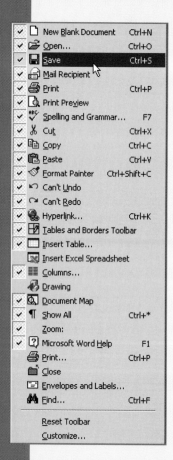

Return a Toolbar to Its Original Settings ➡ p. 23

1. Click on the More Buttons button at the right end of the toolbar.
2. Select Add Or Remove Buttons | Reset Toolbar.

Change the Default Save Folder ➡ p. 26

1. Select Tools | Options.
2. Click the File Locations tab.
3. Click the Modify button.
4. Select (or create and select) a folder and click OK.
5. Click OK.

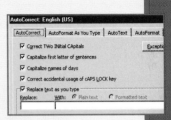

Specify Your AutoCorrect Preferences ➡ pp. 26–27

1. Select Tools | AutoCorrect.
2. Specify your preferences on the AutoCorrect tab, and then click OK.

Put a Word Icon on Your Desktop ➡ pp. 27–28

1. Select Start | Find | Files Or Folders.
2. Type **winword.exe** and press ENTER. If you have more than one hard drive or partition on your computer, be sure to either choose the correct drive or choose My Computer to search all of them.
3. Click the Winword program icon (the blue *W*) and drag it onto the desktop.
4. Click on the label, type **Word**, and press ENTER.

List Word on the Windows Start Menu ➡ p. 29

1. Select Start | Find | Files Or Folders.
2. Type **winword.exe** and press ENTER. If you have more than one hard drive or partition on your computer, be sure to either choose the correct drive or choose My Computer to search all of them.
3. Drag the Winword program icon (the blue *W*) onto the Start button.

If your idea of easy is to just accept things the way they are and make the best of them, you may want to skip over this chapter. But if you're willing to take ten minutes to make Word easier to use from now on and save yourself hours of twiddling time in the future, stay with me.

I'll take you step by step through some simple things you can do to make Word easier and more comfortable for you to use. You won't need to understand everything you do in this chapter, but you'll be happy you took the time (and you'll only have to do these things once).

Starting Off with Your Favorite Font Every Time

You may have noticed by now that every time you start Word or create a new document you get a standard font and font size (as well as a standard page setup, and so on). If you like the way the default font and font size look, and you're happy with the documents produced with them, you don't need to change the defaults—you can skip to the next section. If you like the defaults, just leave them alone. If you don't, you have to change them "by hand."

If you find yourself frequently changing default settings, it's time to set up new defaults. You can change any of Word's default settings from its original selection (the *default* default) to anything else, making your choice the default from that point forward.

Which brings us back to the default font. Out of the box and without any special templates loaded, Word uses a default font and size of Times New Roman, 12 points (see Figure 2.1).

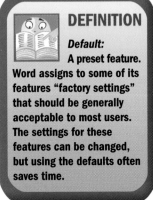

DEFINITION

Default:
A preset feature. Word assigns to some of its features "factory settings" that should be generally acceptable to most users. The settings for these features can be changed, but using the defaults often saves time.

Deciding on a Font

Most people prefer 12 points as a basic font size. For one thing, it's easier on the eyes. For another, it's closer to the size of the characters produced by most traditional typewriters, which still seems to matter (though it probably won't to our children).

The drop-down font list box shows the current font at the insertion point

The drop-down font size list box shows the current size

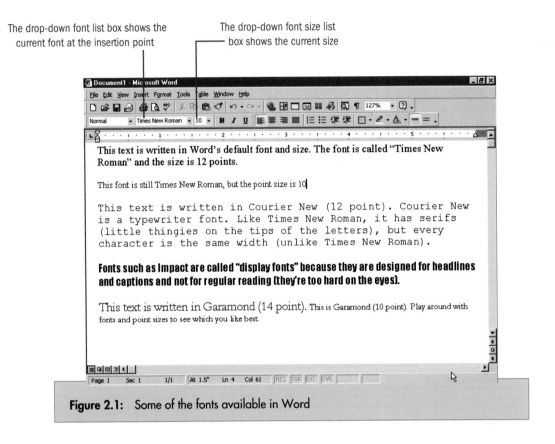

Figure 2.1: Some of the fonts available in Word

Times New Roman is an acceptable typeface for most people. It has serifs, so it's easy to read. However, some people prefer a more typewritten look, especially for first drafts, and may therefore want to use a font like Courier New. You can choose to type with any available font, if there's one you like better. For instance, I like my Garamond font quite a lot. However, it might not translate well to another person's computer (and it doesn't look all that great on the screen), so I stick with 12-point Courier New as my default font.

Not every computer has the same fonts installed (although Windows comes with a few standard fonts, including Times New Roman, Courier New, Wingdings, and a few others). If you open a document on a computer that doesn't have one of the document's fonts, Word substitutes a different font.

DEFINITION

Serifs:
The little thingamajigs on the tips of characters in some fonts, traditionally considered to make a typeface easier to read. Fonts without serifs are referred to by the French term "sans serif." (Not to be confused with Robin Hood's nemesis, the Serif of Nottingham.)

EXPERT ADVICE

Whenever you find yourself doing the same thing repeatedly on the computer, especially in the same type of situation, look for a shortcut or a way to achieve your results automatically. Computers like doing the same thing over and over. Most people don't.

Setting the Default Font

Once you've decided which font you most like working with, you can leave things as they are (if 12-point Times New Roman is fine) or you can set up your new default font. It's easy. Just follow these steps:

1. Start a new document by clicking the New button (the first one on the Standard toolbar).

2. Select Format | Font.

3. Scroll through the Font list box to choose your font. You can select different fonts and see how they look in the Preview area.

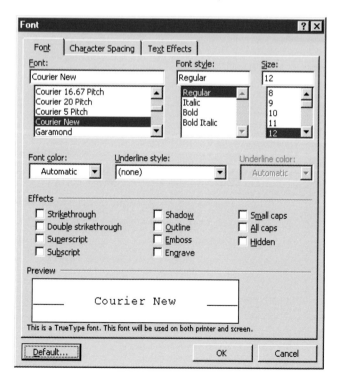

4. Scroll through the Size list box and select a font size. Again, make sure things look OK in the Preview area.

5. When you are satisfied with the font and size, click the Default button. Then click Yes to confirm the change.

Once you're finished, Word displays a dialog box asking you if you're sure you want to make this change. It also tells you that the change will affect all new documents based on the normal template (but there's no need to worry about that part). Just make sure the font and size are correct and then click Yes. There, you've done it. That wasn't so painful, was it?

From now on, every new document you start will get the default font and size you just assigned. Of course, you can always override the default and specify whatever font you want for a whole document or for any selected portion of a document.

Changing Your Toolbars

The idea behind toolbars is to keep the most useful features no more than a single mouse click away, to save you from having to hunt through pull-down menus and so on. It's a great idea, but it doesn't always work that way. First of all, there's so much happening on the screen that all those buttons can be confusing. Second, the toolbar buttons all have little icons on them that are supposed to be perfectly clear, but many of them make no sense at all to a normal person. Third, and most important, the collection of commands assembled on the toolbars is not necessarily the most useful assortment for regular users.

Some of the buttons are there to help sell Word, by illustrating its most advanced or fancy-looking features. Some of those features are things you may never use. Others are features you'll use, but certainly not every day. It defeats the purpose of shortcuts to put arcane features in with saving, printing, and so on.

One of the best new features of Word is the way the toolbars now minimize themselves and try to stay out of the way. Word leaves infrequently used buttons off the toolbars. They're not inaccessible;

Word's menus are also now more responsive, hiding unused features. Just hold your pointer over the down arrows at the bottom of the menu to get the entire menu to pop up, with the formerly hidden choices suddenly visible. If you choose one of the hidden features, it starts showing up on the regular menu again.

you can always click the More Buttons button at the right end of a toolbar and choose any of the missing buttons:

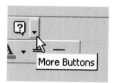

If you do want to deliberately change a toolbar, it's very easy to do now. Again, start by clicking that More Buttons button. Then choose the button called Add Or Remove Buttons at the bottom of the menu that appears. This will bring up a new menu showing all the likely buttons for this toolbar, with the included buttons checked (see Figure 2.2).

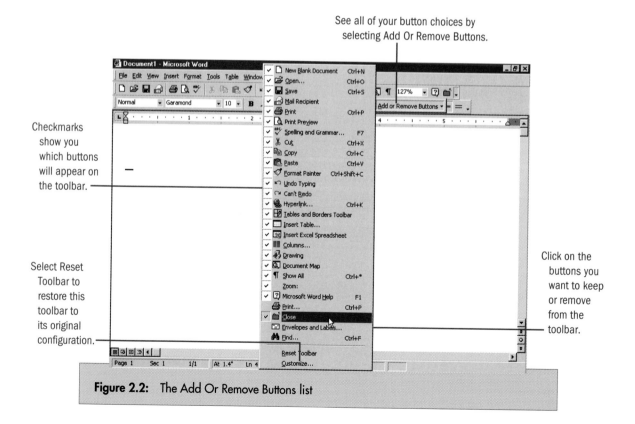

Figure 2.2: The Add Or Remove Buttons list

To add or remove a button, select it. Repeat this process for each button you want to add or remove.

If you wind up changing your mind about your new toolbars and buttons, restoring Word's default toolbars is as easy as customizing them. Simply click on that More Buttons button again and select Add Or Remove Buttons | Reset Toolbars. Back to normal!

Getting Word to Do Things Your Way

The settings described in this section are somewhat a matter of personal preference, so I won't dictate to you exactly what to do. I'll just lay out the options (and their ramifications) and let you decide for yourself. The title of this chapter promises that you will only have to do these things once (set it and forget it), but of course you might change your mind later, in which case you'd need to perform these actions again.

The Options dialog box is Word's nerve center for custom settings. It sports ten different tabs, each of which governs some aspect of Word's setup. Many other dialog boxes in Word (such as the Print dialog box) have an Options button that leads directly to the appropriate tab of the Options dialog box. Here I'll walk you through some of the essential settings.

To begin with, start Word again if you haven't already. Then select Tools | Options. This brings up the Options dialog box (see Figure 2.3).

Losing the Horizontal Scroll Bar

If the View tab is not the one selected, choose it now. In the Window box, consider unchecking Horizontal Scroll Bar. You won't need it much. The idea is to have your text fit on the screen anyway.

Turning Off Background Spell Checking

Whether to allow automatic background spell checking to go on is for you to decide, based on how you prefer to work. Do you prefer to correct typos as they occur, or does that break your concentration? If you fall into the latter category, you can turn off automatic spell checking on the Spelling & Grammar tab in the Options dialog box.

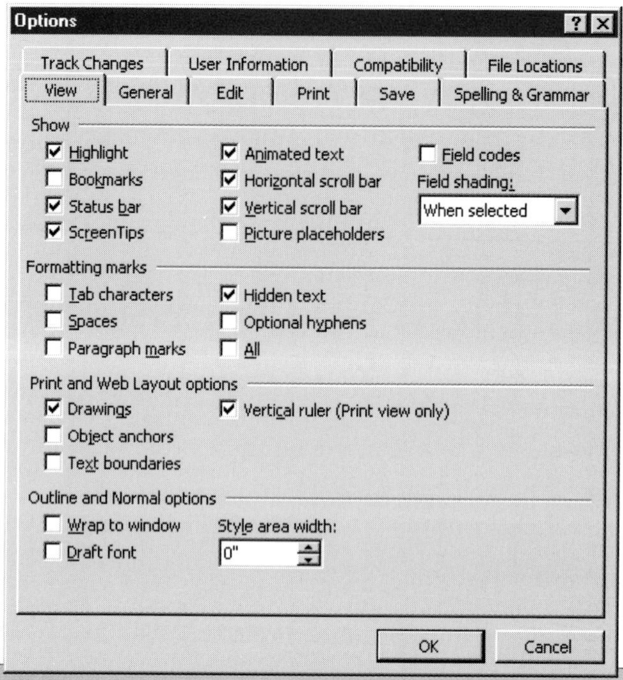

Figure 2.3: The Options dialog box (with the View tab selected)

Click the Spelling & Grammar tab. Then uncheck Check Spelling As You Type. Alternatively, you could check Hide Spelling Errors In This Document, which instructs Word to continue to check your spelling as you type, but to hide the wavy underlines. When you're ready to fix any spelling errors that may have accumulated, you can return to the Options dialog box and uncheck the Hide Spelling Errors In This Document option.

EXPERT ADVICE

If you turn off automatic spell checking and later turn it back on, Word then points out any suspicious words it finds, so from the user's point of view, there's no real difference between the two approaches.

Controlling Text Replacement

Click the Edit tab. There are several editing options you might want to think about changing. First, there's Typing Replaces Selection. Personally, I keep this on because I find it useful, though it can be frustrating to accidentally replace a selection because you brushed the keyboard. Then again, there's always Undo.

Next there's the automatic word selection option, When Selecting, Automatically Select Entire Word. I find this frustrating when I want to select just part of a word, so I turn it off, but many people like it because it makes it much easier to select whole words. It's up to you. You can always double-click a word to select it, either way.

I check Use The INS Key For Paste, not so much because I plan to use the INSERT key to do my pasting, but because I find it so annoying if I accidentally go into Overtype mode (by pressing INSERT when I mean to press DELETE or HOME, for example) and then start running roughshod over my precious text. Yes, you can still go into Overtype if you want, even if you reassign the INSERT key. You can do it by double-clicking the OVR box in the status bar at the bottom of the screen.

I keep Use Smart Cut And Paste checked, but it can occasionally add to your work. This feature mainly deals with stray spaces when you cut and paste text. It's useful most of the time, except when you don't want a space between the inserted text and the text into which you inserted it.

Specifying Your Save and Backup Preferences

Click the Save tab. I don't keep Always Create Backup Copy checked because I dislike having two copies of every document floating around, but if you're worried about losing your work, this is a good fail-safe technique. Allow Fast Saves is a trade-off. I use it because it saves time, but it does result in bigger files. If you're worried about your storage space, uncheck it. For the Save Autorecover Info Every option, choose a nice small number of minutes, such as 10 or 15.

Be sure to save regularly no matter what. Every time you pause or take a break, save your work!

Undo is covered in Chapter 1, and Redo and Multiple Undo are explained in Chapter 3.

UPGRADE NOTE New Save options include the ability to change the document format Word saves in by default and a check box for restricting the features saved in a document to those recognizable by Word 97. Both of these choices will be discussed further in Chapter 6.

EXPERT ADVICE

AutoRecover, found on the Save tab, is a routine that helps if Word or Windows crashes. If that happens, Word restores the most recent auto-saved copy of your document the next time you run Word. In normal circumstances, that backup is deleted when you quit Word, so it's no substitute for saving your document.

Controlling Where to Save Your Documents

As you saw in Chapter 1, Word suggests the My Documents folder when you save a document for the first time. This is a fine place to put documents (obviously), but you may prefer to send your documents elsewhere by default.

To choose a different default folder for documents, click the File Locations tab in the Options dialog box and select Documents in the list. Then click the Modify button. This brings up the Modify Location dialog box, a variation on the familiar Open and Save dialog boxes.

You can change where the dialog box is pointing with the Up One Level button or by using the Look In list, and make a new folder anywhere with the Create New Folder button. When you've chosen the folder you want as your default from now on, click OK.

When you're done with the Options dialog box, click OK.

DEFINITION

AutoCorrect: Word's AutoCorrect feature corrects the spelling of commonly mistyped words as soon as you press enter, tab, or the spacebar, or type any punctuation marks. You add new pairs of words (misspelled and corrected) in the AutoCorrect dialog box.

Choosing Your AutoCorrect Preferences

Some preferences not available from the Options dialog box are those for AutoCorrect. These must be set by selecting Tools | AutoCorrect to access the AutoCorrect dialog box (see Figure 2.4). The main function of this dialog box is to enable you to add new AutoCorrect pairs to the list (typically misspelled words, such as "teh," and their correct spellings, such as "the"). It also gives you fine control over how and when AutoCorrect works. When you've specified all your preferences, click OK.

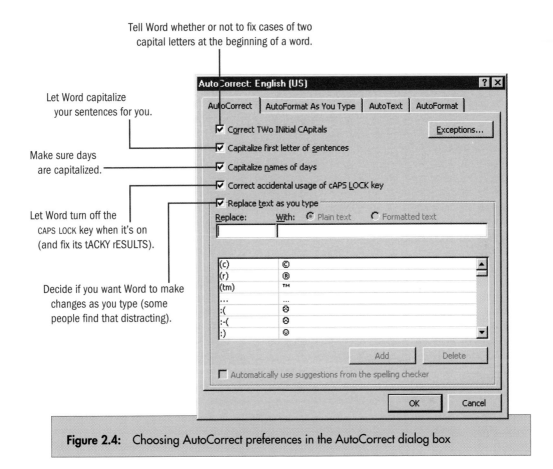

Tell Word whether or not to fix cases of two capital letters at the beginning of a word.

Let Word capitalize your sentences for you.

Make sure days are capitalized.

Let Word turn off the CAPS LOCK key when it's on (and fix its tACKY rESULTS).

Decide if you want Word to make changes as you type (some people find that distracting).

Figure 2.4:   Choosing AutoCorrect preferences in the AutoCorrect dialog box

Putting Word One Click Away

If you use Word all the time, you shouldn't have to fumble around with two or three levels of submenus just to get the darn thing started. Two convenient places to stow shortcuts to Word are on your desktop and in your Start menu.

Putting a Word Icon on Your Windows Desktop

If you use Word all the time, you may want to have a Word icon live on your desktop to make the program easy to start. First, exit

Winword (or Winword.exe) is the actual name of the Word for Windows program.

Word, or at least minimize the window. Now you have to find the Word program. Most likely it's in the Winword subfolder of the MSOffice folder. If so, you can get to it by double-clicking My Computer, then C:, then MSOffice, and then Winword.

But the easiest way to get to Word is to use the Find feature on the Start menu.

1. Click the Start button.

2. Point to Find.

3. Click Files or Folders.

4. In the Find: All Files dialog box that appears, type **winword.exe** and press ENTER. Windows quickly finds the Winword program icon (as well as the folder it's in and some other related icons). If you have more than one hard drive or partition on your computer, you can make sure that you'll find it by selecting My Computer in the Look In list and not just one drive.

5. Click the Winword icon (the blue *W*) and drag it onto the desktop to create a shortcut.

6. An icon called Shortcut to Winword appears, with the little arrow-in-a-box that indicates a Windows 98 (or 95) shortcut. Click on the label under the icon, type **Word**, and press ENTER.

Now you've got a handy desktop icon for Word. You also can make desktop shortcuts for important documents using the same method described here. Just search for the filename of the document you want.

EXPERT ADVICE

If you ever want to double-click a desktop icon that's obscured by several open windows, click the Show Desktop icon on the Quick Launch portion of the Windows 98 taskbar, or right-click on the taskbar first and select Minimize All Windows to get a clear shot at the desktop.

Listing Word on the Windows Start Menu

Another handy place to put a Word shortcut is directly on the Start menu. Once again, you need to get to the program icon, either by hunting for it through folders or (as I recommend) by using the Find feature from the Start menu. Once you've got your Winword icon visible, click it and drag it onto the Start button.

Cleaning Up Your Workspace

All the Office programs try to be as helpful as possible, easy to find and full of suggestions. When the shortcuts and tips are on the money, it's all worthwhile, but other times you may get tired of the extra clutter on your screen. Fortunately, it's easy to tuck away two of the more obtrusive features: the obsequious Office Assistant and the floating Office Shortcut bar.

Closing the Office Assistant Window

When you start Word for the first time, the Office Assistant—a small, animated paper clip—appears in the lower right of the screen. Whenever you ask for help, the Office Assistant opens. Tired of getting advice from a paper clip? Right-click on the Office Assistant and select Choose Assistant from the shortcut menu. You can choose another helper from the Gallery. If you need help with a dialog box, click on the Assistant and it will offer help.

If and when you get tired of seeing the Assistant (or of ceding that much space on the screen for the kibitzing and advice), you can close it by right-clicking on the Assistant and choosing Hide. If you want to bring the little feller back, click the Microsoft Word Help button on

---

EXPERT ADVICE

A typical Office installation puts New Office Document and Open Office Document shortcuts on your Start menu (or, more particularly, on the submenu). If you never use them, you can remove these items by choosing Start | Settings | Taskbar & Start Menu, selecting the Start Menu Programs tab, and then clicking on the Remove button. Select the offenders and click Remove. Or you can simply ignore them.

the Standard toolbar or press F1 and the Assistant appears, asking what kind of help you want.

Turning Off the Office Shortcut Bar

Depending on how Word was installed, you may have noticed the Office Shortcut Bar on the right-hand side of your screen (or elsewhere if you've moved it).

If it's not there, you can run it by choosing Start | Programs | Office Tools | Microsoft Office Shortcut Bar (if you want it). Now, you may find that this toolbar comes in handy, enabling you to start some of your favorite programs or open their documents directly; personally, I find it to be a bit of overkill, and I was relieved when it did not come up automatically after I installed Word 2000, although this outcome appears to differ from one installation to the next (sometimes based on the setup of previous versions of Word). How many different shortcut menus and taskbars and toolbars does one desktop need? So I generally leave the thing turned off. The Office Shortcut bar is not pushy, though. When you quit it (right-click and choose Exit), it asks if you ever want to see it again.

EXPERT ADVICE

Here's one way to fit the Office Shortcut Bar on your screen without giving up precious real estate: click on the shortcut bar's Office logo and choose Customize. Select the View tab and select Auto Fit Into Title Bar Area. This works best if you place the shortcut bar at the top of the screen. Now it fits snuggly within your environment (and only becomes a problem if you have really long document titles).

There's More . . .

What do you want to do now? You're ready to roll. Your copy of Word is set up for your convenience, and you know all the basics of creating documents. From here on out, you should be able to skip through the book, picking out only the information you need right now.

CHAPTER 3

Everyday Formatting and Editing

INCLUDES

- Moving around your document
- Going to a specific place in a document
- Selecting sections of text
- Formatting characters and paragraphs
- Using the Format Painter to copy formatting
- Editing with drag-and-drop and with cut-and-paste
- Finding and replacing text
- Undoing multiple actions

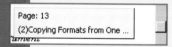

Move Around the Document
with the Vertical Scroll Bar ➡ p. 39

- Click the scroll arrow at the top or bottom of the scroll bar.
- Click the scroll bar above or below the scroll box.
- Drag the scroll box to a new position.
- Click the Select Browse Object button to choose a document element, such as pages (the default), comments, tables, headings, and so on, by which to browse the document.
- Click the Previous Object (by default, it's called Previous Page) button to jump to the previous specified object.
- Click the Next Object (Next Page, by default) button to jump to the next specified object.

Browse for a Specific Object ➡ p. 39

1. Click the Select Browse Object button.
2. Choose a document object: edits, headings, graphics, tables, fields, endnotes, footnotes, comments, sections, or (the default) pages.
3. Click the Previous or Next button to jump through your document, skipping from heading to heading or from table to table, etc.

Go to a Specific Page ➡ pp. 39–41

1. Double-click the left end of the status bar, press CTRL+G, or click the Select Browse Object button and select Go To.
2. In the Go To What box, type a page number.
3. Press ENTER.

Go to a Specific Word ➡ p. 41

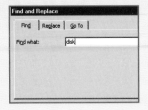

1. Double-click the left end of the status bar and move to the Find tab, press CTRL+F, or click the Select Browse Object button and select Find.
2. In the Find What box, type the word you're thinking of.
3. Press ENTER.
4. Repeat if necessary.
5. Click Cancel.

Select a Section of Text ➡ p. 42

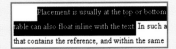

- Click and drag to select any amount of text.
- Double-click to select a word.
- Triple-click to select a paragraph.
- Click the left margin area to select a line.
- CTRL+click the left margin area to select the entire document.
- SHIFT+click or use SHIFT with the arrow keys (or HOME, END, PAGEUP or PAGEDOWN) to extend a selection.

Format a Character ➡ pp. 43–45

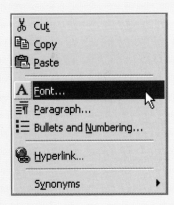

1. Make a selection.
2. Point to the selected text, right-click, and select Font.
3. Choose a font.
4. Choose a size.
5. Select a font style, underline, color, or effect, if desired.
6. Click OK.

Indent a Paragraph ➡ pp. 45–47

1. Place the pointer to the far left of the document.
2. Double-click to select a paragraph, or triple-click to select the entire document.
3. Adjust the indentation pointers on the ruler to add a first-line indent, a hanging indent, or to indent the entire document.

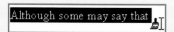

Copy Formatting from Place to Place ➡ p. 47

1. Place the insertion point in (or select) the text that has the formatting you want to copy.
2. Click the Format Painter button on the toolbar. (To apply the format to more than one selection, double-click the Format Painter button.)
3. Drag the Format Painter pointer across the text you want to apply the copied formatting to. (If you've double-clicked the Format Painter button, apply the copied formatting repeatedly and then, when you're done, click the Format Painter button again to turn it off.)

Remove a Selection ➡ pp. 48–49

- To throw a selection away for good, press DELETE.
- To remove a selection from its original location and save it for pasting elsewhere, click the Cut button, or press CTRL+X.

Move a Selection a Short Distance ➡ p. 49

1. Click the selection and hold down the mouse button.
2. Drag the drag-and-drop pointer until the dotted insertion point is located where you want the text to go.
3. Release the mouse button.

Move a Selection Anywhere ➡ p. 49

1. Select the text.
2. To move the selection, press CTRL+X or choose Edit | Cut. To copy the selection, press CTRL+C or choose Edit | Copy.
3. Move the insertion point to the destination.
4. Press CTRL+V or choose Edit | Paste.

Find and Replace Text ➡ pp. 50–52

1. Double-click the left end of the status bar and move to the Replace tab, or press CTRL+H.
2. Type the text you want to find in the Find What box.
3. Click the More button to select any desired search options.
4. In the Replace With box, type your replacement text. Select special characters or formatting to replace with, if you wish.
5. Click Find Next.
6. Click Replace, Replace All, or Find Next. Repeat as often as necessary.
7. Click Close when you're done (or click Cancel if Word fails to find anything that matches).

Undo a Number of Recent Steps ➡ pp. 52–53

1. Click the down arrow on the right side of the Undo button.
2. Scroll through the box that drops down, if necessary.
3. Choose the oldest action to be undone.

This is another read-it-if-you-need-it chapter. If you already know how to move around in your documents, make selections, make changes, and do formatting, you're excused from reading this one—go on to Chapter 4. Otherwise, at least skim through this chapter to make sure you're up to speed. I won't make you do any laborious typing or exercises. I'll just spell out all your options and demonstrate a few.

Editing and Formatting Your Documents

When I said that Chapter 1 covered just about everything you need to know about using Word, I was telling the truth, but once you get past the basics, you'll encounter another set of slightly more refined tasks and goals—things you'll do less frequently but that will become unavoidable. The skills you gained in Chapter 1 are suitable for rough drafts and for harnessing the computer workstation as a writing tool. Now it's time to talk about editing tools, such as those that allow you to make selections, copy formatting, move selections, and replace words—all techniques that are needed to make a document appear complete.

When you're working with computers, there's always a temptation to play with all the available levers all the time. My advice is to do the actual writing first. Get it out there on the page (saved). Then make another pass to fix, change, tweak, correct, and compromise. Tidy up the language. Make your document presentable.

I'm talking about two sets of things, really: editing and formatting— the brain and the body. Editing means changes and corrections to the words themselves. Formatting means determining the appearance of the words (typefaces, emphasis, page margins, and so on). I'll spell out the mechanics (the exact how-to, you-are-getting-sleepy-just-do-as-I-say instructions) in this chapter for each specific task. I recommend skimming it, honestly. When you actually want to do one of the things covered here (such as adding formatting or moving a paragraph), dip back into this chapter. You'll find you can use it as a reference.

Automatic Proofreading

This came up in Chapter 1 (which you may have skipped). If a bunch of the words in your document are underlined with wavy red lines and you don't know what it's all about, the spell checker has automatically checked your document and has some questions about the underlined words. As explained in Chapter 1, just right-click each word and choose an option, or retype the word, or correct the error manually. Chapter 2 tells you how to turn off automatic spell checking. (Choose Tools | Options, select the Spelling tab, and then uncheck Automatic Spell Checking.)

EXPERT ADVICE

If the wavy line is green, Word has a question about your sentence structure (it's the automatic grammar checker piping up). Right-click with your mouse and read the grammar advice before deciding what to do about the supposed problem.

Before You Start Editing and Formatting

To either edit or format your writing in Word, you first need to know how to move around in a document and how to make selections. You probably already know the basics of how to do both, because the rudiments of scrolling, selecting text or objects, or moving around with arrow keys works the same way in Word as it does in most other Windows programs. If you already have a firm grasp of this kind of thing, skip ahead to the section called Basic Formatting and get this chapter over with as fast as you can!

Moving Around in Your Document

For limited movement, use the arrow and other movement keys to the right of the ENTER key on the keyboard. (If your keyboard's Num Lock light is lit, press NUMLOCK to turn it off, and then use the equivalent keys on the numeric keypad, assuming you have one). For traversing large stretches of your document, use the vertical scroll bar. To get somewhere specific, you can try using Go To, Find, or the new Select Browse Object button. (Chapter 12 is full of hints for dealing with long documents.)

CAUTION
Unfortunately, on most keyboards there are INSERT and DELETE keys right next to HOME and END. (They're under END and PAGEDOWN on the numeric keypad.) They have nothing to do with moving and cause you problems. If you accidentally hit one and insert or delete anything, press CTRL+Z right away to undo whatever you did.

DEFINITION

Paragraph:
To Word, a paragraph is anything ending with a paragraph mark, even blank lines and headings. (Click the Show/Hide ¶ button on the Standard toolbar to see these marks in your document.)

Using the Keyboard to Make Short Hops

To move your insertion point a short distance, you should rely mainly on the arrow keys. You can lean on them to get them to repeat. Holding down CTRL while pressing an arrow key magnifies the effect of the key. So, while pressing the RIGHT ARROW key moves the insertion point to the next letter, CTRL+RIGHT ARROW jumps the insertion point to the beginning of the next word; CTRL+DOWN ARROW moves not just to the next line but jumps to the next paragraph. Other movement keys in the same vicinity of your keyboard include HOME, END, PAGEUP, and PAGEDOWN.

Table 3.1 shows what all the movement keys and various movement-key combinations do.

Key or Key Combination	Movement of the Insertion Point
LEFT ARROW	Left one character
RIGHT ARROW	Right one character
UP ARROW	Up one line
DOWN ARROW	Down one line
CTRL+LEFT ARROW	Left one word
CTRL+RIGHT ARROW	Right one word
CTRL+UP ARROW	Up one paragraph
CTRL+DOWN ARROW	Down one paragraph
HOME	To the beginning of the line
END	To the end of the line
CTRL+HOME	To the beginning of the document
CTRL+END	To the end of the document
PAGEUP	Up one screen
PAGEDOWN	Down one screen
CTRL+PAGEUP	To the top of the screen
CTRL+PAGEDOWN	To the bottom of the screen
SHIFT+F5	To its previous location

Table 3.1:   Movement Keys

Using the Scroll Bar to Go Farther

You probably know how to use the basic parts of the scroll bars already, because they work just like the ones in all the other windows that have them (see Figure 3.1):

CAUTION

The insertion point does not move along with the scroll box. If you want to get your insertion point onto the screen you've scrolled to, click on the screen.

- Click the arrow buttons at the top or bottom of the scroll bar to inch along a little bit at a time. You can also hold down the mouse button to scroll continuously.

- Click the areas above or below the scroll box to move your view one screen at a time.

- Drag the scroll box itself along the scroll bar to move yourself to a precise spot in the document (or to make sure you're in the right ballpark before you click the exact spot).

- If you drag the scroll box into position, Word pops up a little box displaying what page you've gotten to.

- Click the Previous Object or Next Object button (these are the double-arrow buttons) to go up or down one page at a time (or one heading at a time, or one graphic at a time, and so on, if you choose a different browse object). These buttons also move the insertion point.

See Chapter 12 for tips on moving around large, complicated documents.

Using Go To to Get to a Specific Place

Another way to jump to a specific place in a document is to use the Go To feature. To access it, select Edit | Go To, double-click the left end of the status bar, or press CTRL+G or F5.

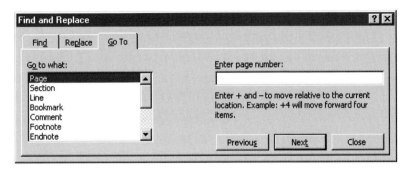

Select the object by which to browse. The choices
are Edits, Heading, Graphic, Table, Field, Endnote,
Footnote, Comment, Section, or Page (the default).

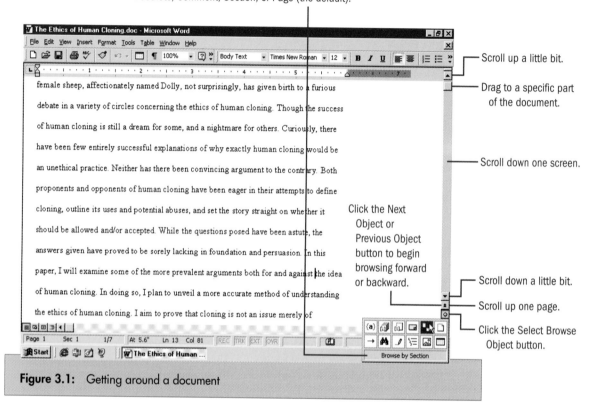

Scroll up a little bit.

Drag to a specific part
of the document.

Scroll down one screen.

Click the Next
Object or
Previous Object
button to begin
browsing forward
or backward.

Scroll down a little bit.

Scroll up one page.

Click the Select Browse
Object button.

Figure 3.1: Getting around a document

In the Go To What box, you can select parts of your document
(other than the top of a page) to go to. By pressing the Next button,
you can skip ahead or back one page at a time.

With Page selected in the Go To What box, type a page number
and press ENTER to go to the top of that page. You can also jump

EXPERT ADVICE

**You can also open the Go To tab in the Find And Replace dialog box by clicking Select Browse
Object and choosing the Go To option (the one at the lower-left).**

forward a number of pages by typing + and that number (such as +2) or back a number of pages by typing - and that number (such as -6). Click Close when you're done using Go To. (The dialog box doesn't close on its own.)

Using Find to Get to a Specific Word

If you're not sure what page you want to go to but you know a specific word or phrase in or near the section you want, use Find. To open the dialog box, select Edit | Find or press CTRL+F. This brings up the Find And Replace dialog box with the Find tab in front.

Type the word or phrase you're thinking of in the Find What text box and press ENTER (or click Find Next) to get to the first example Word finds in your document. To search from the insertion point back to the beginning of the document, first click the More button to expand the dialog box and reveal the advanced options. Then select Up from the drop-down Search list. To search the entire document from beginning to end, select All (see Figure 3.2). Repeat until you get to the selection you want, and then click Cancel to close the dialog box.

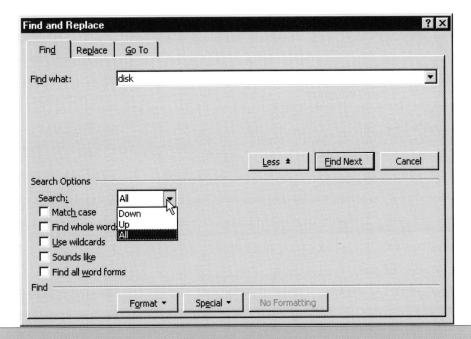

Figure 3.2: The Find tab in the Find And Replace dialog box

Selecting Text

As I mentioned before, you have to have a grip on selecting things before you can edit or format them. Fortunately, there's not much to it. To make simple, short selections, most of the time you'll just click to place the I-beam pointer at one end of the text you want to select, hold the mouse button down, and drag the pointer to the other end. The selected text appears reversed against a colored or dark background.

Word also gives you all kinds of selection shortcuts, some involving keys along with or instead of the mouse. These are described in Table 3.2.

EXPERT ADVICE

You can also open the Find tab in the Find And Replace dialog box by clicking the Select Browse Object button and choosing the Find option (second from the lower-left).

Once you've clicked at a certain point, you can SHIFT+click elsewhere to select everything in between. Likewise, you can position the insertion point, hold down SHIFT, and then use any of the arrow keys or other navigation keys (as explained earlier) to select everything between the original anchor position and the new position of the insertion point.

If You Want to Select an Entire...	Use This Shortcut
Word	Double-click anywhere on the word.
Line	Click the left margin area. (Hold down the mouse button and drag to select several lines at once.)
Sentence	CTRL+click (hold down CTRL and then click) anywhere in the sentence.
Paragraph	Double-click the left margin area, or triple-click on a paragraph.
Document	CTRL+click or triple-click anywhere in the left margin area, or press CTRL+A.

Table 3.2: Selection Shortcuts

Basic Formatting

There are all kinds of things you can do to format your documents and make them more presentable and more persuasive. The most common enhancements are easily available from the toolbars and other doohickeys on the screen.

Using (and Overruling) AutoFormat

DEFINITION

CTRL+clicking: **Holding down CTRL while clicking.**

SHIFT+CLICKING: **Holding down SHIFT while clicking.**

Word strains to offer you additional services with every new release of the program, and it has now reached the level of following you around, making suggestions. You've already seen how it automatically checks your spelling. Word also makes automatic formatting changes if you let it, making numbered lists, turning 2nd into 2nd, automatically creating tables, interpreting e-mail style formatting such as *bold* for **bold**, even making up styles based on your formatting selections, and so on. You can generally override these suggestions by clicking Undo immediately after Word makes the change.

To see what other options you can turn on, or to turn off any of the defaults that you don't like (when you get tired of clicking Undo, that is), select Tools | AutoFormat and choose the AutoFormat As You Type tab in the AutoCorrect dialog box (see Figure 3.3). Then check or uncheck any options and click OK.

There are two forms of AutoFormat: AutoFormat As You Type and plain-old AutoFormat. The former takes action as you're typing, the latter only if you specifically choose Format | AutoFormat. They have many similar features, but the on-demand AutoFormat command does not include borders or tables (tables have their own AutoFormat feature on the Table menu) and can also change or preserve existing style choices.

Controlling Emphasis, Fonts, and Sizes in Your Text

The general approach to formatting text is to select the text you want to format, and then click the button or select the option that applies the formatting you want. If you don't select something first, the formatting applies either to nothing or to the word, the paragraph, or

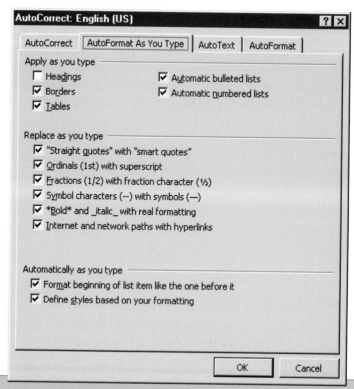

Figure 3.3: If Word is going to be a stickler about formatting, then you might as well tell it your preferences here, on the AutoFormat As You Type tab in the AutoCorrect dialog box.

the entire document in which the insertion point is currently located, depending on the context. So, for example, to make the title of a report bold, you could select the title and then click the Bold button on the Formatting toolbar. To make a single word italic, place the insertion point anywhere in it (or select it) and click the Italic button. The deal is the same for underline.

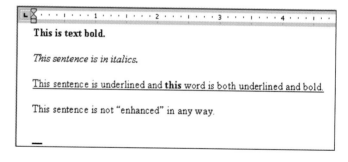

To choose a different font or size for the selected text, click the drop-down font or font size list from the Formatting toolbar, scroll through the list, and choose a font or size. To save you some scrolling, your most recent font selections also appear at the top of the drop-down Font list.

You can do all of these things and more from the Font dialog box, shown in Figure 3.4. To get to it, select Format | Font or right-click anywhere in your text and choose Font from the shortcut menu. Choose various options, mix and match, and check the results in the Preview area of the dialog box. When you're satisfied, click OK.

Indentation

You *can*, of course, indent the first line of a paragraph simply by pressing TAB at the beginning. There's nothing really wrong with this. It's also possible, though, to indent the first line of a paragraph from

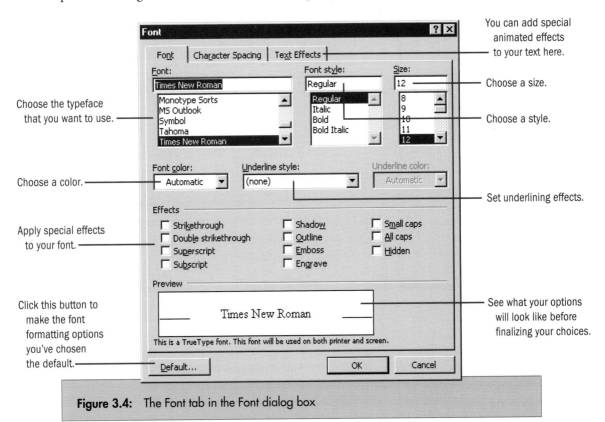

Figure 3.4: The Font tab in the Font dialog box

Remove or restore the Ruler by selecting View | Ruler.

the Ruler, without adding the tab character to the beginning of the line. As you continue to type, each new paragraph automatically gets the same formatting, with the indented first line.

The Ruler has indent handles at either end. The one on the right can be used to indent the right edge of the text from the right margin. The one on the left looks much more complicated:

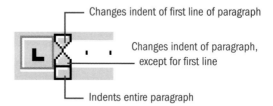

It's really not as tricky as it looks. To change the indent of the first line of the current paragraph, click the upper indent handle (which affects the first line only) and drag it right or left. To indent several paragraphs at a time, select them first. To indent the rest of the lines without moving the first line (called a hanging indent), drag the middle handle (which affects all lines except the first).

Move all three indent handles the same amount by dragging the bottom, rectangular handle. What's confusing is that the middle and bottom handles always move together. The difference is that if you click the middle handle, the top one won't move with them. If you click the bottom handle, it will.

Probably the most convenient use for the indentation handles is for indenting both edges of a paragraph some standard amount, such as a half-inch. (This is common formatting for quotations.)

You can also control paragraph indents by entering exact measurements in the Paragraph dialog box. Select Format | Paragraph or right-click on the text and select Paragraph from the shortcut menu

EXPERT ADVICE

In addition to using the Ruler as a tool, you can also read it as an instrument panel for information about the current paragraph. Move the insertion point into a paragraph to see the indentation, tabs, or even the columns in that particular paragraph.

that pops up. The Paragraph dialog box enables you to do several things at once (change indentation, spacing, and alignment, for example) and to clear up muddled settings by just typing in nice round numbers (see Figure 3.5).

See Chapter 12 for more about outlines.

Copying Formats from One Section of Text to Another

The Format Painter button can copy the formatting of a selection to the next text you select. One of its real advantages is that it lets you easily copy several different types of formatting (font, font size, character formatting, color, indentation, spacing, and so on).

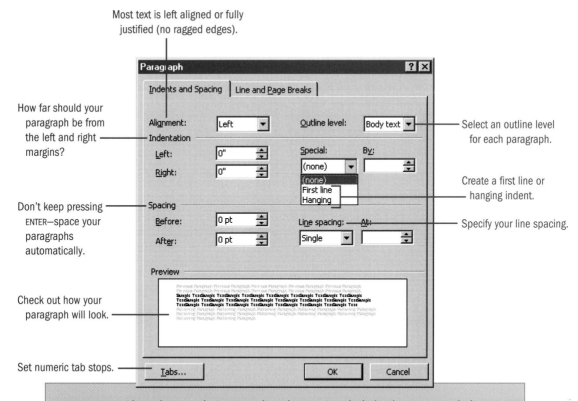

Most text is left aligned or fully justified (no ragged edges).

How far should your paragraph be from the left and right margins?

Don't keep pressing ENTER—space your paragraphs automatically.

Check out how your paragraph will look.

Set numeric tab stops.

Select an outline level for each paragraph.

Create a first line or hanging indent.

Specify your line spacing.

Figure 3.5:   The Indents And Spacing tab in the Paragraph dialog box is a good place to straighten out your indentation if you somehow get things messed up on the Ruler.

Painting a Format

1. Put the insertion point in some text that has the formatting you want (include the paragraph mark if you want to paint paragraph formatting).

2. Click the Format Painter button (or, if you plan to format more than one selection in the same way, double-click it).

3. Click a word or paragraph, or drag with the Format Painter I-beam, to apply the formatting to another selection:

> Now I'm selecting this
> I let go of the mouse bɪ
> the formatting of the p

4. Repeat the process on another area if you've double-clicked the button (it stays active until you click it again).

I call Format Painter the poor person's styles because it enables you to impose a consistent appearance on separated elements in a document. Unlike styles, though, the formatting is dumb and can't be updated everywhere by one simple change.

For more on styles, see Chapters 5 and 12.

Simple Editing

Inevitably, after the first draft of a document, there are corrections to be made, typos to be fixed, last-minute constructive criticism from the boss to be accommodated. Sometimes a document requires a major overhaul. The mechanics of editing consist mainly of deleting stuff, moving stuff around, and replacing stuff.

Deleting vs. Cutting

If you want to be able to track your changes, including cuts, consider turning on "change tracking." "Change tracking" is explained in Chapter 10.

To Word, there is a difference between deleting a selection and cutting it. *Deleting* means removing it completely (although deletions can be undone). *Cutting* means removing it from your document but also keeping a copy in reserve.

Something that has been cut can be pasted anywhere in the current document (or in other documents or even other programs), so long as you do it before copying or cutting anything else. Deleted stuff cannot be pasted. (Cutting and deleting can both be undone, though, with CTRL+Z or the Undo button.) Here's a brief description of these actions:

To delete a selection, simply press DELETE (or BACKSPACE). To cut a selection, press CTRL+X, click the Cut button, select Edit | Cut, or right-click the selection and select Cut. You get the picture.

Moving Things with the Mouse (Drag-and-Drop)

When you want to move a selection a short distance—to another part of the sentence, below a certain nearby paragraph, and so on—Word's drag-and-drop feature is your best bet. When you drag a selection, the pointer has a gray rectangle attached to it.

If you ever need to drag a copy of a selection while keeping the original in place, hold down CTRL while draggin' and droppin'. The little drag-and-drop pointer now sports a tiny plus sign as the only onscreen hint of what you're doing (although the message Copy To Where? instead of the usual Move To Where? appears in the status bar).

When you drag and drop, notice that Word generally keeps the spacing around the old and new places cleaned up, but it sometimes makes mistakes, so you might occasionally have to add a space (or, more rarely, get rid of one).

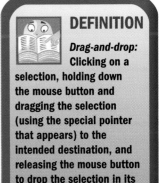

DEFINITION

Drag-and-drop: Clicking on a selection, holding down the mouse button and dragging the selection (using the special pointer that appears) to the intended destination, and releasing the mouse button to drop the selection in its new position.

Moving Things with Cut, Copy, and Paste

There are so many different ways to cut, copy, and paste that I'll put them into a nice handy table for you (see Table 3.3). Just remember that both cutting and copying put the selection on the Clipboard, but copying leaves the original in place—great for creating small variations on the same theme. Paste takes whatever's on the Clipboard and inserts it wherever the insertion point is at the time. Since the contents of the Clipboard stay the same until you empty or fill it up, you can paste the same selection or selections over and over again.

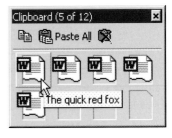

Method	Cut	Copy	Paste
Keyboard	CTRL+X	CTRL+C	CTRL+V
Menus	Edit | Cut	Edit | Copy	Edit | Paste
Formatting toolbar			
Right-clicking the selection	Cut	Copy	Paste

Table 3.3: Cut, Copy, and Paste Options

UPGRADE NOTE Word now allows you to cut, copy, and paste up to 12 items via the clipboard. After you cut or copy more than one item, the clipboard automatically pops up. To paste one item, simply click on the torn Word icon (yellow pop-up boxes show you what each item contains). To paste them all at the same time, click on the Paste All button.

Systematic Changes with Replace

To replace one thing with another once, many times, or everywhere in your document, use Replace. Why would you want to do this? Sometimes you'll decide to change a given piece of terminology with another, you'll want to make a formatting change throughout a document (when you haven't been using styles), or you'll want to clean up a document with extra line breaks in it or other irregularities.

To open the Replace dialog box, double-click the left side of the status bar, select Edit | Replace, press CTRL+H, or, if you're already in the midst of a Find operation (as explained earlier), just click the Replace tab in the Find And Replace dialog box (see Figure 3.6).

As you can see, if you click the More button, you have a lot of options to choose from in the Replace dialog box. Here's what they all do:

- Match Case is handy if you want to replace only those words capitalized exactly like your example word (entered in the Find What box).
- Find Whole Words Only will allow you to find just car and not carpet, for example.
- Use Wildcards lets you find words that start or end with certain letters, using ? to represent any single character and * to represent any number of characters.

EXPERT ADVICE

As with Find, the Replace tab of the Find And Replace dialog box also has its more advanced features hidden. Click the More button to reveal all the options, or the Less button to hide them.

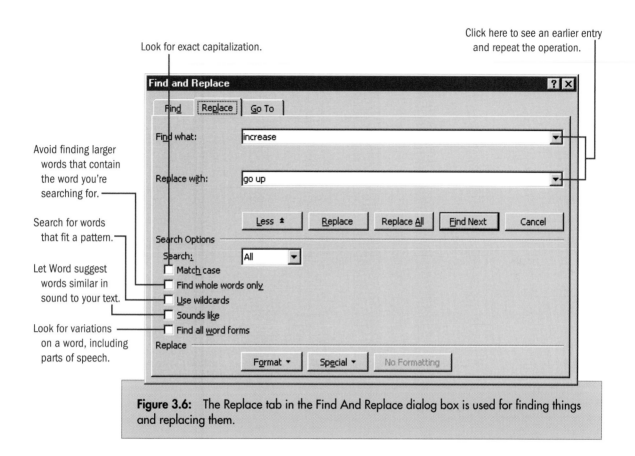

Click here to see an earlier entry and repeat the operation.

Look for exact capitalization.

Avoid finding larger words that contain the word you're searching for.

Search for words that fit a pattern.

Let Word suggest words similar in sound to your text.

Look for variations on a word, including parts of speech.

Figure 3.6: The Replace tab in the Find And Replace dialog box is used for finding things and replacing them.

- Sounds Like sets Word to the task of finding words that sound similar to your example.
- Find All Word Forms lets you find and replace other parts of speech related to the example word. For example, if your example word is increase, Word finds the words increase, increasing, increased, increases, increasification (that last one's a joke), and so forth.
- The Format button allows you to choose a format to find and one to replace it with—any character or paragraph formatting can be found and replaced.
- The Special button has Word look for and/or replace special characters, such as tabs, paragraph breaks, and so on.

CAUTION

If you choose formatting, the next time you use Replace, you'll have to click No Formatting to clear whatever formatting you selected, because your old choices linger on until you change them.

Once you've made your choices, click Find Next to find the first example that matches your Find What text. If it looks like something you want to replace, click Replace. The selection is replaced, and the next example is found. To skip a selection (leaving it unchanged), click Find Next again instead of Replace. To go ahead and change every instance of your example word in the document without seeing each one (which is risky, unless you're sure of yourself), click Replace All.

If Word reaches the end of your document after starting somewhere in the middle, a dialog box appears. Click Yes to continue the search from the beginning, or No to end it there. If Word gets to the end of your document without finding what you want, the Office Assistant (or a dialog box, if the Assistant isn't active) displays a message informing you that Word has finished searching the document and telling you how many replacements were made. Click OK to continue.

When it's done, Word will tell you that you've reached the end of the document (or selection). Click Close (or Cancel, if Word didn't find anything) to close the Replace dialog box. If you've goofed somehow during your replace operation, you can always undo the changes immediately (by pressing CTRL+Z once for each change, or just a single time if you've used Replace All).

You may notice that the Find What and Replace With boxes have drop-down lists attached to them. Word keeps track of the last ten words or phrases you've entered in these boxes during your current editing session. To repeat a find or replace, simply click the button at the right end of the box in question and choose one of the earlier entries.

Undoing Complicated Procedures

You already know how to undo your most recent mistake—just press CTRL+Z, select Edit | Undo, or click the Undo button. If you undo something by mistake (or hit the Undo button too many times), click the Redo button (to the right of Undo) to redo the last undone thing.

If you want to undo something that was done a few actions ago, click the little drop-down arrow to the right of the Undo button. A list of your recent actions drops down.

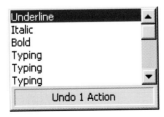

You can scroll through the list if necessary. Select the action you want to undo, and Word turns back the clock to the point of that earlier action. You lose the things you did afterward, even if they were OK, so there's a trade-off involved here.

There's More . . .

You're now safely out of the primer zone. It's time to choose a project. At this point you can think about any of the more complicated tasks you need to accomplish and jump directly to whichever chapter answers your questions. If you're not sure where to look, check the Index—it's pretty thorough, and you don't have to know Word or computer jargon to use it. If you have no challenging tasks to deal with immediately, put the book aside until you do!

CAUTION

If you undo many steps in a single stroke and then change your mind, you have to hit Redo repeatedly to restore all the undone work.

CHAPTER 4

Reusing Files and Recording Simple Procedures

INCLUDES

- Making boilerplate with AutoText
- Reusing a dummy document
- Making a template
- Recording a simple process

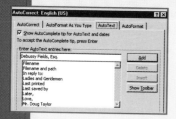

Create Boilerplate with AutoText ➡ pp. 58–60

1. If possible, select the text you want to reuse.
2. Select Tools | AutoCorrect.
3. Click the AutoText tab.
4. Paste (or type) the text in the Enter AutoText Entries Here box.
5. Make sure Show AutoComplete Tip For AutoText And Dates is checked.
6. Click Add.

Insert AutoText Boilerplate ➡ p. 60

1. Start typing the AutoText entry.
2. When the tool tip appears, suggesting the full entry, press ENTER or F3.

Make a Dummy Document to Use as Boilerplate ➡ pp. 61–62

1. Create the document that will serve as the dummy.
2. Select File | Save As.
3. Specify a folder and type a name for the dummy document.
4. Click Save.
5. Strip out (cut) specific information you don't need in the dummy.
6. Include instructions.
7. Save the document again. (Click the Save button on the toolbar.)

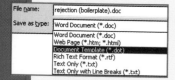

Make a Template from a Document ➡ p. 64

1. Create or open the document to be used as the basis for the new template.
2. Select File | Save As.
3. Type a new name for the template.
4. Click in the Save As Type drop-down list box.
5. Select Document Template (*.dot).
6. Click Save.

Record a Macro ➡ pp. 65–69

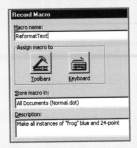

1. Double-click on the word REC on the status bar.

2. Type a name and a description for your macro.

3. Click the Keyboard button.

4. To create a shortcut for the macro, experiment with keyboard combinations until you find one that's not already taken. (Try ALT+SHIFT+*something*.)

5. Click Assign.

6. Click Close.

7. Carefully execute the procedure.

8. When you're done, leave the insertion point in a sensible place for repeating the macro.

9. Double-click REC again. (If you make any mistakes, use Undo and then repeat from step 1.)

I've said it before and I'll say it again: Computers are no good unless they can save you some work (at least in the long run). A lot of writing projects are routine, especially in the office or in any organizational setting (volunteer groups, clubs, subversive underground cells). This means you can often reuse text for ordinary situations. Reusable text is known as boilerplate.

One common example of boilerplate text is letterhead. For that matter, even a simple name and address can qualify as boilerplate. Another typical kind of boilerplate is a form letter, such as a publishing house's rejection letter, sadly enough.

But boilerplate is just the name of the solution, not a specific command or method in Word. There are several common ways to create boilerplate text and use it. Each method is more or less appropriate for different situations.

Creating Boilerplate with AutoText

A simple boilerplate can be made with AutoText. Longer boilerplate text can be made by saving a dummy copy of a document and keeping it around as a basis for later documents. Word also has *templates,* which are more sophisticated versions of this type of blank, dummy document, but you don't need to mess with them unless you have some pretty sophisticated goals in mind.

EXPERT ADVICE

Boilerplates are "good for you," but you might not want to bother with them. Fine with me. This isn't the dentist's office where I make you feel guilty. Use them only when you're fed up with repetitive typing and feel that "there's gotta be a better way."

Word has had an AutoText feature for many versions now (formerly, the Glossary), but I didn't think much of it then. The idea is that you preload certain text that you might want to use frequently or even regularly (sound familiar? yes, it's boilerplate again). Problem was, it seemed to require too much setup and then too many extra keystrokes to insert the AutoText entries, so I never really used it. However, it seems now that AutoText entries will present themselves as tool tips (those little floating light-yellow signs) if you start typing them.

If you're actually typing something else, no problem. Just keep going. If you *do* mean to insert the AutoText entry, you can just press ENTER or F3 to accept the suggestion.

Not sure which keystroke to use to OK an AutoText entry? Use whichever hand motions feel more comfortable.

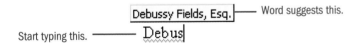

Start typing this. ——— *Debus*

Word suggests this.

So how do you *create* AutoText entries? That's also pretty easy:

1. Type the text, format it the way you want it to appear, and then select it.
2. Select Tools | AutoCorrect and click the AutoText tab.

You only have to do this step once to make all your AutoText entries easy to OK.

Your entry appears twice, once as the name of the AutoText entry, and the second time as the entry itself (see Figure 4.1).

3. This is the most important step: make sure Show AutoComplete Tip For AutoText And Dates (at the top of the AutoText tab) is checked. Click it if it's not.

4. To finish up, click Add to inaugurate your new AutoText entry.

Make sure this is checked.

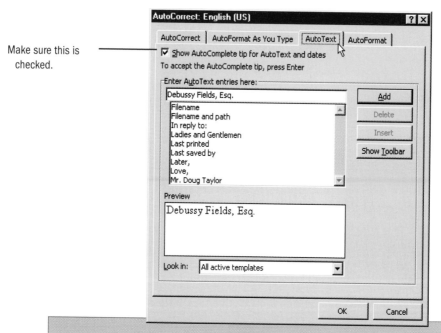

Figure 4.1: A new AutoText entry is born.

EXPERT ADVICE

If you make an AutoText entry and find it useless or even intrusive, you can come back to this dialog box (Tools | AutoCorrect, AutoText tab), select the offending AutoText entry, and click the Delete button.

Using a Dummy Document as Boilerplate

I won't call something a *template* unless it's a bona fide Word template, because I don't want to confuse you by sometimes using a term that has a specific meaning for Word as well as a meaning with broader applicability. (But to me, any document saved and used as a basis for spin-offs is a template.)

Real document templates are explained in the upcoming section, "Making a Real Template."

The most important thing I can tell you about this type of operation is that you should *make a copy of the document first*—before you strip out the specific information and turn your sample document into a dummy. Why? Because you'll start gutting some key document, keeping only the parts that are needed for the dummy, and then, if you're anything like me, you'll just go right ahead and *save* the dummy without thinking, without specifying Save As—you'll have accidentally replaced that key document with an empty husk. This is much worse than accidentally deleting a document, because the document actually still exists but the old contents are scattered randomly all over your hard disk. If anything like this does happen to you, get hold of a useful file-recovery program, such as Norton Utilities, with which you can sometimes piece together fragments by searching the entire disk for key words (not much fun, but often better than rewriting).

Making a Copy First

Begin by opening the document on which you want to base your new dummy. And how do you make a copy? With Save As, of course (as explained in Chapter 1). Quickly, then:

1. Select File | Save As. This brings up the Save As dialog box (see Figure 4.2).

2. Select a folder in which to store the dummy file.

EXPERT ADVICE

In the Save As dialog box, select Tools | General Options and click the Read-Only Recommended check box, to help subsequent users remember not to save changes to the dummy document.

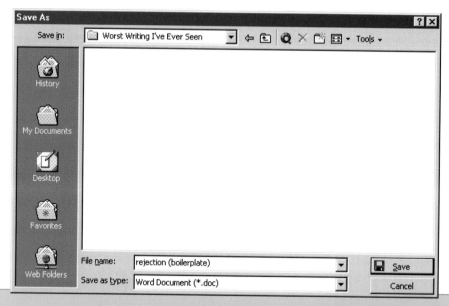

Figure 4.2:   Typing a name for a dummy document copy in the Save As dialog box

3. In the File Name box, type a new name for the document, one that you'll recognize later when you need to use it as a basis for a new copy.

4. Click the Save button.

Then go ahead and strip out any specific information in the document, saving only the material you plan to reuse. It's a good idea to leave some kind of instructions in the parts of the dummy that will have to be filled in for a particular copy, to make sure you don't later leave any embarrassing gaps (see Figure 4.3). When the dummy document is ready, save it again. (Click the Save button on the toolbar.)

Making a Copy Again When the Time Comes

The same sort of advice holds when the time comes to use the dummy document to create copies: use Save As to save the dummy as a new

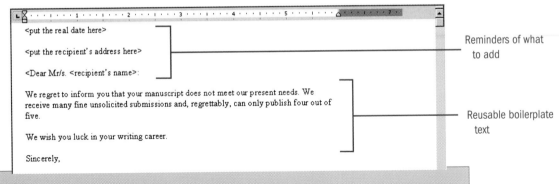

<put the real date here>

<put the recipient's address here>

<Dear Mr/s. <recipient's name>:

We regret to inform you that your manuscript does not meet our present needs. We receive many fine unsolicited submissions and, regrettably, can only publish four out of five.

We wish you luck in your writing career.

Sincerely,

Reminders of what to add

Reusable boilerplate text

Figure 4.3: A dummy document containing comments that tell the user what details to add

document before filling in the details. It's too easy to accidentally work only on the dummy, and then either have to clean it up again next time or—worse yet—supersede some work by repeatedly saving over the same copy.

Once again (with feeling): Open the dummy document. Select File | Save As. Type a distinct name for your new document. Click the Save button. There—your dummy document is safe for next time.

Making a Real Template

Even bothering to think about—let alone learn anything about— Word's actual *template* feature could inherently complicate your life and turn a simple writing task into a philosophical discourse about types and tokens. However, templates *do* have their advantages. The main advantage is that they're very hard to accidentally overwrite. Once you've preserved your boilerplate document as a template, it's designed to spin off new documents without altering the original. So, if you really want to save a copy of a sample document as an actual Word document template:

1. Select File | Save As.
2. Type a new name for the document.

3. Click in the Save As Type box and select Document Template.

4. Then click Save.

DEFINITION

Template:
A special type of document used as a basis for new documents. Any document can be saved as a template. Use the New command on the File menu to specify which template to use for a new document.

Once you choose the Document Template type, Word should automatically point at your Templates folder in the Save As dialog box. If it doesn't, switch to that folder yourself (it's most likely inside the Microsoft Office folder).

If you want to include self-updating information (such as a date field) in a template, you'll want to use the Insert | Field command, as touched on in Chapter 8. Some of the built-in templates and *wizards* (special kinds of templates that interview you and automatically create documents for you) use these kinds of fields, as do mail merge documents. (Mail merge is torn down to size in Chapter 9.)

Creating a New Document Based on a Template

When the time comes to start a new document based on your template, don't start by clicking on the New button on the Standard toolbar. That button's great, but it skips the stage where you get to choose a template. (Actually, that's why it's great.) Instead, follow these steps:

1. Select File | New. This brings up the New dialog box (see Figure 4.4).

2. Select your template, and click OK. (The other tabs in this dialog box include built-in templates that come with Word.)

Word will start a new document based on your template.

Word categorizes its templates by function.

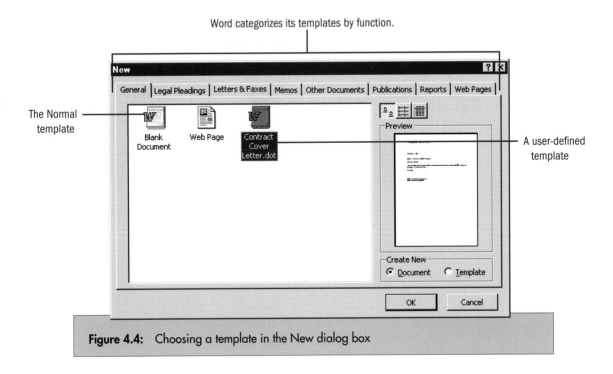

The Normal template

A user-defined template

Figure 4.4: Choosing a template in the New dialog box

Macros: Recording a Few Simple Steps

I hope my mentioning *macros* in the heading didn't scare you off. This section just covers *simple* macro recording and playback, but I won't *make* you do it. If the idea gives you the creeps, you're exempt. Off to Chapter 5 with you.

All along I have been emphasizing that anything you find yourself doing over and over could probably be delegated to the computer. Take this idea a step further now, and think about playing around with the macro recorder a little. A macro can record the typing of a piece of boilerplate and then play it back at any point. Since there are easier ways to make and use boilerplate text, you won't need to call on macros for that purpose. But there are other repetitive computer and Word tasks

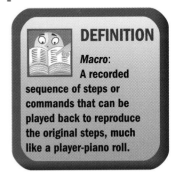

DEFINITION

Macro:
A recorded sequence of steps or commands that can be played back to reproduce the original steps, much like a player-piano roll.

EXPERT ADVICE

For immediate "instant macros," don't forget that once you do something you know you're going to repeat a few times (but may not need as a macro in the future) you can always use the Redo button, located on the Standard toolbar, or simply hit CTRL+Y.

---

besides just typing. For example, certain editing tasks become repetitive, especially when you are cleaning up a document or converting some of the contents of an old document into a new format.

Do Your Housecleaning First

To record a macro, you have to run through the task sequence manually with the macro recorder turned on. Then the computer can imitate what you did whenever you invoke the macro. To make the recording process go smoothly, make sure that the portion of the document you'll be working on when you record is free of errors and is typical of the kind of passage you'll be using the macro on. If you think your *computer* takes everything literally, wait until you record a macro. If it could record you scratching your nose, it would include that in the steps it saves.

Actually, the macro recorder can be somewhat forgiving: it ignores backspaces and canceled steps, but why take chances?

If you have to add little correcting steps while recording a procedure, the macro recorder will pick all of that up and replicate those extra steps each and every time. Recording a macro is sort of like performing an ancient religious ceremony that must be started over if a single step goes astray. Practice the sequence a few times to get it together before letting the cameras roll.

EXPERT ADVICE

It is possible to "pause" while recording a macro, perform steps that will go unrecorded, and then resume (without affecting how long the macro will take to play back), but that period of discontinuity is likely to destroy the usefulness of the macro unless you dot all your i's and cross all your t's.

Lights, . . . Camera, . . .

Put the insertion point in the sort of place it will be when you want to run the macro (so you don't end up recording the steps to get it into position), and then double-click on the word REC on the status bar. (This is a welcome shortcut for selecting Tools | Macro and then clicking Record New Macro.)

This will bring up the Record Macro dialog box (see Figure 4.5). Type a name for your macro—something descriptive (otherwise, months later, you might wonder what "rplcoldrptdts" might stand for). Take note that macro names cannot have spaces in them. If you like, you can also type a description of the macro in the Description area near the bottom of the dialog box.

Then click the Keyboard button in the Assign Macro To area. This brings up the Customize Keyboard dialog box (see Figure 4.6).

Press some combination of keys. If the key combination you tried is already in use, its action will appear under the words Currently Assigned To. When you've got a good one, click Assign. Then click Close.

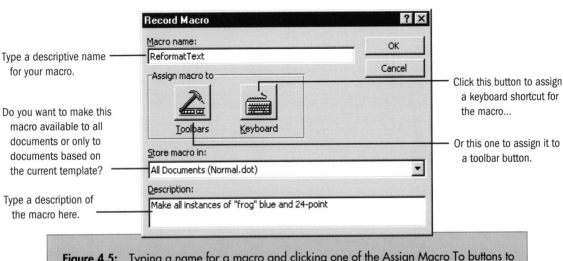

Type a descriptive name for your macro.

Do you want to make this macro available to all documents or only to documents based on the current template?

Type a description of the macro here.

Click this button to assign a keyboard shortcut for the macro...

Or this one to assign it to a toolbar button.

Figure 4.5: Typing a name for a macro and clicking one of the Assign Macro To buttons to create a handy shortcut

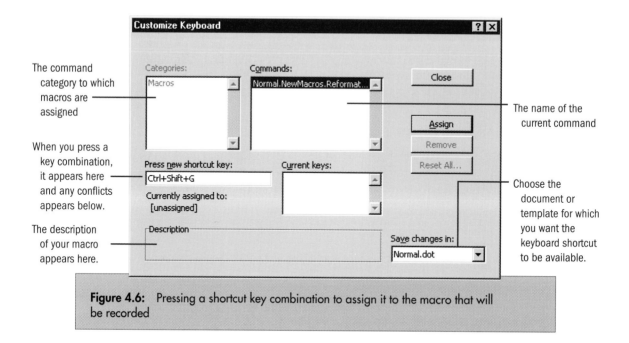

The command category to which macros are assigned

When you press a key combination, it appears here and any conflicts appears below.

The description of your macro appears here.

The name of the current command

Choose the document or template for which you want the keyboard shortcut to be available.

Figure 4.6: Pressing a shortcut key combination to assign it to the macro that will be recorded

Action!

Stop | Pause

You're now recording a macro. Quiet on the set! You'll notice a few reminders on your screen. First of all, there's a miniature Macro Recorder toolbar floating on the screen. (Actually, only the word Stop is really visible in its title bar.)

This toolbar sports a Stop button and a Pause button. The word REC on your status bar should now be bold. Also, your mouse pointer now appears as a pointer-and-cassette combination, as shown here, both to remind you that you're recording and that the Macro Recorder can't record text selection done with the mouse. (It can

---

EXPERT ADVICE

Definitely create some kind of shortcut to the macro. Usually the keyboard shortcuts are the least obtrusive. (Your best bets for unused key combinations are ALT+SHIFT with letters.) I'd advise you to add a macro to a menu or a toolbar only if it's something you're really going to use all the time.

record menu selections and choices in dialog boxes made with the mouse, though.)

Perform your procedure carefully. Leave the insertion point in the best place to repeat the process when you're done (in case you'll want to use the macro over and over without repositioning the pointer between each use). When you're done, click the Stop button on the Macro Recorder toolbar or double-click REC again. Closing the toolbar does not stop the recording.

Playback Time

When you want to use the macro, position the insertion point where you want the macro to take effect, and then press the key combination. (If you forget your key combination, then choose Tools | Macro | Macros, select the one you want, and click the Run button.) Repeat as needed.

There's More . . .

Now that you know how to make boilerplate and save yourself some typing, how about creating an AutoText entry for your name and address (or anything else you have to type frequently or regularly)?

Chapter 5 deals with the special formatting requirements for reports and formal documents. If that's not your cup of tea, decide what's the next pressing goal you want to achieve with Word, and head for the chapter that gets you to it. If nothing's that pressing, get your nose out of the book and go talk to someone.

Producing a Simple Report

INCLUDES

- Adding headers, footers, and page numbering
- Assigning headings
- Using simple styles
- Creating a title page
- Using automatic indentation
- Changing alignment, line spacing, and margins
- Creating numbered and bulleted lists
- Using the Shrink to Fit feature

FAST FORWARD

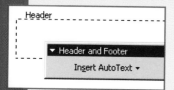

Add a Header or a Footer ➥ pp. 75–77

1. Select View | Header and Footer. (To make a footer, click the Switch Between Header And Footer button.)
2. Type the text you want in your header (or footer). Press TAB to move to the center and right side.
3. Click the Page Number button if you want to add a page number.
4. Click the Date button if you want to add the date (which will be automatically updated every time the document is opened).
5. Click Close.

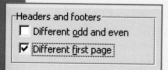

Start a Header or Footer on Page Two ➥ pp. 77–78

Follow the steps in the previous Fast Forward item for adding a header or footer.

1. Select File | Page Setup (or click the Page Setup button on the Header And Footer toolbar).
2. Click the Layout tab of the Page Setup dialog box.
3. Check the Different First Page check box.
4. Click OK.

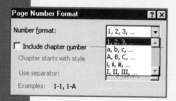

Number Your Pages ➥ pp. 78–80

1. Select Insert | Page Numbers.
2. Choose a position and an alignment for your numbers.
3. If you want a special numbering format, click the Format button. (If not, skip to step 5.)
4. Choose a format from the Number Format drop-down list box, and then click OK.
5. Click OK.

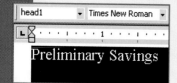

Create a Style ➥ pp. 80–81

1. Format a paragraph.
2. Select it.
3. Click in the Style box on the Formatting toolbar.
4. Type a name for your new style.
5. Press ENTER.

Change a Style on the Fly ➡ pp. 83–84

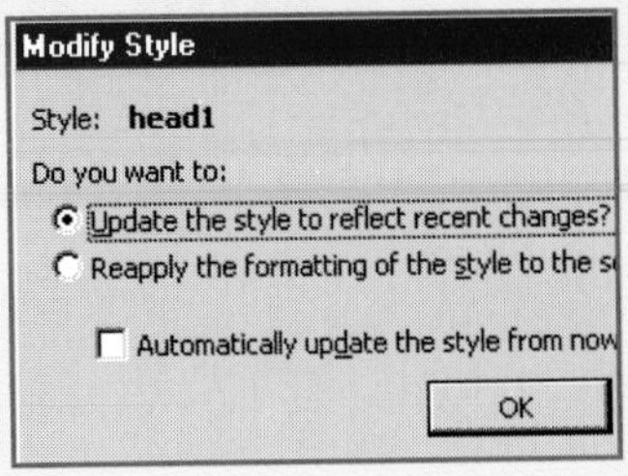

1. Make your changes to the paragraph that's currently formatted with the style.
2. Click in the Style box on the Formatting toolbar (or press CTRL+SHIFT+S).
3. Press ENTER.
4. Make sure that Update The Style To Reflect Recent Changes? is selected in the Modify Style dialog box that appears.
5. Check Automatically Update The Style From Now On if you want Word to update the style for you any time you change the format of text in that style.
6. Click OK.

Change a Paragraph's Line Spacing ➡ pp. 86–87

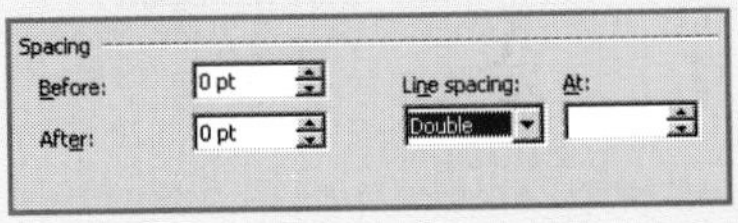

1. Select Format | Paragraph.
2. Select the Indents and Spacing tab.
3. Click in the Line Spacing drop-down list box in the Spacing area of the Paragraph dialog box.
4. Select one of the options.
5. Click OK.

Create an Automatic Paragraph Indent ➡ pp. 87–88

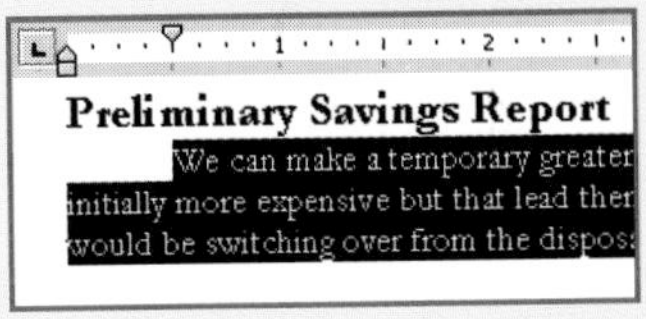

1. Place the insertion point in a typical paragraph.
2. Click on the First Line Indent marker (the upper one) at the left end of the Ruler, and drag it to the indentation level you want.
3. Click in the Style box on the Formatting toolbar (or press CTRL+SHIFT+S).
4. Type a new name for your paragraph style.
5. Use Replace to search for the Normal style and replace it with your new style wherever you want to add it throughout the document.

Change a Paragraph's Alignment ➡ pp. 89–90

After placing the insertion point in a paragraph (or selecting several paragraphs):

- Click the Align Left button on the Formatting toolbar to return to left-justified, ragged-right alignment (the default).
- Click the Center button to center the selection.
- Click the Align Right button to impose right-justified, ragged-left alignment.
- Click the Justify button to align the selection at both margins (with full justification).

Specify Margins ➡ p. 90

1. Select File | Page Setup.
2. Click the Margins tab of the Page Setup dialog box.
3. Enter the top, bottom, left, and right margins you want.
4. Click OK.

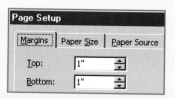

Create a Numbered List ➡ pp. 91–92

1. Start a new paragraph with the number 1, followed by a period (or hyphen or closing parenthesis), and a space (or tab).
2. Type the first item in the list.
3. Press ENTER. Word starts the next paragraph with the number 2.
4. Type each item in the list, pressing ENTER after each one.
5. Press ENTER twice when you get to the end.

Create a Bulleted List ➡ pp. 91–92

1. Click the Bullets button on the Formatting toolbar.
2. Type the first item in the list.
3. Press ENTER. Word starts the next paragraph with another bullet.
4. Type each item in the list, pressing ENTER after each one.
5. Press ENTER twice when you get to the end.

Once your document is past that rough-draft stage and you've polished it up with the basic niceties of formatting and editing adequate for most purposes such as internal documents and informal reports, then you're finished, and you should stop worrying about how it looks. Then again, there's a slightly higher level of polish you might want to achieve for reports, handouts for presentations, and the like—you know, those situations in which you might need the edge that a cleanly designed document can give you.

Adding a Header or Footer

For any document with more than a couple of pages, a header or a footer is a must. Imagine what would happen if the document were dropped on the floor, its pages scattered and mixed with other paperwork. How much easier it would be to reassemble if every page had a small header identifying the document and the page number!

Why the View Menu and Not the Insert Menu?

To add a header or a footer (or both), you have to pull down the View menu and select Header and Footer. Why is this command not on the Insert menu? Because every document by default has a footer and header. Accessing them through the View menu allows you to edit those blank footers and headers.

This drops you temporarily into Print Layout view (as indicated by the vertical ruler on the left side of the window and the symbolic representation of the edges of the page), with the header active and a little Header and Footer toolbar, shown next, floating partly over the header and partly over the grayed-out contents of the document.

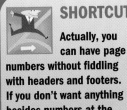

SHORTCUT

Actually, you can have page numbers without fiddling with headers and footers. If you don't want anything besides numbers at the top or bottom of each page, skip to "Numbering the Pages."

If you intend to create or edit a footer, click the Switch Between Header and Footer button. You'll be taken to an analogous area at the bottom of the page.

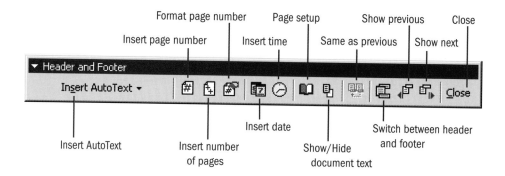

Naturally, the details of the text, the insertions, and the formatting of your header (or footer) will depend on your needs. See Figure 5.1 for an explanation of how to make one specific type of header.

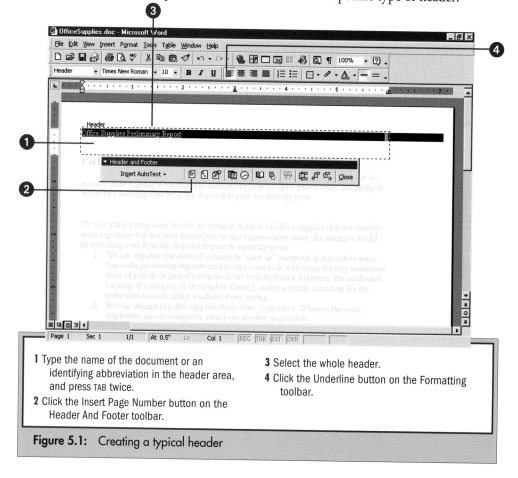

1 Type the name of the document or an identifying abbreviation in the header area, and press TAB twice.

2 Click the Insert Page Number button on the Header And Footer toolbar.

3 Select the whole header.

4 Click the Underline button on the Formatting toolbar.

Figure 5.1:   Creating a typical header

When you're done with your header or footer, click the Close button on the Header And Footer toolbar. This will return you to Normal view (unless you were in Print Layout view to begin with).

Starting Headers and Footers on the Second Page

Normally you don't want a header or footer on the first page of a document. The first page of a document usually has a clear title or other identifier.

Making a title page is explained later in this

If you want no header or footer on the first page of your document:

1. Select File | Page Setup or click the Page Setup button on the Header and Footer toolbar. This brings up the Page Setup dialog box.

2. Click the Layout tab if it's not already in front.

3. Check the Different First Page check box (see Figure 5.2).

4. Click OK.

Tell Word where you want the section to start.

For more on formatting documents with sections, see Chapter 12.

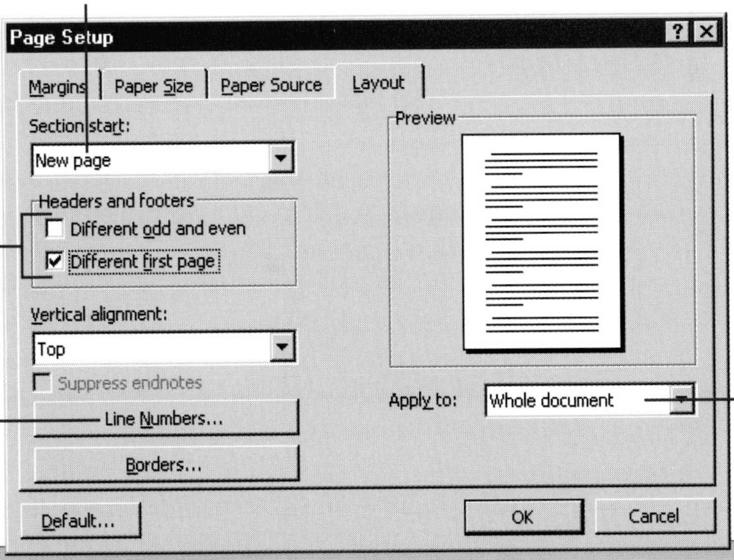

Do you want the same header or footer information on every page in your document?

Do you want your changes to apply to the entire document, or to the document from this point on?

Only worry about this if you'll need to number every line in your document.

Page Setup

Margins | Paper Size | Paper Source | Layout

Section start:
New page

Headers and footers
☐ Different odd and even
☑ Different first page

Vertical alignment:
Top

☐ Suppress endnotes

Line Numbers...

Borders...

Preview

Apply to: Whole document

Default...   OK   Cancel

Figure 5.2: Checking the Different First Page check box to have a header start on page 2

EXPERT ADVICE

It's generally a good idea to give headers and footers a smaller font size than the body text of your document. Doing this ensures that there's never any confusion at the top of the page.

To see the results, select View | Header and Footer. You'll see the now-blank header area for page 1. Notice that the label at the top of the header area on page 1 is First Page Header. Click the Show Next button on the Header and Footer toolbar. You'll be taken to the top of page 2, shown in the following illustration, where you'll see the header you created earlier. (This one is still labeled Header, as will be true for all pages except page 1. Click Close.

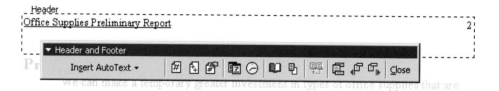

Numbering the Pages

If you want to add page numbers without any of the other accoutrements of headers and footers, or if you want some elaborate type of page numbering, there's a separate command dedicated to page numbering. (Yes, you could also create a header or a footer and then only insert a page number.)

Positioning the Page Number

To number your pages, select Insert | Page Numbers. This brings up the Page Numbers dialog box, shown in Figure 5.3.

Choose a position for the page numbers (Top Of Page or Bottom Of Page) and an alignment (Left, Center, Right, Inside, or Outside). You can also decide whether or not to have page numbers appear on

How should the numbers be justified, and should justification be the same on each page?

Choose a location for your page numbers.

Preview your numbering settings.

Turn this off unless you want page numbers on the first page.

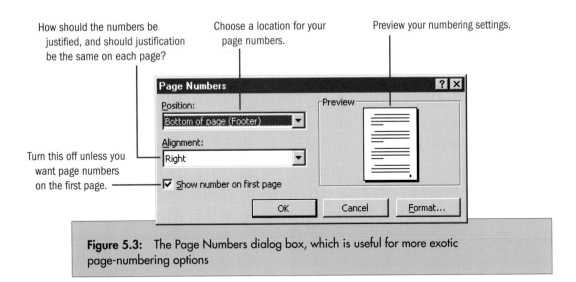

Figure 5.3: The Page Numbers dialog box, which is useful for more exotic page-numbering options

the first page. If you want some special kind of numbering (such as Roman numerals, letters, or a combination of chapter and page numbers), click the Format button. This brings up the Page Number Format dialog box, shown here:

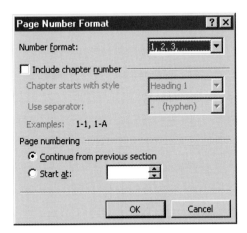

Choose the number format you want from the drop-down list box, and then click OK. When you're satisfied with your page-numbering selections, click OK in the Page Numbers dialog box.

Numbering Pages in Relation to a Total (for example "Page 2 of 19")

To include page numbers expressed in relation to a total number of pages, insert your page numbering in a header or footer (using View | Header and Footer, as explained earlier in this chapter) and follow the steps outlined in Figure 5.4.

This process will insert the total number of document pages in your header or footer. It will also automatically update the total if the number of pages in your document changes.

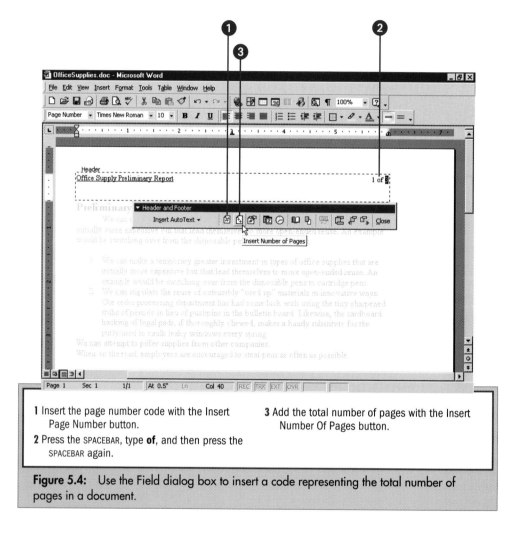

1 Insert the page number code with the Insert Page Number button.

2 Press the SPACEBAR, type **of**, and then press the SPACEBAR again.

3 Add the total number of pages with the Insert Number Of Pages button.

Figure 5.4:   Use the Field dialog box to insert a code representing the total number of pages in a document.

Using Styles to Impose a Simple Design

If you want to make your document really presentable, you should experiment with different fonts and sizes for the text. There is an easy way to do this. The basic principle is to make similar elements look similar. You start by defining different styles for the different types of elements in your document, such as headings. Then you assign the appropriate style to every text element in your document. This enables you to change the appearance of every instance of a particular element at once, simply by changing the style.

The most common design element in a document is the heading. Sometimes you will have a document with only a single level of heading, and at other times your documents will have several levels.

Defining a Style

Defining a style for a document is easy. Simply format some text manually with the font, size, and emphasis (bold, italic, and so forth) you want. You can also choose other paragraph formatting, such as spacing, alignment, and indentation, all of which are explained later in this chapter. Then, with the insertion point still in the text you want formatted, click in the Style box at the left end of the Formatting toolbar, type a name for your new style, and press ENTER. The following illustration shows a heading style being defined:

EXPERT ADVICE

Word comes with a set of heading styles, called Heading 1, Heading 2, and so on. They're not very elegant, but they'll do in a pinch. If you make up your own heading styles, be sure to give them names that differ from the preexisting styles.

Keep in mind that when you create a style this way, it is associated *only* with your *current* document and not with the Normal template. This means that any subsequent documents produced with the Normal template will not have that style.

Assigning a Style

Once you've created a style, you can assign it quite easily to any selection (or paragraph, depending on the style). See Figure 5.5 for an explanation of how to assign styles.

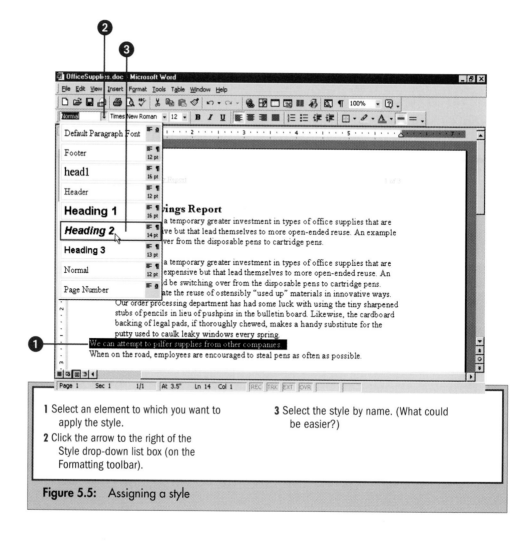

1 Select an element to which you want to apply the style.

2 Click the arrow to the right of the Style drop-down list box (on the Formatting toolbar).

3 Select the style by name. (What could be easier?)

Figure 5.5:　Assigning a style

Changing a Style

If you decide that you want to try a variation on the style, simply select any example of the style and make manual changes to the format. (You'll usually use the Formatting toolbar to do this.) Then select the style name in the Style box and press ENTER. Word will display the Modify Style dialog box, shown here, which offers you two options.

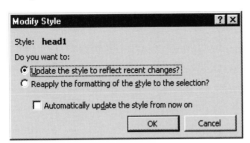

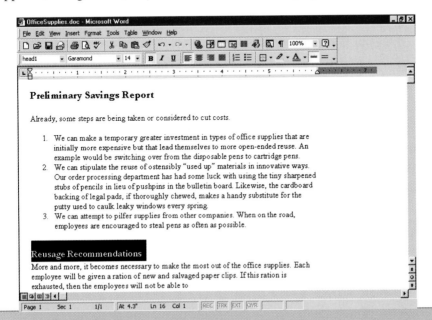

CAUTION

Changing the format of an existing style to create a new style means replacing the original formatting choices, so don't do this unless you're prepared to lose the old style in favor of the new.

Make sure that the first option (Update The Style To Reflect Recent Changes?) is selected, and then click OK. All the other elements using this style will change to reflect the new formatting you just applied (see Figure 5.6). If you choose to automatically update the

Figure 5.6: A report showing a revised heading style with 14-point type, instead of the 16-point type the head 1 style originally had

style from that time on (there's a check box in the dialog box that controls this option), then any further changes to the style will take effect without your being prompted. It won't, however, affect the way in which other styles are revised.

Making a Title Page

Some documents are *so* serious and formal that they require a separate cover page that announces the document's title and the names of the people responsible. Because of all the blank space that usually appears on such a page, the usual way to lay out a title page is to center the text on it vertically. This is a little tricky in Word because, by default, the vertical alignment of text on a page applies to the document as a whole.

There is a way to get around this problem: divide the document into two sections. Word will allow you to assign different vertical alignments to separate sections of the same document. For our purposes, the first section will consist of only the title page, and the second section will contain the rest of the document.

1. Make sure you're in Normal view (select View | Normal).
2. Position the insertion point at the beginning of the first line of text that will appear after the title page. (This is usually just under the title, or at the top of the page if there is no title yet.)
3. Select Insert | Break, which brings up the Break dialog box.

EXPERT ADVICE

You must undo the Different First Page choice for headers/footers if you're adding a title page to your document. Otherwise, you'll have a title page, then a headerless/footerless page, then headers/footers starting on the second normal page.

4. Click on the Next Page option in the Section Break Types area and click OK. An end-of-section marker will appear just before the regular text of the document (after the title, if there is one already).

5. Move the insertion point up before the break.

Preliminary Savings Report

6. Select File | Page Setup. This brings up the Page Setup dialog box. Click the Layout tab if necessary.

7. Check the Different First Page check box. (You don't want headers or footers on the title page, do you?)

8. Click in the Vertical Alignment box (just below the Headers And Footers area) and select Center from the drop-down list.

9. Click on OK.

Your layout is done, although you may still need to add more material to the title page to give it the extra *oomph* you're looking for. For instance, you may want to center the title paragraph so it sits neatly on the page. Figure 5.7 shows the first two pages of a report in print layout view at 39 percent size so that you can see the centered title page and the first page of the report with a header.

EXPERT ADVICE

If you create the section break *after* there's already a "different first page," that feature will repeat in the second section (though you can go to the second section and turn it off again).

Page number

Report text

Title

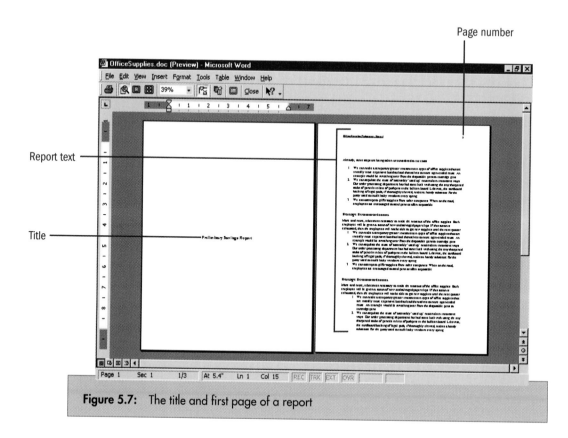

Figure 5.7: The title and first page of a report

Changing the Line Spacing

Some documents, especially early drafts, work best if they are double-spaced. If you pass around a document (on paper) to others for comments, double spacing will allow your colleagues to jot down their oh-so-helpful advice between the lines. To change the spacing of a portion of your document, first select the portion you want to change. (Merely placing the insertion point in a paragraph will enable you to change the spacing of only that paragraph. Select the entire document with CTRL+A if you wish to change the spacing of it all.)

Simply click the Double Space button on the Formatting toolbar to double-space the document. When it's time to return a document to single spacing, click the Single Space button on the toolbar.

If you want some kind of spacing other than double spacing, or if you are using the default toolbars, select Format | Paragraph. This brings up the Paragraph dialog box (see Figure 5.8). Click the Indents and Spacing tab if necessary. Then click in the Line spacing drop-down list box in the Spacing area and select Double or one of the other options. Then click OK.

If you haven't done so already, I recommend adding the Double Space and Single Space buttons to your Formatting toolbar for easy access. (For more on customizing your toolbars, see Chapter 2.)

TIP
The Paragraph dialog box is also the place for setting up extra spacing before and/or after a paragraph.

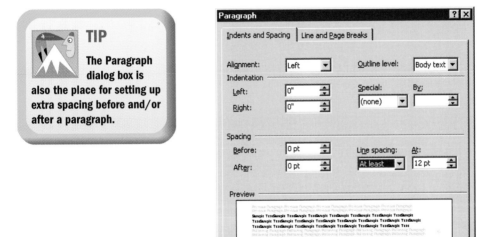

Figure 5.8:   Choosing a different line spacing in the Paragraph dialog box

Automatic First-Line Indents

You can always indent the first line of a paragraph manually by pressing TAB at the beginning of the paragraph. You can establish a first-line indent for all future paragraphs by dragging the First Line Indent marker on the Ruler into position. But the only way to have the first line of regular paragraphs indent automatically without causing all the other elements (including headings) to also be indented is to establish a special style for body text, distinct from the Normal style that every paragraph gets by default if it isn't given a specified style.

EXPERT ADVICE

In fact, if Tabs And Backspace Set Left Indent is checked in the Edit tab of the Options (Tools | Options) dialog box, then any time you press tab at the beginning of a paragraph, Word will interpret it as a request for a first-line indent and will change the indentation marker on the Ruler automatically. This feature first appeared in version 7.0 of Word.

Chapter 12 has more on some of the trickier aspects of styles.

After you establish this special style (as shown in Figure 5-9), to indent any paragraph just select the body style (or whatever you called it). You can also define other styles, such as your heading styles, so that the paragraph that immediately follows automatically gets the body text style.

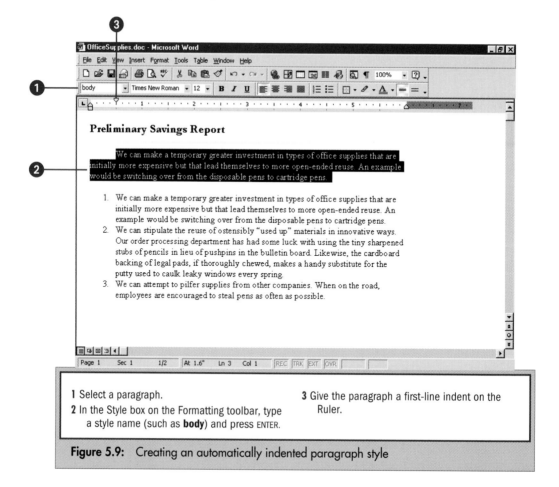

Figure 5.9:   Creating an automatically indented paragraph style

1 Select a paragraph.

2 In the Style box on the Formatting toolbar, type a style name (such as **body**) and press ENTER.

3 Give the paragraph a first-line indent on the Ruler.

Changing a Paragraph's Alignment

By default, normal paragraphs in Word are left-aligned, meaning that they are aligned along the left side and "ragged" (not aligned) along the right. Changing the alignment of a paragraph or of any selection is a snap. Say you want to center a heading (or a caption, or a quotation, or whatever). Click in the text, and then click the Center button on the Formatting toolbar. (The Justify button aligns text along both the left and right margins at the same time by varying the amount of spacing between the words, and to a lesser extent between the letters themselves.)

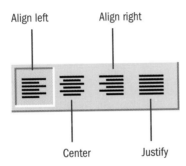

Align left   Align right

Center   Justify

A new feature in Word, called Click and Type, now allows you to enter text, graphics, tables, or other items in a blank portion of your document with the paragraph alignment of your choice. Pass the cursor over a blank portion of your document (you need to be in either Web Layout or Print Layout view) and the Click and Type pointer will change its appearance to represent right, left, or center alignment. This is convenient in that you don't need to keep pressing

EXPERT ADVICE

When centering text, make sure there's no tab indentation or extra spaces at the beginning of the line. If there is, the text will be off center.

ENTER to get to the center of the document or mess with your alignment settings, Click and Type does it for you. Just put the cursor where you want your new content and double-click.

Setting Up Margins

CAUTION

If your document has sections, make sure that you've placed the insertion point in the section you want to affect before setting new margins.

By default, Word gives you 1-inch margins at the top and bottom of each page and 1¼-inch margins at left and right. Specifying different margins is a snap, though. To change your margins, follow the steps in Figure 5.10.

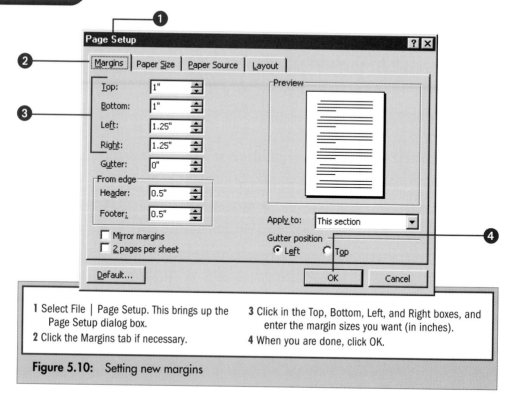

1 Select File | Page Setup. This brings up the Page Setup dialog box.
2 Click the Margins tab if necessary.

3 Click in the Top, Bottom, Left, and Right boxes, and enter the margin sizes you want (in inches).
4 When you are done, click OK.

Figure 5.10: Setting new margins

Creating Numbered and Bulleted Lists

With numbered and bulleted lists, you can often take an argument or explanation and boil it down to a set of easy-to-grasp key points. Word can handle either kind of list automatically, adding a number or bullet to each new item in the list. It will *increment* the numbers (increase them by one each time) automatically as well. If you cut and paste items in a numbered list, Word will renumber them for you. Note that this will not happen if you have AutoFormat turned off.

In fact, if you type a new paragraph starting with a number, as soon as you press ENTER Word will assume that you are starting a numbered list and will turn the number you typed into one of its magical elements that's not really a character (meaning you can't select or delete it directly since it actually resides in the paragraph mark).

There will be times when you won't want what you typed to be treated as a numbered list. To turn off this option for the moment, go to the AutoFormat As You Type tab of the AutoCorrect dialog box (available from the Tools menu) and deselect Automatic Numbered Lists. When you're ready to activate this feature again, just make sure that the box is checked.

To start a numbered list from the Formatting toolbar, click the Numbering button. To start a bulleted list, click the Bullets button. The button you clicked will appear pushed in, the way the Bold, Italic, and Underline buttons do when they are clicked. Type the first item in your list, and then press ENTER.

Each new paragraph will get a number or bullet, depending on which button you clicked. When you get to the end of your list, press

DEFINITION

Bulleted list: **A list of items, each of which is (most commonly) preceded by a dot (centered, not on the baseline like a period), although other symbols (squares, pointing fingers, faces, shapes, etc.) can be used.**

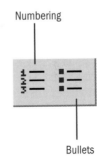

Numbering

Bullets

EXPERT ADVICE

Numbered and bulleted lists will end if you press enter twice. If you want extra spacing between list items, select the list, choose Format | Paragraph, and enter the amount for spacing before or after each paragraph.

ENTER again and then click whichever button you clicked on to start the list. The button will become unpressed, and the previous paragraph style will again prevail. Rearranging the items in a numbered list is a snap:

1. Select the item(s) you want to move.

2. Either drag the selection to a new location, or cut it and then paste it in the new location (as described in Chapter 3).

3. When you complete a move, the numbers will correct themselves "automagically."

Fine-Tuning Automatic Lists

To choose different numbering or different indentation styles for your lists, you have to get your hands a little dirty (though you still don't really have to understand how Word handles the items). Right-click on any paragraph in the list you want to micromanage and choose Bullets and Numbering from the menu that pops up. (This method can also be used to start a new bulleted or numbered list.) This brings up the Bullets And Numbering dialog box (see Figure 5.11).

For a list you've just typed, the appropriate tab should come up automatically. For lists within lists, check out the Outline Numbered tab. The Bulleted tab gives you a choice of dingbats; the Numbered tab offers a choice of numbering styles. Click Customize to change the formatting of your bullets or numbers and to opt against the default hanging indent, if you so choose.

On each of the tabs, you can also click on the Customize button to gain even more control over the fine points of the list style. For example, clicking Customize on the Numbered tab brings up the Customize Numbered List dialog box, whose most important option is Start At. This option allows you to change the starting number of the list (a feature that is great for continuing a list after an intervening paragraph). The determined user can also affect the type of numbering, the characters (such as periods or parentheses) used before and/or after the numbers, the alignment of the numbers, the indentation, the space after the numbers, and the ubiquitous hanging indent.

DEFINITION

Hanging indent: When the first line of a paragraph is indented less than the rest of the lines. (The first line "hangs" further to the left than the rest of the paragraph.) This is also called a negative indentation.

Choose or edit a numbering style on this tab.

Choose or edit a bullet style on this tab.

Choose or edit an outlining style on this tab.

You can customize existing styles.

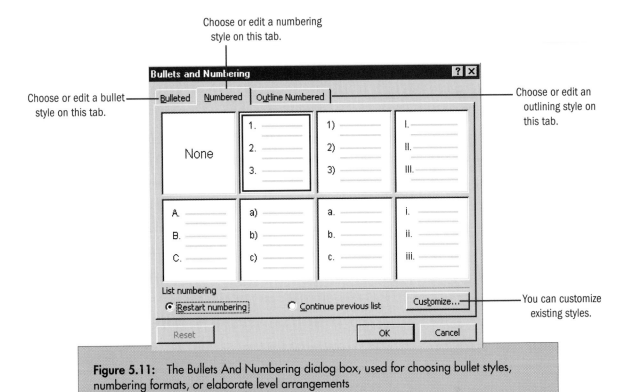

Figure 5.11: The Bullets And Numbering dialog box, used for choosing bullet styles, numbering formats, or elaborate level arrangements

Using Shrink to Fit to Avoid Nearly Empty Pages

It never fails that a document you're about to print will turn out to go just barely onto that ninth page, wasting paper now and when you make 27 photocopies of your report for the meeting. That last page, with only a sentence and a half on it, looks a little lame, too. One of Word's cooler features—Shrink to Fit (also known as Shrink One Page)—solves this problem. You can get to this feature by clicking on the Print Preview button.

CAUTION

Shrink to Fit won't do anything if there's more than a few lines on the final page.

EXPERT ADVICE

It's a good idea to save your document (by clicking the Save button) before making any major formatting changes.

Click the Shrink to Fit button and Word will change the formatting of your document as subtly as possible. It fiddles with line spacing, font sizes, and so on, to squeeze out that little overrun and force your document to end near the bottom of the previous page. If you don't like the results, press CTRL+Z to undo them immediately.

There's More . . .

If this chapter has not satisfied your report-designing ambitions, try skipping ahead to Chapter 12, where you'll find the keys to designing elegant, sophisticated (or very long) documents, for advice on producing and maintaining professional-quality publications.

CHAPTER 6

You Need a Universal Translator

INCLUDES

- Getting someone else's document onto your computer
- Opening documents created with other word processing programs
- Opening a document that Word can't translate
- Saving a document that was imported from another word processing program
- Saving Word documents in other formats
- Saving Word documents in common formats

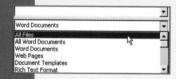

Open a Non-Word Document in Word → pp. 102–104

1. Start Word.
2. Click the Open button on the Standard toolbar.
3. Browse around your disk, your desktop, or other disks connected to your computer via a network, until you find your file.
4. Click in the Files Of Type list box and choose All Files (unless you can already see the document you want to open).
5. Double-click on the document you want to open.

macfile.mcw

Open a Document of any Type → pp. 105–106

- If the document icon looks like a Word document icon, double-click on it and Word will start up (if it isn't already started) and open the document.
- If the document is not a Word document, Word may still be able to open it.

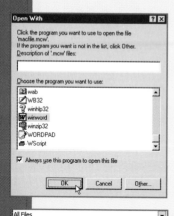

Open a Document in a Format Windows Doesn't Recognize → p. 106

1. Double-click the document icon.
2. Choose WINWORD in the Open With dialog box that appears.
3. Click OK.

Open a Document that Word Can't Translate → p. 107

- Try opening the document in another word processing program, such as WordPad.
- Ask the person who gave you the document to save it in a format that Word can understand (such as Text Only).

Save an Imported Document in Word
Format ➡ p. 107

1. Select File | Save As.
2. Choose Word Document in the Save As Type drop-down list box.
3. Click Save.

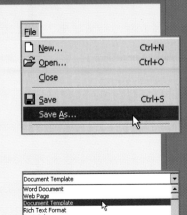

Save a Word Document in Another Format ➡ p. 108

1. Select File | Save As.
2. Click in the Save As Type drop-down list box and choose the format you want.
3. Type a different filename for the document.
4. Click Save.

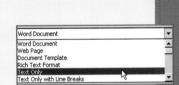

Save a Document in a Universal
Format ➡ pp. 108–109

1. Select File | Save As.
2. Choose Text Only or Rich Text Format in the Save As Type box.
3. Type a different filename for the document.
4. Click Save.

Look around your office or wherever you use your computer. Although you might have many computers around you, they might not be the same type as yours: for instance, some may be Macs. The other IBM-type PCs may not have Windows installed, and even the ones that do may have other word processing programs on them, such as WordPerfect. Now think about all the computers outside your workplace that produce documents of every type and stripe. Inevitably, the time will come when someone will hand you a disk that contains a document created on a different computer or in some other word processing program and ask you not only to put the document on your computer or print it out, but also to edit the dang thing in Word for Windows.

Can't Get There from Here

CAUTION

Always use your virus scanning software to check disks you get from others as soon as you insert them into your computer. No matter how "nice" your friends or coworkers are, your computer can still pick up a nasty virus from their disks if you don't practice safe disk swapping. Once you've copied a file from a diskette, remove it from the disk drive so your computer doesn't try to "boot up" using it next time you start it up.

It's almost as if someone has handed you a wax cylinder from Thomas Edison's day and asked you to make a cassette tape copy of the music encoded thereon. Computer generations evolve about every 18 months, so this analogy is not too far-fetched. Oh, and by the way, can you take this huge stone with hieroglyphics carved on it, scan it in, run a character-recognition program, update the information, and have a report on my desk by 5:00? Thanks.

Fortunately, the little elves at Microsoft have worked long and hard to make Word compatible with a wide range of earlier and competing word processing formats, as well as with documents created on other types of computers. Your approach to the translation issue depends on whether you're trying to work with someone else's document or trying to give someone with a different system a copy of one of your documents. I cover both sides of the transaction in this chapter.

EXPERT ADVICE

If you get a disk from someone with a Macintosh computer, try asking him to give you the files on a PC formatted disk. Most Macs can read PC disks, but the reverse is not as common.

Getting the Document onto Your Computer

Generally, someone will hand you a document on a disk (although more and more often nowadays documents are arriving via e-mail or in some other electronic form), and you'll need to import it somehow into Word. If the disk is from a PC, go ahead and put it in your disk drive. Then open the floppy drive window. (Double-click My Computer, and then double-click the floppy drive icon.) Drag onto your desktop the document (or documents) you need to import into Word (see Figure 6.1). The original files will stay on the disk unless you hold down SHIFT while dragging.

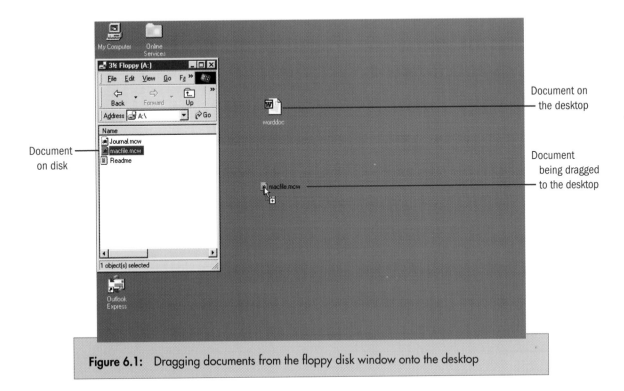

Figure 6.1: Dragging documents from the floppy disk window onto the desktop

DEFINITION

Import:
To open in one program a document that was created in another.

If you put a shortcut to your disk drive on the Start menu, you can open a disk easily from anywhere, instead of having to use My Computer to access your floppy drive icon. To add the shortcut, just drag the disk icon onto the Start button.

Files that arrive as e-mail attachments will be stored in a folder designated by your e-mail program. In most e-mail programs, you can select where you want file attachments to end up. Good locations include your desktop, a temporary folder (usually called Temp), or a folder specially created for attachments.

Downloading Files from the Internet or an Intranet

Another way to get files onto your computer is to download them from the Internet (or from your company's internal intranet). With Word, you can now simply enter the URL of the file you want into the Open dialog box, and Word will download and open the file for you.

See Chapter 14 for more about setting up FTP locations and downloading files.

If you have access to an FTP site (an Internet file-archive site), you can select it from the normal Open dialog box. Click the Open button or select File | Open. Then, click the Look In drop-down list box, scroll down to FTP Locations, and choose one of the locations there (or set up your own by clicking Add/Modify FTP Locations). Then browse through folders and select a document to open as if the file were on your own computer. See Chapter 14 for more on transferring files to and from Internet (and intranet) sites.

Word Also Works as a Web Browser

The more conventional way to download files from the Internet (or from intranets) is to use an FTP (File Transfer Protocol) program or a Web browser (such as Internet Explorer or Netscape Navigator). As the Windows desktop evolves, more and more programs will have the ability to browse the Net built in, as Word now does. This means that you can actually jump around from one Internet site to another, following links if necessary. When you reach the file you want, Word will open it on the screen.

Moreover, Word can also understand and handle embedded hyperlinks, including links to resources out there on the Internet, to those on local networks (intranet or otherwise), and to objects stored on your own computer (see Figure 6.2). If you work with a document that includes a link to a file, you can just click the link to open that file in

DEFINITION

Download:
To transfer a file from a remote computer to your local computer.

Intranet:
A private network based on the protocols used to run the Internet.

URL (uniform resource locator):
A unique address identifying a specific file or resource on the Internet or on an intranet.

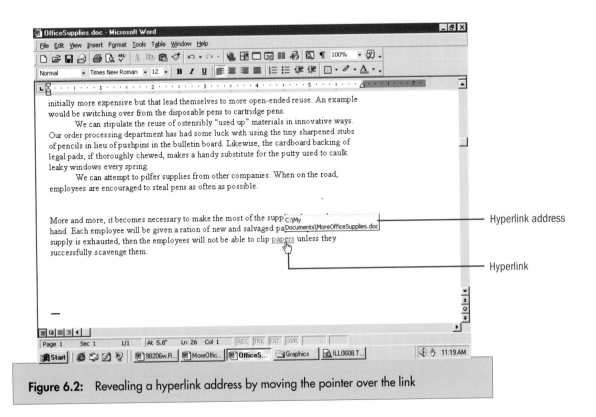

Figure 6.2:   Revealing a hyperlink address by moving the pointer over the link

Word (if it can be opened—see "Trying to Open the Document," coming up).

In fact, when you type a file path or URL into a document, AutoFormat As You Type can automatically change it into a clickable hyperlink (see Chapter 3 for how to set your AutoFormat preferences).

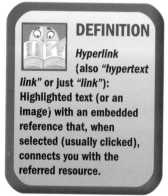

DEFINITION

Hyperlink (also *"hypertext link"* or just *"link"*): Highlighted text (or an image) with an embedded reference that, when selected (usually clicked), connects you with the referred resource.

Converting Web Documents to Word Format

Many of the documents accessible via the Internet (and on many private intranets) are created and stored in HTML (hypertext markup language) format. Fortunately, Word recognizes and can handle HTML documents, so if you download one via the Open dialog box by clicking a link leading to it, Word will automatically convert the document to its own format and display it on the screen. When you save it, you'll have the choice of saving it in HTML or Word format (as discussed later in this chapter).

Trying to Open the Document

You can often open a document that was created in one of the common word processing formats by just using the normal file opening routine to import it into Word. Word will recognize the format and automatically convert the document on the fly. Here's how it works.

First, click the Open button on the Standard toolbar. This brings up the Open dialog box. Click on the Up One Level button a few times to work your way up to the desktop (or wherever you've got the file stored).

The main window in the Open dialog box typically shows only those files whose extensions are .doc, which is the extension that Word automatically gives to its document files. (File extensions might not be visible in this window, but they are there nonetheless, and Windows still uses them to help determine file type.) Many documents besides those created in Word have that extension. But an equal number of documents have different extensions or no extension at all. To see all the documents on your desktop, regardless of their extensions, click in the Files Of Type drop-down list box and choose All Files (see Figure 6.3). Documents of every type will then appear in the window.

Then simply go ahead and select the document you want to open and click the Open button. Most of the time, Word will know what to do and will go ahead and open the document without giving you any trouble. It may take awhile, though. As Word performs the conversion, you'll see a message in the status bar telling you that Word is converting your document.

SHORTCUT
Double-click the document in the window of the Open dialog box to open it.

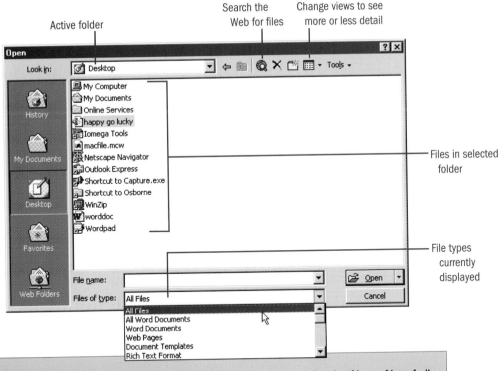

Figure 6.3:　Changing the display in the Open dialog box from only .doc files to files of all formats

If your document has an unusual file format or a misleading extension, Word may pop up the File Conversion dialog box, shown here, asking you to specify the format of the original file. Choose the one you think is correct and click OK.

Open a file as Plain Text —

Select an encoding option for the file you're trying to open —

Preview the conversion results —

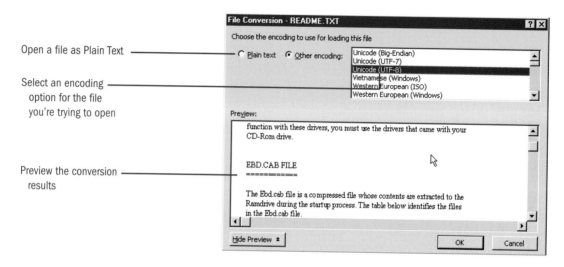

If you attempt to open a file of a type that Word doesn't recognize, you'll see a dialog box asking you which filter you want to use to open the file. If all else fails, try Text Only, but doing that doesn't always produce a readable document. Your best bet is to ask the original creator of the document to try saving it in a different format—one that both her word processing program and yours understand. For more on that option, see "Saving a Document in a Lingua Franca," later in this chapter.

Clickin' or Draggin' the Document Icon

In Windows, the easiest way to open a document is to double-click its icon. You don't have to have Word already running to do this. Windows will start up whatever program is needed to open the item you double-click on. For this to work smoothly with Word, however, the icon must be a Word document icon (a blue-edged rectangle with a blue *W* inside).

Double-Clicking on a Word Document Icon

If you double-click on a Word document icon, Word will start (if it's not already running) and automatically open that document.

Word can handle any document created in an earlier version of the program (any version number earlier than 9.0) with no trouble. It won't even mention to you that it's translating the document. If you need to return the document to someone who is using a version of Word earlier than 6.0, make sure to save it again in that person's original format before giving it back (as explained in "Saving in Another Format," later in this chapter).

CAUTION

A document can look like a Word document without being one by having the ".doc" extension. Word will still attempt to open the document, but it may fail or open the document as "garbage" if the document's format is not one that Word can translate.

Double-Clicking on a Non-Word Document Icon

If a document appears to have been made in another word processing program, such as WordPerfect, double-clicking on it will start that program instead. If the document is unrecognized, it will sport the generic Windows icon.

If you double-click the icon, a Windows dialog box called Open With will appear. This dialog box asks you to choose the program you want to use to open the unrecognized document (see Figure 6.4).

Scroll through the list of programs in the Choose The Program You Want To Use list box, and click on winword. Don't check Always Use This Program To Open This File unless you know all the ramifications of doing so. Then click OK. If Word is unable to interpret the document correctly, it will open the document up but render its contents as unreadable garbage.

macfile.mcx

EXPERT ADVICE

The appearance of a document icon is based on its (usually) hidden extension. (This means that a WordPerfect document whose filename ends in .doc will appear to be a Word document.) If you miss those old DOS extensions, you can turn them on again in the View tab of the Options dialog box that can be accessed from the View menu of any folder window.

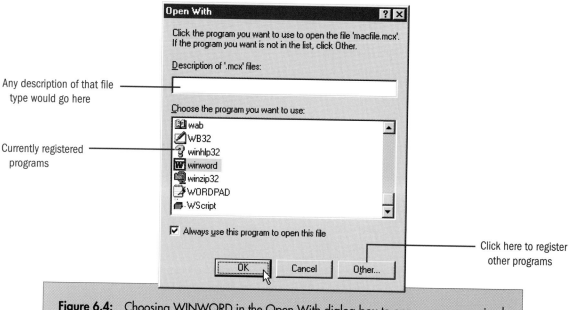

Any description of that file type would go here

Currently registered programs

Figure 6.4: Choosing WINWORD in the Open With dialog box to open an unrecognized document

Click here to register other programs

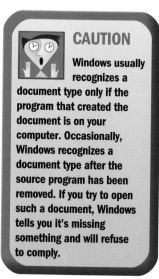

CAUTION

Windows usually recognizes a document type only if the program that created the document is on your computer. Occasionally, Windows recognizes a document type after the source program has been removed. If you try to open such a document, Windows tells you it's missing something and will refuse to comply.

Right-Clicking on an Unrecognized Document Icon

The easiest way to open an unrecognized document in Word is to right-click the document icon, and then choose Open With from the menu that pops up. This also brings up the Open With dialog box that is shown in Figure 6.4. Again, if Word is unable to interpret the document correctly, you'll have unreadable garbage on the screen.

Dragging a Document Icon onto the Word Icon

An easy way to open a document created in another word processing program is to drag the document icon onto the Word program icon (or, ideally, onto a Word shortcut on your desktop). Word will start up (if it's not already running) and open the document, if it's able to. Chapter 2 explains how to put a shortcut to Word on your desktop.

If Word Is Unable to Open a Document

There will be times when you will receive a document that you simply can't open. There are two things you can try in such a situation: First, try to open the document in some other program, such as WordPad or another word processing program. This intermediate step might provide the missing link. Save the open document in WordPad (or your other word processing program) as a Word document (give it a different name). Expect more minor flaws and inaccuracies in the format than would occur in a normal import.

If that doesn't work, ask the owner of the original document to save it in a format that you both have in common. You can scroll through the Files Of Type drop-down list box in the Open dialog box to see what formats Word speaks. Ask the other person to check his or her Save As dialog box (or the equivalent) for formats that the source program can produce. Look for formats in common. At the very least, you should both be able to handle text files (though you'll lose all your formatting). Better yet, you might both be able to save in Rich Text Format, which will preserve most of the formatting.

If you open a document in another program, you might have to clean up a lot of extraneous coding from the document's native format.

Saving Imported Documents

Word remembers the format of an imported document. If you just click the Save button or select File | Save when you are done working with the document, Word will keep the document in its original format. To turn the thing into a Word document (which is worth doing, in my opinion, if you need to keep it around), select File | Save As.

When the Save As dialog box comes up, choose Word Document in the Save As Type drop-down list box. Then click Save. From then on, your file will be a bona fide Word document.

See "Saving a Document in a Lingua Franca" later in this chapter for more on Rich Text Format.

EXPERT ADVICE

If you open a document created in an earlier version of Word (such as Word 2.0), you can save it directly in Word 2000 format by using the plain old Save command or button (as opposed to Save As).

Saving in Another Format

The kindest thing you can do is save your Word document in the exact format that the other person uses. Word can imitate a large set of other word processing programs for this purpose. (The results are not always 100 percent accurate, but what is?)

To save a Word document as another type of document, select File | Save As. Then click in the Save As Type drop-down list box, and choose from the many other formats available. Type a new name for your document (to preserve the original copy in Word format) and then click Save.

You can also use this technique to convert Word documents to the popular HTML Web-document format for publication on a Web site or for internal availability on a company intranet (see Chapter 13 for more on converting documents to HTML).

See Chapters 13 and 14 for more on creating and publishing Web documents.

Saving a Document in a Lingua Franca

In the worst-case scenario, you and your coworker will have word processing programs that have no formats in common. In that case, you can still save your document in Text Only format (which is usually a better choice than Text Only With Line Breaks, since it preserves the original paragraphs). Every word processing program on the planet can read text documents, but all your formatting will be lost. A better choice is Rich Text Format, which Word can produce. It's a kind of plain text format with a lot of special codes to indicate

---

EXPERT ADVICE

If Word can't produce a document in exactly the format that your colleague's word processing program expects, offer him the list of formats that Word can produce and see whether his word processing program can import any of them.

different types of formatting. If your colleague's word processing program understands RTF (as it's called), you're in business.

Either way, select File | Save As, drop down the Save As Type list box, and choose the common format (Text Only or Rich Text Format). Give the document a different name, to avoid eradicating the original, and click Save.

Sending and Uploading Files

The flip side of downloading and converting files from the Internet is sending or uploading files to remote sites. Just as you can now download files by entering the appropriate URL into the Open dialog box, you can also upload a file (send it to a remote server) by selecting File | Save As. In the Save In box, scroll down to FTP Locations and choose a site (or set one up with Add/Modify FTP Locations).

See Chapters 10 and 11 for more about sending and uploading files. See Chapter 14 for more about setting up FTP locations and uploading files to Web sites.

Then, browse through folders for the right place to save the document, type a filename, and click the Save button.

There's More . . .

By now you're probably tired of Word. This might be a good place to knock off for a while. You can take a rest or move on. The next chapter tells you what to do if you've lost track of a document on your computer. After that, the rest of the book covers how to handle heavy-duty tasks, how to create highly organized documents, and how to make and publish Web pages.

CHAPTER 7

Finding Stuff You've Lost on Your Computer and the Net

INCLUDES

- Using Word's Find feature to find a document
- Using Windows' built-in Find feature to find a document
- Checking the Recycle Bin
- Searching the Internet with the Web Search button
- Searching an intranet with Web Fast Find

Search for Documents from Within Word ➔ pp. 114–117

1. Click the Open button on the Standard toolbar. In the Open dialog box select Tools | Find.
2. Click the Delete button if you don't want to use the supplied criterion.
3. Choose a property, a condition, and a value in the Define More Criteria area.
4. Click the Add to List button.
5. Repeat steps 3 and 4 as often as you need to.
6. Choose a folder in the Look In drop-down list box. Click the Find Now button.

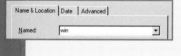

Search for a Document in Windows ➔ pp. 118–119

1. Click on Start | Find | Files or Folders.
2. Click the Name & Location tab.
3. Type a filename or part of a name in the Named box.
4. Choose a drive to start searching in the Look In list box.
5. Check Include Subfolders unless you only want to look in the root of the drive.
6. Click the Find Now button.

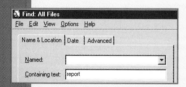

Search by Contents ➔ p. 120

1. Click on Start | Find | Files or Folders.
2. Click the Name & Location tab.
3. Type the text you're looking for in the Containing Text box.
4. Click the Find Now button.

Save the Results of a Search ➡ p. 120

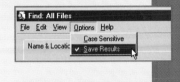

1. In the Windows Find dialog box, select Options | Save Results.
2. Select File | Save Search.

Check the Recycle Bin
for Missing Files ➡ pp. 121–122

1. Double-click the Recycle Bin on the desktop.
2. Scan the list of files (you can sort them by deletion date or alphabetical order).

Search the Web from Within Word ➡ p. 122

1. Click the Web Search button on the Web Toolbar (it's also on the Open dialog box). Microsoft's all-in-one search page will open.
2. Choose a search engine and then type your word or phrase in the box provided. If you find the file you're looking for, then Word will download and open the file for you.
3. Try another search if you don't find what you want, or review the search engine's advanced options.

Documents get lost inside computers. It's a fact—sad, but true. Yes, it helps if you maintain an organized folder structure and if you're always careful to save your documents in the correct folders. But no matter what, sometimes files just aren't where you think they are. Fortunately, program developers have started to recognize this fact instead of catering to an idealized user (geeky, just like them), and you now have several decent ways to hunt for missing documents.

It always happens at the worst time, too. Just when someone from accounting is hollering for some backup paperwork, or when your boss needs to see that report you thought you were done with last October. That's when you can't find what you need. Don't let the pressure get to you. Keep cool, follow the steps in this chapter, and you'll find your missing work.

Searching for Documents from Within Word

Word's document-finding feature, Find, is available from the Open dialog box. Click the Open button on the Standard toolbar to get to the Open dialog box. Then go to the Tools menu on the right side of the Open dialog box and select Find. This brings up the Find dialog box (see Figure 7.1).

In the Find Files That Match These Criteria area (the top half of the dialog box), there should be one criterion listed (based on what was selected in the Files Of Type list box in the Open dialog box). The default criterion is usually Files Of Type Is Word Documents (which I know doesn't sound grammatical). Word is building a list of criteria by which to filter the possible documents and come up with a short list of documents that meet all your requirements. The list always starts with Word Documents, but you can add as many additional criteria as you like and even remove this one basic criterion

DEFINITION

Criterion:
A rule or test applied to a set of objects under consideration. Only those objects that match the criterion or criteria—for example, Word documents created before a certain date and containing some specific text—will be selected.

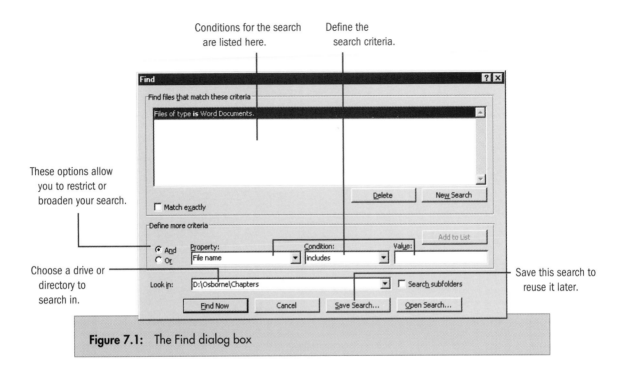

Figure 7.1: The Find dialog box

as well as others you've added. To remove a criterion, just select it and click the Delete button.

Describing the Document to Search For

You can add more criteria to the list if it will further limit the number of documents that will match, helping you zero in on your missing document sooner. To do so see the explanation in Figure 7.2. Repeat this process as often as necessary to refine your search.

EXPERT ADVICE

To search for a document based on text it contains, add this criteria: Text Or Property (in the Property box), *includes* (in the Condition box), the text to look for (in the Value box). A search that includes this kind of criteria can take a while.

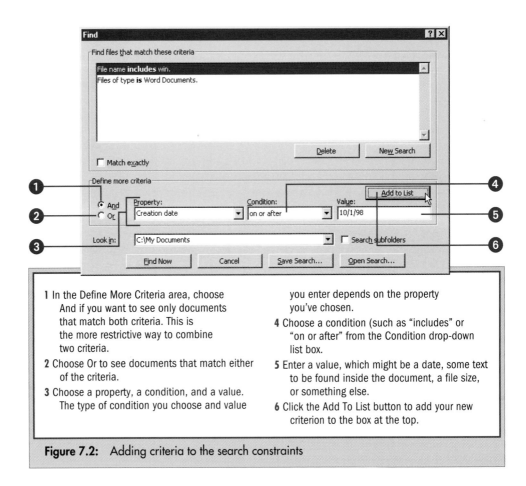

1 In the Define More Criteria area, choose And if you want to see only documents that match both criteria. This is the more restrictive way to combine two criteria.

2 Choose Or to see documents that match either of the criteria.

3 Choose a property, a condition, and a value. The type of condition you choose and value you enter depends on the property you've chosen.

4 Choose a condition (such as "includes" or "on or after" from the Condition drop-down list box.

5 Enter a value, which might be a date, some text to be found inside the document, a file size, or something else.

6 Click the Add To List button to add your new criterion to the box at the top.

Figure 7.2: Adding criteria to the search constraints

Figure 7.2 shows a Find dialog box that has had "File name includes win" added and in which a third criterion—creation date on or after 10/1/98—is in the process of being added.

Specifying Where to Search

At the bottom of the Find dialog box, you can specify a folder in which to start the search, though if you leave it at C:\ you can be sure that your whole hard disk will be searched. Check the Search Subfolders option. If you uncheck it, the search will end in the Look In folder. With it checked, all folders inside the Look In folder, and all folders inside them, and so on, will also be searched.

Starting the Search

To begin the search, click the Find Now button. The Find dialog box will disappear and the documents Word finds will appear in the Open dialog box, shown here. Word will display all the documents it finds, and the folders they live in, in the same window in the Open dialog box.

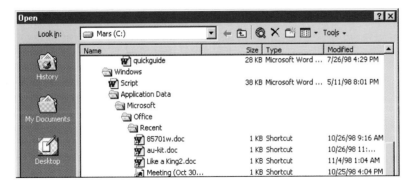

Complicated Searches

Word's Find feature can be rather complicated and confusing, so here's a more complicated example to give you some realistic practice.

Let's say you're looking for a document created before October 1998, whose title has the word *report* in it somewhere, and in which the word *widget* appears in the text. Choose File | Open and then follow the steps in Figure 7.3.

EXPERT ADVICE

If you don't have a Web Fast Find page set up on your network, you can still use the Windows Find File feature described earlier in this chapter to search other computer drives accessible from your network.

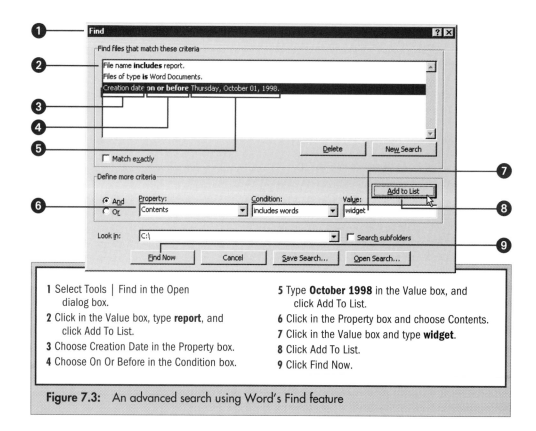

1 Select Tools | Find in the Open
   dialog box.
2 Click in the Value box, type **report**, and
   click Add To List.
3 Choose Creation Date in the Property box.
4 Choose On Or Before in the Condition box.

5 Type **October 1998** in the Value box, and
   click Add To List.
6 Click in the Property box and choose Contents.
7 Click in the Value box and type **widget**.
8 Click Add To List.
9 Click Find Now.

Figure 7.3:   An advanced search using Word's Find feature

Searching for Documents with Windows' Find Feature

An alternative to Word's Find feature is the powerful Find feature that comes with Windows itself. You might use this Find feature when you haven't started Word yet, or you might end up preferring it to Word's approach.

To try the Windows Find feature, click the Start button, choose Find, and then choose Files Or Folders.

Searching by Filename

In the Find dialog box that appears, type a filename or part of a name and then click the Find Now button. Find will start searching. While

it's working, the image of a magnifying glass will move in a circle with an image of a document appearing and disappearing underneath it.

A window will open at the bottom of the dialog box, and files will start appearing in it as they are found (see Figure 7.4). You can stop the search at any time (if, for example, you see the document you're looking for) by clicking the Stop button. The window that shows the found documents behaves as any Windows folder window does: the icons in it can be double-clicked, copied, and so on.

To change the search criteria or start a new search, click the New Search button. Windows will warn you that this will clear the results of the first search. Click on OK. (If you do want to save the results of your first search, see "Saving the Results of a Search," later in this section.)

SHORTCUT

If you have a folder window open, pressing CTRL+F will open the Find dialog box. You can also right-click on any file or folder and choose Find from the menu that pops up.

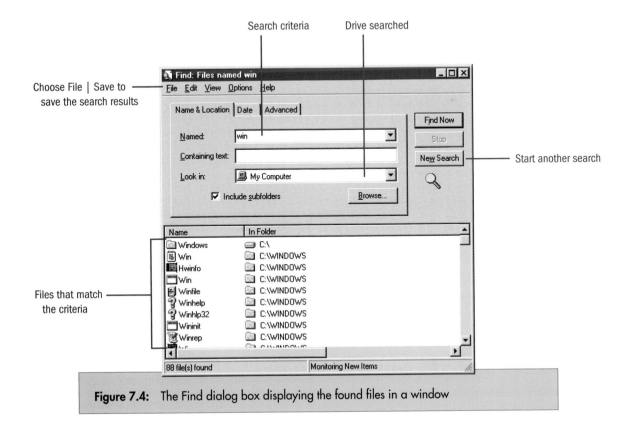

Figure 7.4: The Find dialog box displaying the found files in a window

Searching by Date or Contents

To constrain the search based on the document's creation date or the date on which it was last modified, click the Date tab in the Find dialog box. Provide the information requested, and click the Find Now button.

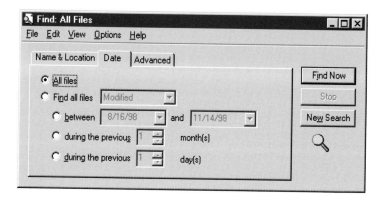

To search for a document based on some text that is contained within it, enter the text you're looking for in the Containing text box. Click the Advanced tab to specify types of files (for instance, Microsoft Word documents only) in the Of Type box, and you can specify size limitations in the Size Is box.

Saving the Results of a Search

If you have the funny feeling that you're going to end up wanting to reuse the results of this search sometime in the near future, you can save them. Because the window that shows the results of a Find search works just like any other folder window, you can save it and use it as if it were a folder. To do this, from the Find dialog box select Options | Save Results and then File | Save Search. Windows will save an icon on your desktop called Files named Such-And-Such, which you can double-click on whenever you want to access those found files again.

Checking the Recycle Bin

If your document is missing because it has been deleted (or thrown in the Recycle Bin) accidentally, it won't show up when you try to find it either within Word or in Windows. So, as a last resort, you should open the Recycle Bin and look inside. To do so, double-click the Recycle Bin icon on the desktop.

A window much like a folder window will open, showing the deleted files (see Figure 7.5). The files are probably in alphabetical order. (If they're not, click the Name button at the top of the window to sort the files by name.) Scan through, scrolling if necessary, until

Choose File | Empty Recycle Bin to permanently
remove all files and recover disk space.

Choose File | Restore to restore
a selected file or files.

Click here to sort
by name.

Click here to sort by
file location.

Deleted files

Click here to sort by
file size.

Click here to sort
by file type.

Click here to sort by
deletion date.

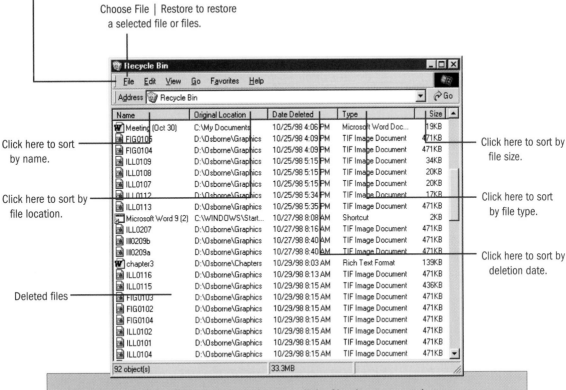

Figure 7.5: The Recycle Bin window, showing all the files that are gone but not yet forgotten

you see the file you're looking for. If you find it in there, simply drag it out of the window onto the desktop, and then put it in a safe place so that you won't lose it again.

If you haven't found that missing document by now, it's gone. Check any backup disks you might have made from your computer, as well as any stray disks. There are file recovery programs (such as those included with the Norton Utilities package) that can scour your hard disk for scraps of obliterated files containing key words, so if you have the patience for such an approach, you still might recover some of the missing file.

Searching the Web from Within Word

 To look for a document that is somewhere out there on the Net, even if you don't know its filename or location, click the Web Search button on the Web Toolbar (it's also on the Open dialog box). This opens up a Microsoft central all-in-one search site. Enter key words into any of the search boxes and click a Search button. If you find the document or file you're looking for, Word will download and open it for you.

Searching an Intranet with Web Fast Find

If your computer is part of an internal network, and if the network's administrator has set the network up as an intranet, enabling most Internet software to work over the local connection, *and* if that sysadmin is also trying to accommodate Microsoft Office 2000 as completely as possible, then she or he may have installed a Web Fast Find page. This is the local equivalent of a Web search page, but its database will include only references to files on your local intranet.

There's More . . .

The remaining chapters all deal with various specific projects you might want to undertake with Word. Don't slog through them until or unless you actually need the specific help they provide.

CHAPTER 8

Designing and Reusing Forms

INCLUDES

- Planning a form
- Constructing a form
- Basing a form on a table
- Massaging a form into shape
- Adding lines and shading to a form
- Making an interactive onscreen form
- Filling out an on-screen form

Add Information to the Top of a Form ➡ p. 127

Before you insert the table that will make up the main part of your form, type the information you need at the top of the form, including the name of the form, the name of the organization the form is for, and any necessary instructions.

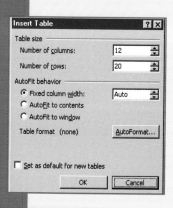

Insert a Table ➡ p. 127

1. Choose Table | Insert | Table.
2. Type the number of columns and rows.
3. Click OK.

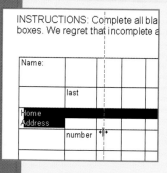

Fit the Text into Your Form ➡ pp. 127–129

- Click in a table cell to add text. Press Tab to move from cell to cell.
- Experiment with different font sizes.
- Drag column dividers to widen or narrow columns.
- Select and change individual rows for fine adjustments.
- Merge cells to create wider areas.
- Add and delete columns.

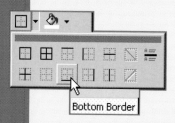

Add Borders (Lines) to a Form ➡ pp. 131–133

1. Right-click on any toolbar and choose Tables And Borders.
2. Select a cell or cells.
3. Choose a line weight.
4. Click a border button to apply a border to the selection.
5. Repeat as necessary.

Add Shading to a Form ➡ p. 133

1. Select a cell or cells.
2. Choose a shading color from the Tables And Borders toolbar.
3. Repeat as necessary.

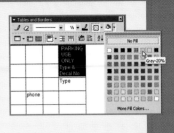

Make an Onscreen Form ➡ pp. 134–135

1. Right-click on any toolbar and choose Forms from the menu that pops up.
2. Insert text fields, check box fields, and drop-down fields as needed.
3. Protect the document.
4. Save it as a template.

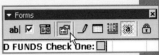

Use an Onscreen Form ➡ p. 138

1. Choose File | New.
2. Choose the template for the onscreen form.
3. Click OK.
4. Have the user fill out the form.
5. Save the form.
6. Print the form, if necessary.

All organizations, from the glacial bureaucracy to the entrepreneurial home-office sole proprietorship, rely on forms. Nobody really likes forms much. They never give you enough room. They represent paperwork in its purest form. But face it: without 'em, the whole world would run on Post-it® notes and cocktail napkins.

The simplest forms, such as straightforward invoices, require no special tricks for assembly. You just type some categories, leave room or make long underlines for the user to fill in the blanks, and presto! You've created a form. Beyond this rudimentary level, though, the creation of a form requires you to know a bit about tables and how to apply borders (lines) on the page. If you're truly ambitious and forward-looking, with a little extra effort you can create onscreen forms, complete with automated check boxes and drop-down lists of choices.

Planning Your Form

See Chapter 12 for more information about the fanciest document design techniques.

The first step in creating a form with Word is to sketch out a dummy on paper. That's right—step away from your computer, grab a piece of scrap paper, and pick up a pencil. Try to determine the following:

- How many lines of information will your form need?
- How many items should go side by side?
- Where will you want boxes and bordered areas?
- What wording will you use and what text should be the most prominent?

Tables (and other techniques for drawing them) are discussed in other contexts in Chapter 12.

You don't have to polish the thing at this stage—you're just trying to get an idea of your design.

Constructing Your Form

Tables are essential for keeping columns aligned and creating boxed areas (cells). For a simple form, a relatively small table with just a few columns and rows will do the job without requiring a lot of tweaking. For a complicated form, you can either create several tables and massage them separately or start with one mega-table and work on various parts of it to create the different areas. If you're going to make one big table, start by figuring out the largest number of boxes or areas that will need to go side by side on a single line. This is how wide the table will need to be.

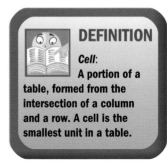

DEFINITION

Cell: A portion of a table, formed from the intersection of a column and a row. A cell is the smallest unit in a table.

Adding a Title and Other Information at the Top

Before you go ahead and insert a table, type the information you need at the top of the form, such as the name of the form, the name of the organization the form is for, and any necessary instructions.

PARKING PERMIT APPLICATION
Spudco Industries, Worldwide

INSTRUCTIONS: Complete all blanks in this form and check (☑) applicable boxes. We regret that incomplete applications cannot be processed.

Now you're ready to insert a table.

Inserting a Table

When you need a small table, it's easiest to just draw tables with the pop-up menu options. Follow the steps in Figure 8.1.
Voilà! There's your table.

SHORTCUT

You can also just draw the row and column dividers using the Pencil tool. More on that in Chapter 12.

Fitting Text into the Table

Now it's time to start entering the text for the form and playing with the font sizes and column widths to get things to fit. Click inside the cell in which you want to include text. Type your text and move from

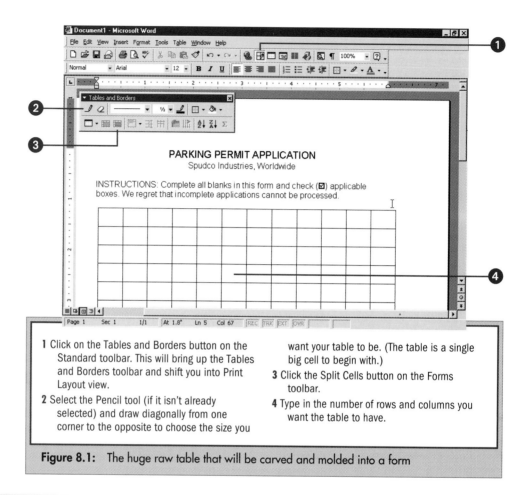

1 Click on the Tables and Borders button on the Standard toolbar. This will bring up the Tables and Borders toolbar and shift you into Print Layout view.

2 Select the Pencil tool (if it isn't already selected) and draw diagonally from one corner to the opposite to choose the size you

want your table to be. (The table is a single big cell to begin with.)

3 Click the Split Cells button on the Forms toolbar.

4 Type in the number of rows and columns you want the table to have.

Figure 8.1:   The huge raw table that will be carved and molded into a form

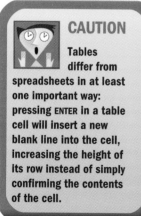

CAUTION

Tables differ from spreadsheets in at least one important way: pressing ENTER in a table cell will insert a new blank line into the cell, increasing the height of its row instead of simply confirming the contents of the cell.

cell to cell with the TAB key. Work your way down from the top and be generous with rows. The table columns are all quite narrow at this point, but in most of the rows of your form you won't need to use all the columns, so you can widen columns when necessary to make important text fit. To widen a column, put the mouse pointer over a column divider and then drag it (see Figure 8.2).

When you drag a column divider, the columns on either side of the divider are resized accordingly. If you don't want the column to the right to be resized, press SHIFT as you drag the column divider.

When it comes time to format the text in a table, you can select an entire column by holding down ALT and clicking in the column. Another method is to place the insertion point at the top of the

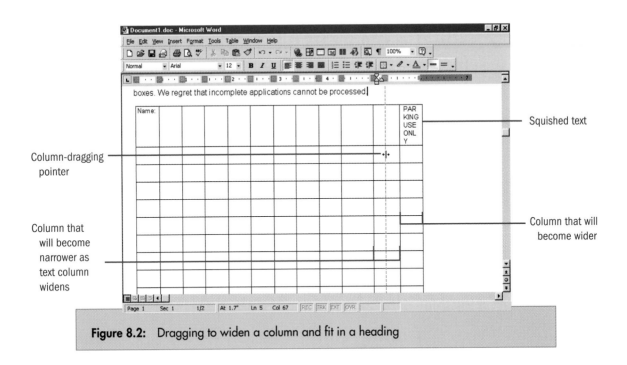

Column-dragging pointer

Squished text

Column that will become narrower as text column widens

Column that will become wider

Figure 8.2: Dragging to widen a column and fit in a heading

column and, when the pointer turns to a black downward-pointing arrow, click to select the column. To select an entire row at once, position the cursor in the left margin near the row, and click as though you were selecting a line of text. Now you can format the selected columns or rows.

You may need to adjust the size of text entries in individual cells to get things to fit nicely. Normally, any text too wide for a cell will wrap as it would in a paragraph, adding as many new lines as necessary until the text fits. The row height will automatically expand to accommodate the extra lines of text. To change the text size, select the text and type a new size in the Font Size box on the Formatting toolbar.

As you work your way down the form, you will come to rows in which you want to widen an individual cell without widening the entire column throughout the table. To do this, select the row (click just to the left of the row) and then drag the column divider. Only cells in the selected row(s) will be affected.

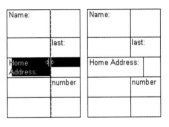

Combining Cells to Make Larger Areas

In some rows of your form, you'll need a few large columns instead of the number of columns you have specified in your table. One way to do this is to select several cells and merge them into one. To do so, just select the cells by clicking in the first and dragging through to the last one, and then choose Table | Merge Cells.

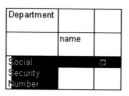

Work your way to the bottom of the form, manipulating the cells until the text areas sort out into the form you envisioned.

Adding and Deleting Rows and Columns

No matter how careful you were in making the initial estimates of the numbers of rows and columns needed for your form, you'll probably need to add or delete a few before you're done. To select a row, click in the margin just to the left of it. To select a column, press ALT and click in the column. To delete a selected row or column, choose Table | Delete | Rows or Table | Delete | Columns.

Inserting a row or column is also easy:

1. Select a row or column, but this time select the row above or the column to the left of the point at which you want to insert the new area.

2. Click the Insert Table button on the Standard toolbar. In this context, clicking the button inserts a row or column into the table. To insert a column after the last column of a table, hold down ALT and click to the right of any cell in the last column before clicking the Insert Table button.

3. Click the Insert Column button.

SHORTCUT
To add a row at the end of a table, place the insertion point in the last cell of the current last row and press TAB.

The Insert Table button turns into the Insert Column (or Insert Row, depending on the context) button when you are working inside an existing table.

Adding Lines to a Form

In Word, lines are called *borders*, which gives you a hint about how they're applied. You can add borders to any or all sides of most document elements, such as a paragraph or a selection. For your form, you'll generally apply borders to table cells (though you might sometimes apply borders to the text floating inside a cell).

Remember, gridlines don't print. They're just there to show you the outlines of the table.

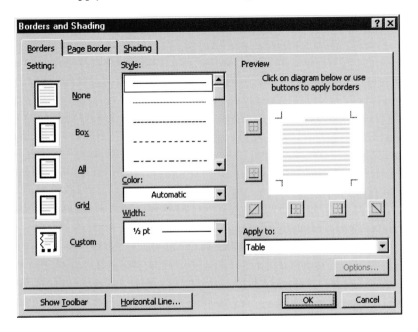

If you want to apply a uniform format to the entire table or to format only a single cell or a selection, do the following:

1. Right-click in the table and choose Borders and Shading from the pop-up menu.

2. Make your choices from the Borders and Shading dialog box that appears.

3. Choose the item to format if nothing has been selected (Table, Cell, or Paragraph in the Apply To list at the lower right of the dialog box).

EXPERT ADVICE

Word now adds borders automatically when you create a new table. If you plan on adding different styles of borders to your forms, it may be a good idea to follow the steps in applying uniform formats to the entire table and select None in the Setting area. This way you can start with a clean slate.

When formatting rows and columns, there are easier steps to take. See Figure 8.3, which shows a fill-in-the-blank line being created.

When you want a different type of border, click on the Line Style drop-down list box at the left end of the Tables And Borders toolbar and choose which one you want to apply. Again, make sure to select

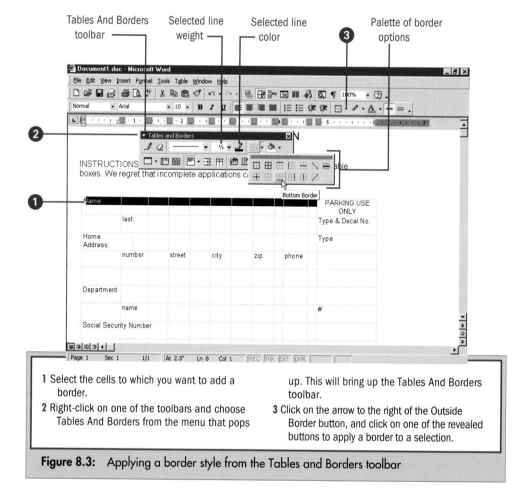

1 Select the cells to which you want to add a border.

2 Right-click on one of the toolbars and choose Tables And Borders from the menu that pops up. This will bring up the Tables And Borders toolbar.

3 Click on the arrow to the right of the Outside Border button, and click on one of the revealed buttons to apply a border to a selection.

Figure 8.3: Applying a border style from the Tables and Borders toolbar

---

EXPERT ADVICE

Sometimes a selection of cells will behave strangely (it may include stray cells or skip needed ones) after you've moved column dividers or merged cells. If this happens, select individual cells in the area and apply the borders one by one.

---

the cells whose borders you want to modify first. If you add a border to a cell or set of cells by mistake, it's easy to remove it. Keep the cells selected (or select them again). Then click the No Border button (located on the bottom row of the palette, showing gridlines but no borders) on the Tables And Borders toolbar.

Shading Selected Areas

What good would a form be without some shaded for-office-use-only areas? Shading is also a good way to emphasize the heads of some sections. You add shading from the drop-down list box at the right end of the Tables And Borders toolbar. Once again, if you're shading a whole table or a single cell, you can do this by choosing Borders And Shading from the shortcut menu that pops up when you right-click within a table. Once the Borders And Shading toolbar appears, click the Shading tab.

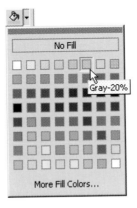

Just select the area you want to shade, and then choose a shading option. (The values in the list refer to the percentage of black on white.) You can also add color as you see fit.

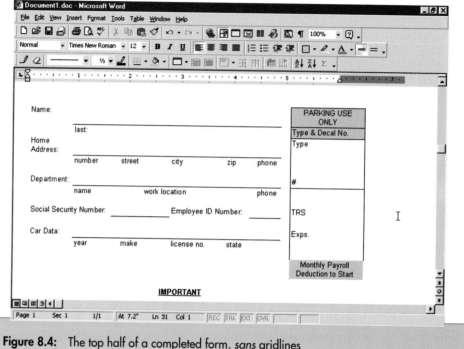

Figure 8.4: The top half of a completed form, *sans* gridlines

Viewing a Completed Form

The best way to judge a form (besides printing it out) is to turn off the dashed gridlines that show the structure of the underlying table. To do so, choose Table | Hide Gridlines. The gridlines will disappear and your form will snap into focus (see Figure 8.4, above).

Turn off the Tables And Borders toolbar when you're done (right-click on it and uncheck Tables And Borders). There's little enough room on the screen as it is!

Making an Onscreen Form

Most of you are done with this chapter now and should get out while you can. If you're interested in the slightly more arcane topic of onscreen forms, though, read on.

The purpose of an onscreen form is to save paper and to provide a sort of interactive guidance system that helps the form-user fill out the form efficiently and accurately. (Does it really work that way? Beats me. It might take a while to pay off because people will find it unfamiliar at first, but with the recent focus on intranets and online collaboration, you're likely to see more of this sort of thing in the future.) Also, a form of this sort can have protected areas, so that the subject filling out the form can't accidentally overwrite or change the contents of the form.

If you're willing to attempt this, start by bringing up the Forms toolbar (right-click on any toolbar and choose Forms from the menu that pops up). The compact, floating Forms toolbar appears, shown here, with an assortment of cryptic buttons.

CAUTION

Shading usually looks different on a printed copy than it looks on the screen, so consider test-printing some different shading choices before you settle on a type of shading for your form. The 10 percent to 20 percent values are the most legible ones.

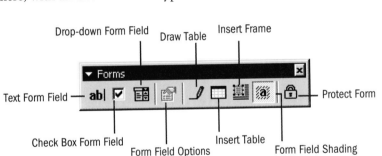

The Forms toolbar has its own copy of the Insert Table button, and you can use it to create fairly wide tables:

1. Move the Forms toolbar over to the left of your screen.
2. Click the Insert Table button and drag across the waffle-patterned grid that appears in order to highlight the number of rows and columns you want.
3. Release the mouse, and the empty table will be in your document.

For any area of the form that requires the user to enter text (as opposed to those for which a check box or drop-down list would be more appropriate), click in the appropriate cell and then click the Text Form Field button. A shaded box will appear in the cell.

DEFINITION

Onscreen form: A form designed to be viewed and filled out on a computer screen. Once the blanks are filled in, forms of this type can then be printed out, if desired, or they can simply be passed on and stored electronically.

Form field: An area in a form designed to hold a specific type of data. Text form fields allow text to be entered, check box form fields allow options to be checked or unchecked, and drop-down form fields allow the user to select from a list of choices.

Inserting Check Boxes

The Text Form Field Options dialog box allows you to control the maximum length of the text entry, among other things.

Check boxes give users simple yes or no options, making a form easy to fill out. To insert a check box, click the Check Box Form Field button. Then, to control whether or not the box is checked to begin with, make sure that your insertion point is on the check box field you created, and then click the Form Field Options button of the toolbar (see Figure 8.5). In the Check Box Form Field Options dialog box that appears, click on Checked in the Default Value area to have the check box checked by default.

You can also add explanatory text to the form that will appear in the Word status bar at the bottom of the screen when the user puts the insertion point on the check box field. To do so follow these steps:

1. Click the Add Help Text button in the dialog box.

2. Select the Status Bar tab from the Form Field Help Text dialog box that pops up.

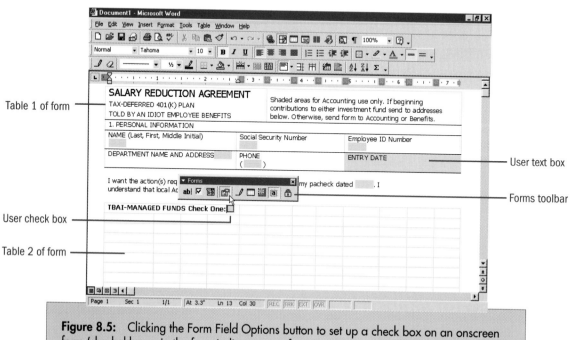

Figure 8.5: Clicking the Form Field Options button to set up a check box on an onscreen form (shaded boxes in the form indicate areas for user entry)

3. Type your explanatory text in the box provided.

4. Click OK.

Inserting Drop-Down List Boxes

To insert a box that can drop down a list of allowable choices for the user, follow these steps:

1. Click the Drop-Down Form Field button on the Forms toolbar.

2. Click the toolbar's Form Field Options button, and the Drop-Down Form Field Options dialog box appears.

3. Type each option in the Items In drop-down box, clicking on the Add button after every entry.

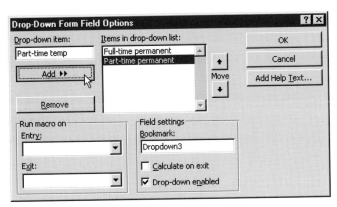

Protecting an Onscreen Form

As I mentioned earlier, to make an onscreen form function properly, you have to protect it. Not only does this prevent the people who are filling out the form from accidentally changing the fixed part of it, it also enables all the form field boxes to work the way the form designer intended them to. To protect the form, click on the Protect Form button on the Forms toolbar (or choose Tools | Protect Document).

Saving an Onscreen Form as a Template

If you want to use an onscreen form time and again, it's best to save it as a template. Then, when you want people to fill out a copy of the

CAUTION

The form template must be saved in the Templates folder if you want it to show up as an option when a user chooses File | New. Be sure that the Save In area of the Save As dialog box is pointed to that folder after you choose Document Template.

form, you just have them create a new document based on the template. The document will work the way the original form did, and when you save the results, the template will be unaffected.

To save a completed blank form as a template, do the following:

1. Choose File | Save As and type a filename for the form in the Save As dialog box.

2. Choose Document Template in the Save As Type drop-down list box.

3. Click Save.

Using an Onscreen Form

When the time comes to use an onscreen form, choose File | New (don't click on the New button on the toolbar, because that will not let you choose a template). In the New dialog box that appears, choose the template for the form, and then click OK.

Then simply have the user fill out the form. All the interactive elements should work as advertised. When the form has been completed, save it as a normal Word document. You can then print out the entire form with its contents, or, if you prefer, you can print just the entries without the form itself. To do that,

1. Choose Tools | Options and click on the Print tab.

2. Check Print Data Only For Forms in the Options For Current Document Only box.

3. Click OK.

I hope it was worth all the effort.

Creating Forms for the Web

If you make an onscreen form with Word, you can convert it to HTML (as discussed in Chapter 6), and then post it to the Web or display it on a local intranet. This way, users can interact with your form using any Web browser, instead of just with Word. The trick, however, is getting Web forms to *do* anything. For this, you will need help developing ActiveX routines from someone who understands the local network and available applications. See Chapter 14 for more about publishing on the Web and on intranets.

There's More . . .

You've just threaded your way through one of the trickier types of document to create with any word processor: a form. Using Word's flexible table features or its more involved form-field features, you can now throw together a credible form in a very short time. Chapter 9 covers what for some people is an even more intimidating bugaboo: merging names and form letters in a mass mailing (though, to be fair, my technical editor keeps assuring me that this should not be an intimidating topic, and that Word really does make it easy). Still, my advice is to escape to Chapter 10 while you can!

Preparing a Mass Mailing

INCLUDES

- Deciding when to use mail merge
- Creating a data source
- Putting together a form letter
- Filtering a data source to include only some of the data
- Using an existing data source
- Using an address book as a data source
- Merging directly to a printer
- Creating envelopes and mailing labels for a mail merge

Start a Mail Merge ➡ pp. 146–147

1. Start a new document.
2. Choose Tools | Mail Merge.
3. Click on the Create button in the Mail Merge Helper dialog box, and choose Form Letters.
4. In the dialog box that appears, click the Active Window button.

Create a Data Source ➡ pp. 147–149

1. Click on the Get Data button in the Mail Merge Helper dialog box and choose Create Data Source.
2. Add and remove field names as needed in the Create Data Source dialog box.
3. Click OK.
4. Save your data source.
5. Click the Edit Data Source button in the dialog box that appears.

Enter the Data in a Data Source ➡ pp. 149–150

1. Create a data source as explained in the previous Fast Forward item.
2. Type the contents of a field in the Data Form dialog box.
3. Press TAB to move to the next field.
4. Repeat steps 2 and 3 until the record is complete.
5. Click the Add New button to start a new record.
6. Repeat steps 2 through 5 until you've entered all the records.
7. Click OK when you've finished.

Add a Merge Field to the Main Document ➡ pp. 151–152

1. Click the Insert Merge Field button on the Mail Merge toolbar, and choose the field you want to insert.
2. Include normal spacing and punctuation around and between merge fields.
3. Repeat as necessary.

Merge the Data Source and the Main Document ➡ pp. 152–155

1. Prepare a Data Source and a Main Document.
2. Click the Mail Merge button on the Mail Merge toolbar.
3. Click the Merge button in the Merge dialog box.

Merge a Form Letter with an Existing Data Source ➡ p. 156

1. Click the Get Data button in the Mail Merge Helper dialog box and choose Open Data Source.
2. If the data source is not a Word document, choose All Documents in the Files Of Type drop-down list box.
3. Choose a data source and click on Open in the Open Data Source dialog box.

Merge to E-mail Addresses ➡ pp. 158–159

1. Click on the Merge To drop-down list box in the Merge dialog box and choose Electronic mail.
2. Click the Setup button.
3. In the Merge To Setup dialog box, choose the merge field from the data source (the address book) that contains the e-mail addresses of the recipients.
4. Type a subject line.
5. Check Send Document As An Attachment if you want the letters to be sent as Word documents and not as plain e-mail text.
6. Click OK.

Merge to Fax Recipients ➡ p. 159

1. Click on the Merge To drop-down list box in the Merge dialog box and choose Electronic Fax.
2. Click the Setup button.
3. In the Merge To Setup dialog box, choose the merge field from the data source (the address book) that contains the fax numbers of the recipients.
4. Click OK.

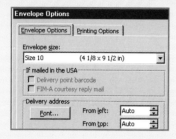

Create Envelopes for a Mailing ➡ pp. 160–162

The following steps assume you have a main document on the screen and have created a data source.

1. From within the main document, click the Mail Merge Helper button on the Mail Merge toolbar.
2. Click the Create button in the Mail Merge Helper dialog box, and choose Envelopes.
3. In the dialog box that appears, click the New Main Document button.
4. Back in the Mail Merge Helper dialog box, click the Get Data button and open a data source.
5. In the dialog box that appears, click the Set Up Main Document button.
6. In the Envelope Options dialog box, choose your envelope type.
7. Click OK.
8. In the Envelope Address dialog box, click the Insert Merge Field button and choose merge fields to construct an address.
9. Type punctuation and spaces as needed.
10. Click OK.

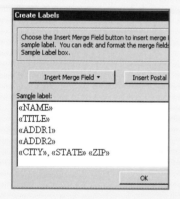

Create Mailing Labels ➡ pp. 163–164

1. From within the main document, click the Mail Merge Helper button on the Mail Merge toolbar.
2. In the Mail Merge Helper dialog box, click the Create button and choose Mailing Labels.
3. In the dialog box that appears, click the New Main Document button.
4. Back in the Mail Merge Helper dialog box, click the Get Data button and open a data source.
5. In the dialog box that appears, click on Set Up Main Document.
6. In the Label Options dialog box, choose the labels' manufacturer in the Label Products drop-down list box.
7. Choose the labels' product number in the Product Number list box.
8. Click OK.
9. In the Create Labels dialog box, click the Insert Merge Field button and choose merge fields to construct an address.
10. Include punctuation and spaces as needed.
11. Click OK.

Yes, the dreaded mail merge. Sending a form letter to everyone on a mailing list (or to just some of the people on the list) is probably one of the toughest computery tasks that normal, busy people such as you ever have to do. If it were a little more tricky, you'd be able to palm the job off on some computer jockey. It's one of those procedures that invariably turns up some ridiculous problem. Something always goes wrong.

If your mailing list already exists in some database program (such as Access, dBASE, or FileMaker Pro), you might be better off doing the mail merge in that program rather than in Word. Granted, the form letter will be a little trickier to put together. (The reporting features of database programs make you think in terms of page layout, and can be tricky if you're used to the paper and typing metaphors used in Word.) But it will still be easier, I predict. Your experience may differ, though, and Word definitely *can* handle outside data sources.

In fact, Word has a pretty helpful automated routine that walks you through the steps of creating a mail merge. As with all such procedures, it gets trickier if you stray from the main path. It can also get a little confusing because there are something like 30 different dialog boxes you might be faced with, depending on exactly what you do. Don't worry—I'll guide you through everything carefully.

When to Merge

A mail merge is not the sort of operation to get into lightly. If you need to send the same letter to a relatively small number of people, three or four or so, you'll probably be better off just creating boilerplate and then making changes to each letter individually. You'll find that only if you have a large number of recipients or a complicated letter will the additional overhead of setting up the mail merge be justified. With a mailing list of 10 names or more, mail merge is definitely the way to go.

Another factor to consider is whether you'll be sending letters out to the same set of people again. If you are, the time invested in creating the mailing list will pay off when you need to reuse it.

What's Involved in a Mail Merge?

It might also be worth your while to create a data source in Word if you have other uses for a database of names and addresses but don't have a full-fledged database manager program.

The mail merge process in Word is somewhat flexible, and it's possible to start or continue the process from several different points, but here is the typical sequence of procedures:

1. Start a main document and enter the dummy letter into which all the specific information will be poured.

2. Create or open a data source that contains the specific information to be added to each merged document.

3. Finish the main document, inserting references to the information in the data source.

4. Merge the data source with the main document to create a set of merged documents.

Starting a Mail Merge

DEFINITION

Main document: In Word's mail merge procedure, the prototype into which all the data from a mailing list is merged to create each specific letter (usually a form letter).

To kick things off, choose Tools | Mail Merge. The Mail Merge Helper dialog box appears, with instructions in a small area at the top (see Figure 9.1). Click the Create button and choose Form Letters.

Word displays a dialog box offering you the choice of either making a form letter (main document) from your current document or starting a new document. If you've just started Word or have already started a blank new document, click the Active Window button. If the current document is one you don't want to use for this mail merge, click the New Main Document button.

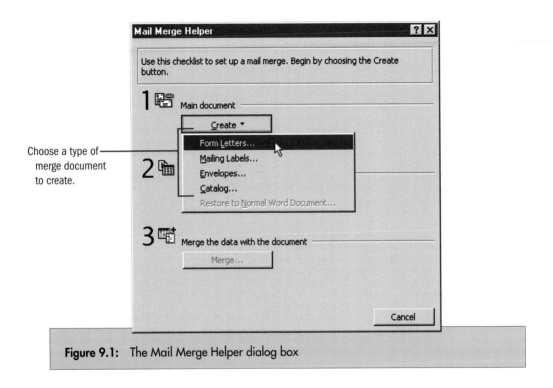

Choose a type of merge document to create.

Figure 9.1: The Mail Merge Helper dialog box

If you want to base your form letter on an existing letter, open that document first, save a copy of it (use File | Save As) under a different name, and then start the mail merge process. When Word asks which document to use, click Active Window.

Assembling a Data Source

Next you need to make a data source for the merge. This involves establishing the structure of the data source (that is, what information will go into it) and the more tedious job of data entry. (Quick, where's your assistant?)

If you already have a data source, either in the form of a Word document or in a database program, skip ahead to "Merging with an Existing Data Source" later in this chapter. (If the data source is a

DEFINITION

Data source: A document containing data organized into fields and records, as in a database. A record is one complete set of related data (such as a person's name, address, and phone number). A field is an individual category of data (such as an address).

EXPERT ADVICE

If you installed Microsoft Query (it's not part of the Typical installation, so you'll know it if you did), then you can use the Query Wizard to pull the data from your external data source.

Word document, it has to be formatted as a data source and not simply as a list of information.)

Creating the Data Source Document

Click the Get Data button next to step 2 in the Mail Merge Helper dialog box, and choose Create Data Source. The Create Data Source dialog box appears (see Figure 9.2).

Word starts you off with a reasonable list of field names (categories): Title, FirstName, LastName, and so on. You can remove any field name you won't need by highlighting it and clicking the Remove Field Name button. To add a field name, type it in the Field Name box, and click the Add Field Name button.

Try to make the categories as narrowly defined as possible, so that in the future you can sort or choose from the records based on a specific

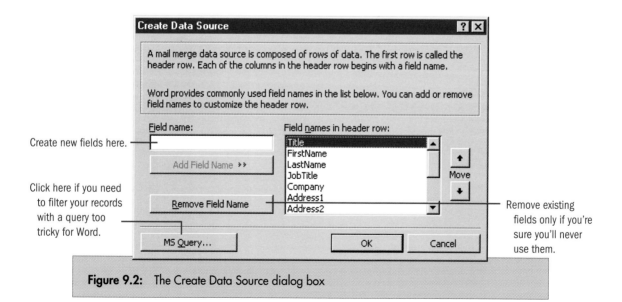

Figure 9.2: The Create Data Source dialog box

field (such as the city a person lives in, as opposed to a complete address). One useful field to include is a salutation field, indicating how to address the person at the beginning of a letter.

When you've finished, click OK. Word automatically displays the Save As dialog box so that you can give your data source a name. Type a name you'll remember later (perhaps including the word *data*), note where you're saving the document, and click Save. Don't mix up your data source documents and your main merge documents. Giving them distinctive filenames can help keep them straight. You might also want to create a special Merge folder for all your merge-related documents.

Word then notices that your data source has no contents yet and displays a message box asking you whether you want to work on remedying that or jump over to the main document (the form letter). Stay on the data source track for now by clicking the Edit Data Source button.

Entering the Data

Word next displays the Data Form dialog box (see Figure 9.3). The dialog box is called Data Form because it represents a form you can fill out to enter the records into your data source. (Word is actually creating a table behind the scenes, but it presents this dialog box to you to make the data entry easier.)

This is that tedious data entry phase I told you about. A great character-building task for someone just starting out in your field, right? The mechanics are easy, though. Just type the person's title (Mr. or Ms., usually), press TAB, type the person's first name, press TAB, and so on. Skip any fields that don't have values by pressing TAB again. Once you have created a couple of records, you may want to review ones you did earlier. You can move from record to record using the left- and right-pointing arrowhead buttons at the bottom of the dialog box, or you can jump all the way to the beginning or end of the record set using the outer two buttons.

When you get to the bottom of the list of fields (the list will scroll as you go), click the Add New button to enter the next record. Repeat ad infinitum. Click OK when you've finished.

CAUTION Only remove field names that you're absolutely sure you won't need. It doesn't cost you much to retain a category, even if it's blank most (or all) of the time. (You can add fields at a later date, but it's a hassle).

You can edit the main document now instead of doing the data entry. To do so, click the Edit Main Document button and skip ahead to the next section, "Creating a Form Letter." (You'll still have to enter the data sometime, though.)

CAUTION It's very easy to click the OK button when you really mean to add another record. If that happens, the Data Form dialog box will close. To bring it back up, click the Edit Data Source button in the Mail Merge toolbar of the main document.

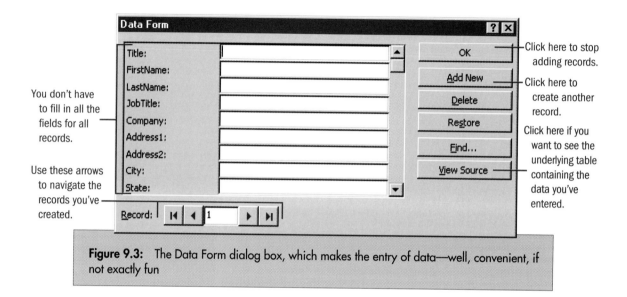

Figure 9.3: The Data Form dialog box, which makes the entry of data—well, convenient, if not exactly fun

Creating a Form Letter

You'll next be presented with the empty document window of your so-called main document, with a special Mail Merge toolbar, shown here.

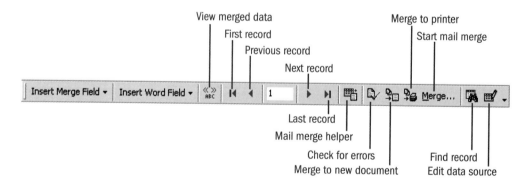

This is a complicated-looking toolbar, but you can ignore most of it for now. The buttons from View Merged Data over to Last Record are not relevant at this stage (and you may very well never need them). The Mail Merge Helper button is a good one to remember, since it gets you back to that main dialog box, which, with its steps 1,

2, and 3, guides you through the mail merge process. The next four buttons start the final step, the actual merge, but it's too soon for that. The Find Record button won't come in handy unless you have an enormous data source. The last button, Edit Data Source, is a convenient way to flip over to the data source.

Typing the Text that Won't Change

Most of your form letter will be like any other letter or document—plain text. Type or insert your letterhead. To add a date code that will automatically show the date of the mail merge:

1. Choose Insert | Date and Time from the main menu bar.
2. In the Date and Time dialog box that appears, choose the format you prefer.
3. Click in the Update Automatically check box to insert the data as a power field.
4. Click OK.

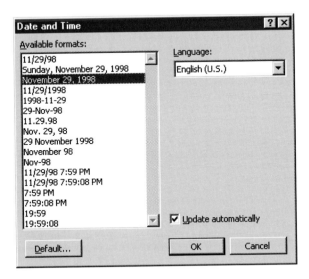

Adding Merge Fields

When the time comes to enter the parts of the form letter that will need to change for each person you're sending the letter to (such as the name and address), click the Insert Merge Field button on the Mail Merge toolbar and choose the first field you want to insert.

Word will insert the name of each merge field, enclosed in guillemets (<<>>). Remember to include normal spacing and punctuation between and around the merge fields. If you want the resulting text to be formatted in a particular way, choose the merge fields and format as you would normal text. Write the contents of the letter, including merge fields where appropriate. When you've finished, save the form letter.

Performing the Merge

When you've got your data source completed and the main document drafted, you're ready for the actual merging of the two documents. Click the Mail Merge Helper button on the Mail Merge toolbar to start the third act of this drama.

DEFINITION

Query:
A request for only those records that meet specified criteria, usually from a database.

Controlling Which Records Are Included in the Merge

Some form letters don't go to every person on a mailing list. For example, overdue notices might go out only to customers with a number greater than 60 in their InvoiceOverdue merge field. Or you might want to send your letter only to the people on your list who live in Chicago. If you want to send your letter to everyone on your mailing list, skip ahead to "Producing the Form Letters."

To be more selective, click the Query Options button in the step 3 area of the Merge Helper dialog box. Then click on the Filter Records tab. Word displays yet another dialog box full of empty boxes (see Figure 9.4).

If you want to add more criteria to your filter, repeat the process in the next line. The default conjunction between the criteria is And, but you can change it to Or if you want to combine the results of the two comparisons, rather than further narrow the results. For example, if you include the criteria "City Equal To Chicago And InvoiceOverdue Greater Than 60," your letter will be sent only to those recipients who match both criteria. If you include the criteria "City Equal To

Pull down the Field drop-down list and choose the field (or first of several fields) from the data source that governs who's in and who's out.

The Comparison box suggests Equal To. Choose other types by clicking on the drop-down list.

Click this tab if you want to sort the records you've got.

"And" queries generally retrieve fewer records than "Or" queries.

If the Compare To box becomes live, refine your merge by specifying criteria that fields must meet.

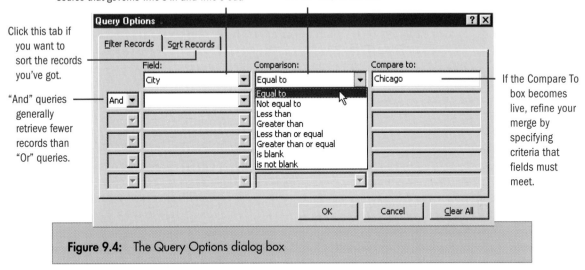

Figure 9.4: The Query Options dialog box

Chicago Or City Equal To San Francisco," the letter will go to people in the data source who live in either city.

If your mailing list was entered in no particular order *and* you want your form letters to come out in some order, you can sort the records in the data source.

1. Click on the Sort Records tab in the Query Options dialog box.

2. Choose up to three different merge fields for the mailing to be sorted on. For each you can choose ascending (A to Z for nonnumeric fields) or descending (Z to A for nonnumeric fields).

3. Click on OK. You'll be returned to the Mail Merge Helper dialog box.

Why would you need to sort on more than one field? Well, you could do so as a further way of sorting when two records match in the first sort field—a kind of tie-breaker. For example, you might want to sort records based first on City, then on LastName, and finally on FirstName, to make sure that even people with the same last name are sorted properly by first name.

If you've put off entering the data for your data source, you must do so now. Click the Edit button under step 2 in the Mail Merge Helper dialog box and choose the data source name (it should be the only choice). Then jump back to "Entering the Data."

Clearing a Query

Once you've established the criteria for a query, those criteria will be used to filter your records for subsequent merges until you clear them. To do so, click the Clear All button in the Filter Records tab of the Query Options dialog box.

Producing the Form Letters

Now that you've got all your ducks in a row, click the Merge button in step 3 of the Mail Merge Helper dialog box. Generally, you'll want to merge your form letters into a new document. Your other options—in the Merge To list box—are to merge directly to the printer or to e-mail. Before actually merging, however, you can save yourself some later grief by checking to see whether anything's gone wrong in the process (though, honestly, if you've stuck close to the guidelines, everything ought to be fine).

Checking for Errors Before Printing

When you're ready to actually perform your merge, you can stage a dry run to check for errors (see Figure 9.5).

Back to the Merge

Once you have clicked the Merge button, Word creates a new document that contains all the resulting letters, each one based on the form letter but with actual information from the data source merged in, record by record. Each letter is separated from the previous letter by a section break that also functions as a page break.

The simulated merge does not produce
a merged document or send anything
to the printer (if you're merging
directly to the printer, this option
is the safest bet).

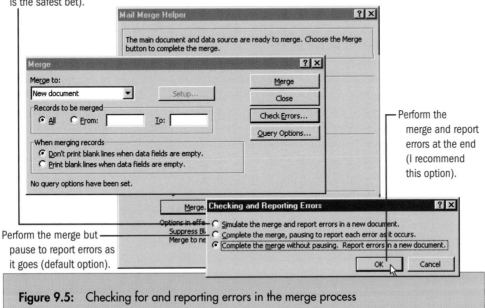

Perform the
merge and report
errors at the end
(I recommend
this option).

Perform the merge but
pause to report errors as
it goes (default option).

Figure 9.5: Checking for and reporting errors in the merge process

1. Click the Check Errors button in the Merge dialog box (or on
   the Mail Merge toolbar).

2. Choose an option and click OK. This returns you to the Merge
   dialog box.

3. Click the Merge button to start the merge process.

What to Do with Merged Documents

CAUTION

If there's something wrong with your main document, do not correct each letter manually! It might be tempting to do this and avoid the hassle of running another mail merge, but trust me, you're better off redoing the merge.

OK, now you have umpteen documents back-to-back, each very similar. What do you do? Usually, you'll just want to print them. There's no real need to save the results when they're so repetitive, take up so much disk space, and can be re-created at the drop of a hat.

But before you print, you should inspect the results to make sure they look OK. This is the main reason for not printing them directly while merging. If there's anything wrong with the resulting merged documents, close the file without saving it and make corrections to the main document, the data source, or the query used to generate the merge.

Diversions from the Straight and Narrow

I've just outlined the most straightforward approach to mail merge, but you can actually perform the steps in many different orders, and some situations require slightly different procedures. I'll run through the most common variations now.

Merging with an Existing Data Source

If your data source already exists, you still need to create a main document to begin with, as explained in the "Starting a Mail Merge" section of this chapter. Then click the Get Data button in the step 2 area of the Mail Merge Helper dialog box, and choose Open Data Source.

For more on finding files from within Word, see Chapter 7.

The Open Data Source dialog box (which looks very much like the normal Open dialog box) appears. Browse through the folders, if necessary, to find the data source document, and select it. If your data source is not a Word document, click the Files Of Type drop-down list box and choose All Files. Then click Open.

Now you have to put together your form letter, so skip back to the section in this chapter about "Creating a Form Letter" for instructions.

Merging with an Address Book

If you have a working address book in Windows that is tied in to Microsoft Outlook or to some other workgroup software, you can use the addresses stored there (or some subset of them) as your data source.

You still need to create a main document to begin with, as explained in "Starting a Mail Merge." After doing so, click the Get Data button in the step 2 area of the Mail Merge Helper dialog box, and choose Use Address Book. The Use Address Book dialog box will appear, asking you to choose which address book to use.

CAUTION

Be sure to filter the addresses in your address book so that only specific people get the form letter (unless you really want to send it to everyone in the book). Filtering is explained in "Controlling Which Records Are Included in the Merge."

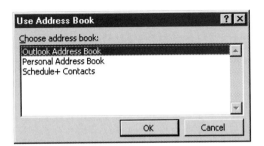

Choose the address book you want to use, such as your Personal Address Book, and then click OK. The next little dialog box you have to get past is the Choose Profile box. Most likely, the suggested default will be correct and you can click OK. It depends on how your computer, and possibly your network, is set up. If you're not sure what to do, ask whoever maintains the shared computer resources where you work.

Now you have to put together your form letter, so return to the section on "Creating a Form Letter" for instructions.

Using a Separate Header Source

Some data sources lack header information and require that you use or set up a separate header source file that contains only the names of the

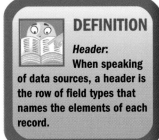

DEFINITION

Header:
When speaking of data sources, a header is the row of field types that names the elements of each record.

merge fields to be used in your merge. If you are saddled with this type of data source (or if you have many types of data that can share a single header organization), after you've created the main document, click the Get Data button in the step 2 area of the Mail Merge Helper dialog box and choose Header Options. This will bring up the Header Options dialog box.

If a header source document already exists, click the Open button and open it in the Open Header Source dialog box that appears. If a header source document does not already exist, click the Create button and create one on the fly. The procedure is essentially the same as that for creating a data source (but without the painful data entry), as explained in "Creating the Data Source Document," earlier in this chapter.

Next you have to put together your form letter, so turn back to "Creating a Form Letter" for instructions.

Merging to E-mail Addresses

SHORTCUT

To merge directly to your printer, click the Merge To Printer button on the Mail Merge toolbar.

It's possible to send out a mailing via e-mail if you have valid e-mail addresses for all the recipients (you'll also, naturally, need access to e-mail through a network or an Internet service provider). This is similar to using an address book as your data source (see "Merging with an Outlook (or Other) Address Book," earlier in this chapter). To send the merged mailing electronically, click the Mail Merge button on the Mail Merge toolbar, click the Merge To drop-down list box in the Merge dialog box, and then choose Electronic Mail. The Setup button in the Merge dialog box will become active. Click it to display the Merge To Setup dialog box, and choose the merge field from the data source (the address book) that contains the e-mail addresses of the recipients in the Data Field With Mail/Fax Address list box.

EXPERT ADVICE

If you run into memory problems while performing a mail merge, you should try merging directly to your printer (after proofreading your main document very carefully). This approach will often get around the memory problem.

Type a subject line for the e-mail messages in the Mail Message Subject Line box, and check Send Document As An Attachment to have the merged letters attached to e-mail as Word documents. If you don't check this option, the contents of the merged letters will be sent as plain text e-mail. Then click OK. Back in the Merge dialog box, click the Merge button.

Merging to Fax Recipients

You can also send a mailing via fax if your correspondents don't mind. (Be courteous about this—many people really hate getting unsolicited faxes, as the price of fax paper can make for expensive junk mail.)

1. Click the Merge To drop-down list box in the Merge dialog box.

2. Choose Electronic Mail. The Setup button in the Merge dialog box will become active.

3. Click the Setup button to display the Merge To Setup dialog box.

4. Click the Data Field With Mail/Fax Address drop-down list box and select the merge field that contains the recipients' fax numbers. (Most of these options only apply to e-mailing, not faxing. You needn't worry about checking Send Document As An Attachment if you're faxing, and the subject header works only for e-mail.)

5. Click OK when you've indicated the field with the fax number in it.

6. Click the Merge button in the Merge dialog box.

Returning to a Partially Completed Mail Merge

This chapter explains how to perform a mail merge as one continuous series of dialog boxes and choices. In reality, it's a long and sometimes arduous process that often involves a lot of data entry somewhere in the middle, and it's possible that it will take several days to get it together. Given this amount of work, it's important that you save all your documents before quitting Word.

When you return to the mail merge the next day, open the main document. Then click the Mail Merge Helper button on the Mail Merge toolbar. This will return you to where you left off. If you start with any other document and choose Tools | Mail Merge, you'll be starting a completely new merge, and you don't want that.

Creating Envelopes for Your Mailing

Once you've successfully merged your form letter with your mailing list, you still need to mail the resulting letters (that is, unless you're faxing or using electronic mail). From within the main document, click the Mail Merge Helper button. Click the Create button in the step 1 area, and choose Envelopes.

EXPERT ADVICE

Word will pick up your return address from its User Info data. If you want to use a different address, choose Tools | Options, and click the User Info tab. Then enter your name and address and click OK. Be sure to change it back later if necessary.

Word will display a dialog box giving you the option of either opening a new document or turning the current one into an envelope document.

1. Click the New Main Document button.
2. Click the Get Data button in the Mail Merge Helper dialog box.
3. Choose Open Data Source.
4. Choose a document (the same data source you used for the form letters) in the Open Data Source dialog.
5. Click Set Up Main Document when the next dialog box appears.

Choosing an Envelope Type

In the Envelope Options dialog box that appears, choose your envelope type (see Figure 9.7). Most of the time, you'll be using a Size 10 envelope (4 1/8 by 9 1/2 inches), also called a No. 10 envelope, and won't have to change a thing. If you're using some other envelope type, click the Envelope Size drop-down list box and choose the correct type.

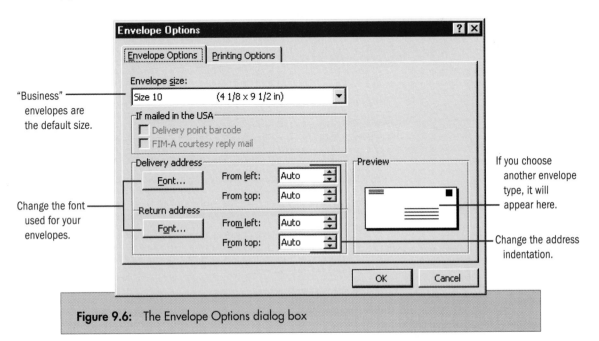

Figure 9.6:   The Envelope Options dialog box

Indicating How the Envelopes Will Be Fed into the Printer

Word can usually figure out the orientation for feeding your envelopes to your printer, even if the printer doesn't have an envelope feeder.

If your printer requires you to feed your envelopes manually or in some unusual way (that is, if your printer doesn't have an attached envelope feeder and you have to insert the envelope right down the middle), click the Printing Options tab of the Envelope Options dialog box.

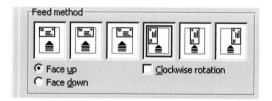

From the choices illustrated in the dialog box, click on the envelope orientation that matches the way your printer works. In the Feed From drop-down list box, choose a method of feeding the envelopes into the printer.

Merging the Envelopes

When you're ready to perform the merge, click OK in the Envelope Options dialog box. The Envelope Address dialog box will appear (see Figure 9.8).

Now complete the merge as you would a normal mail merge. Word will produce an output document consisting of all the envelopes and show them to you in page layout view. The envelopes are separated by page breaks. If they look OK, print them.

EXPERT ADVICE

If you've already been working on another type of main document, Word offers to change the current document type or create a new main document. If you choose New Main Document, click on Get Data and set up the data source as before.

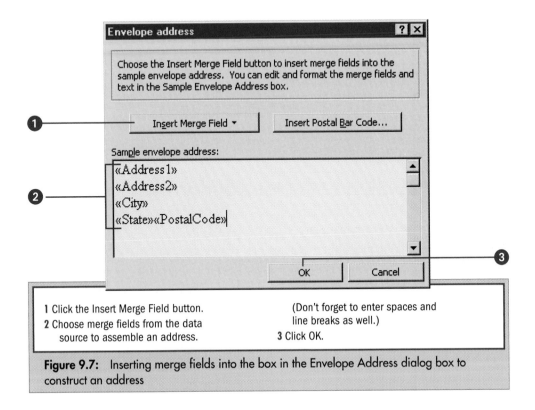

Figure 9.7: Inserting merge fields into the box in the Envelope Address dialog box to construct an address

Creating Labels for Your Mailing

An alternative to printing envelopes is to print mailing labels and then stick them onto envelopes. This is helpful if you have the labels and lack a convenient way to print envelopes.

If you have a dot matrix printer, start by clicking the Dot Matrix option button in the Label Options dialog box.

1. From within your main document, click the Mail Merge Helper button.

2. In the Mail Merge Helper dialog box, click the Create button in the step 1 area and choose Mailing Labels.

3. Click the New Main Document button.

4. Click the Get Data button in the Mail Merge Helper dialog box.

5. Choose Open Data Source.

6. Choose a document (the same data source you used for the form letters) in the Open Data Source dialog box and click Open.

7. When the next dialog box appears, click Set Up Main Document.

8. The Label Options dialog box will appear. Look at the packaging your mailing labels come in and note the manufacturer (it's Avery, nine times out of ten) and the product number.

9. Choose the manufacturer in the Label Products drop-down list box and choose the product number in the Product Number list box. Click OK. Now you can skip ahead to Setting Up the Address.

Dealing with Nonstandard Labels

If your label type is not listed, or if your labels are made by some fly-by-night company, click the New Label button on the right side of the Label Options dialog box. The New Custom laser dialog box appears, showing a detailed diagram of a single label type with all the pertinent measurements pointed out.

If you need to print a label for a single document, see Chapter 11.

Start by typing a name for the label. Next, you'll have to measure your labels if all the information isn't on the packaging. Enter the actual dimensions for your labels (you will see the diagram change in response to the numbers you enter). When you finish defining the new label, click on OK in the New Custom laser dialog box, and then click on OK in the Label Options dialog box.

Setting Up the Address

Once you've specified your labels, the Create Labels dialog box appears. Use the Insert Merge Field button to choose merge fields from the data source and assemble the address to go on the labels. Don't forget to include spaces, punctuation, and line breaks as necessary. Then click OK.

Completing the Merge

Proceed with the merge as usual. Word will produce an output document showing the merged labels. If everything looks OK, print the labels.

There's More . . .

Well, you've made it through probably the most challenging and difficult procedure you'll ever have to do with Word! Congratulations. You deserve a break now. The next chapter deals with sharing documents (on local networks and intranets) and tracking changes.

CHAPTER 10

Sharing Documents and Tracking Changes

INCLUDES

- Protecting a document for changes or comments
- Keeping track of changes
- Accepting or rejecting changes
- Adding comments
- Reviewing comments
- Routing a document to a list of people
- Working with a routed document

Protect a Document ➥ pp. 168–169

1. Choose Tools | Protect Document. This will bring up the Protect Document dialog box.
2. Choose Tracked Changes Or Comments.
3. Type a password if you want. (Be sure to remember it!)
4. Click OK.

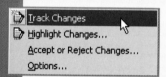

Start Tracking Changes ➥ pp. 169–170

Either

- Right-click in the TRK box in the status bar to display a pop-up menu, and choose Track Changes.

Or

- Double-click in the TRK box.

Review Changes ➥ pp. 170–171

1. Right-click in the TRK box in the status bar to display a pop-up menu, and choose Accept Or Reject Changes.
2. In the dialog box that appears, do *one* of the following:

   - Click Accept All and then Yes in the dialog box that pops up.
   - Click Reject All and then Yes.
   - Click one of the Find buttons to review each change in turn.

3. Review each change as Word identifies it, clicking either Accept or Reject as appropriate.
4. Click Close when you get to the end of the document.

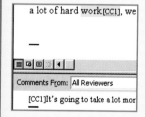

Add a Comment to a Document ➥ pp. 172–173

1. Position the insertion point.
2. Choose Insert | Comment.
3. Type the text of your note.
4. Click Close.

Review Comments ➨ pp. 173–174

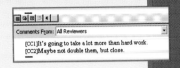

1. Choose View | Comments.

2. Choose All Reviewers or an individual's name in the Comments From drop-down list box at the top of the comments pane.

3. To incorporate suggested wording from a comment, use cut (or copy) and paste as you would with normal text.

Routing a Document ➨ pp. 174–177

1. Choose File | Send To | Routing Recipient.

2. Choose a profile to use (the default is Outlook) and click OK.

3. Click Address to start adding names to your routing slip.

4. Select names in the Address Book dialog box, clicking on To after you select each one.

5. Click OK.

6. Write a message in the Message Text box.

7. Decide whether to give the document to everyone at once or one at a time.

8. Click Route to route the document right away.

Review a Document Routed to You ➨ p. 177

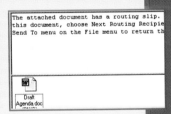

1. Open the e-mail message containing the document.

2. Read the message text.

3. Double-click the embedded Word document icon.

4. Review the document and make changes or suggestions as needed.

5. Choose File | Send To | Next Routing Recipient.

6. Click OK.

Computers and networks are supposed to allow people to work together seamlessly. As we all know, this utopian ideal is still far from a reality. However, Word has several features that allow a group of people to collaborate on a document by circulating successive drafts and keeping track of changes and who has said what. Think of it as a paper trail without the paper.

Each of these procedures—tracking changes, attaching comments, and routing—can be done separately. For example, you can give someone a copy of a draft document by handing them a disk (instead of routing a file via e-mail) and still keep that person's changes distinct from the original text.

With the growth of intranets over the last few years, it's becoming more and more likely that you'll be expected to collaborate with workers whom you may not even see regularly. Tools such as these help you coordinate your work with others without getting hopelessly lost in all the changes.

Protecting a Document

When you've drafted a document and are getting ready to solicit comments from your colleagues, you can take the precaution of *protecting* the document (See Figure 10.1). If you Protect The Document For Tracked Changes, any changes that anyone makes to

---

EXPERT ADVICE

There are other features in Word that you may want to explore if you collaborate on word processing projects or work with onscreen documents. You can keep multiple versions of a document stored in a single file by choosing File | Versions (and filling in the dialog box that appears to identify the new document version).

EXPERT ADVICE

To jazz up your onscreen documents, you can use color text with the Font Color button on the Formatting toolbar. (You can also animate it with the Text Effects tab in the Font dialog box—but check with your colleagues first, to see if they like animated marquees running around the text on their screens!) See Chapter 13 for more on formatting onscreen documents.

---

the document from that point on will be marked as revisions (as explained in the next section). If you Protect The Document For Comments, no one will be able to make changes directly to the document or to anyone else's comments, but anyone will be able to add comments. (Comments are explained later in this chapter.) Read on and learn more about both tracked changes and comments before you decide which type of protection to choose.

If you're really concerned about security, you can enter a password. Make sure you remember it! (Capitalization counts.)

Creating and protecting online forms is explained in Chapter 8.

Tracking Changes

The purpose of tracking changes is to make it easy to tell what text was changed in a document. By default, deleted text is struck through but left visible. Added text is underlined. Both are colored. Also, a

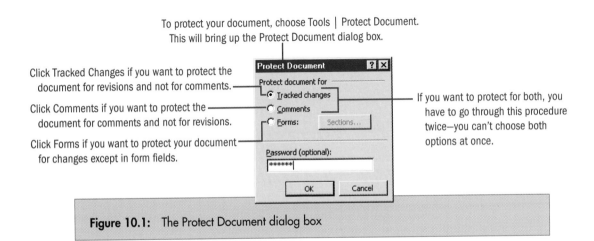

To protect your document, choose Tools | Protect Document. This will bring up the Protect Document dialog box.

Click Tracked Changes if you want to protect the document for revisions and not for comments.

Click Comments if you want to protect the document for comments and not for revisions.

Click Forms if you want to protect your document for changes except in form fields.

If you want to protect for both, you have to go through this procedure twice—you can't choose both options at once.

Figure 10.1: The Protect Document dialog box

vertical line appears in the left margin next to any line that has changes. Word assigns a different color to each contributor.

Turning On Change-Tracking

If you want your revisions to a document to be tracked as changes, choose Tools | Track Changes | Highlight Changes before you start editing. In the Highlight Changes dialog box that appears, click Track Changes While Editing. Make sure Highlight Changes On Screen is checked to make sure you can see the change-tracking. Click OK.

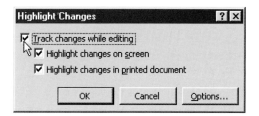

SHORTCUT

You can double-click in the TRK box on the status bar (or right-click it and select Track Changes), to start tracking changes.

Making Changes

After Tracking Changes has been turned on, edit the document as you normally would. For example, to change a phrase, first highlight it and then type over it. Instead of seeing the old text replaced by the new text, as usual, you'll see that the old text is struck through and the new is underlined, and both are in color.

so with a ~~little luck~~ <u>lot of hard work</u>, we'll be

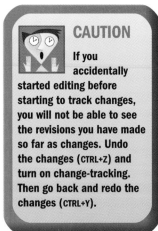

CAUTION

If you accidentally started editing before starting to track changes, you will not be able to see the revisions you have made so far as changes. Undo the changes (CTRL+Z) and turn on change-tracking. Then go back and redo the changes (CTRL+Y).

Reviewing the Changes

At some point, when all the shouting has died down, you'll want to accept or reject the changes or suggestions that your coworkers have made. First, save the document, in case you want to change your mind later. Next, right-click in the TRK box and select Accept Or Reject Changes in the shortcut menu that pops up.

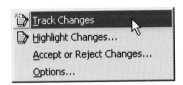

This brings up the Accept Or Reject Changes dialog box. If you've already looked the changes over and want to incorporate them all, go ahead and click the Accept All button.

If all the suggested changes were worthless and you prefer your original pristine prose, click the Reject All button. Either way, Word will ask you to confirm your choice. Click Yes, unless you have a sudden attack of doubt.

If you're somewhere in between these two frames of mind, click one of the Find buttons to review the changes one at a time (see Figure 10.2).

SHORTCUT

If you have a lot of changes to be reviewed, consider turning on the Reviewing toolbar (right-click any toolbar and choose Reviewing). Then you can search for changes or change the change-tracking status at any time.

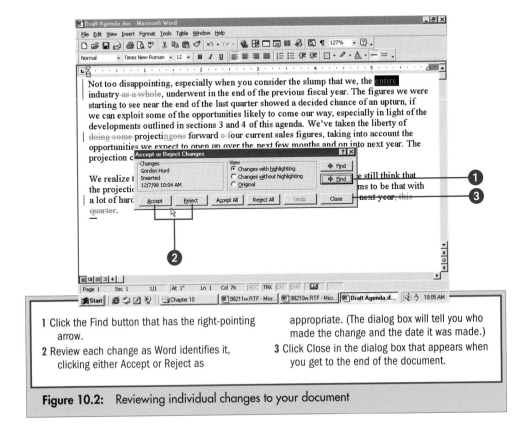

1 Click the Find button that has the right-pointing arrow.

2 Review each change as Word identifies it, clicking either Accept or Reject as

appropriate. (The dialog box will tell you who made the change and the date it was made.)

3 Click Close in the dialog box that appears when you get to the end of the document.

Figure 10.2: Reviewing individual changes to your document

EXPERT ADVICE

Sometimes it's easier to read an edited document if you first hide the changes. To do so, uncheck the Highlight Changes On Screen check box in the Highlight Changes dialog box. Word will still track changes and you'll be able to see the highlighting when you turn it back on.

Adding Comments to a Document

Christian Crumlish:
It's going to take a lot more than hard work.

Another way that others can kibitz—I mean, help you with suggestions—is by adding comments. Comments are the electronic equivalent of those sticky yellow notes with which people would otherwise decorate your manuscript. You can find notes easily—the word to which they're nearest will be bright yellow, and a vertical line will appear in the margin of the line on which they appear. If you position the cursor over the yellow word, it will turn a brighter shade of yellow and the name of the commentator and the text of the comment will all appear in a floating tool tip.

If this isn't obvious enough for you, you can click the Show/Hide button on the Standard toolbar and each comment will appear marked in text with the initials of the person who made it. If you double-click the initials or select View | Comments, you'll be able to see the comments in their own window at the bottom of the screen.

DEFINITION

Comment: A note added to a Word document and anchored to a specific place in the text. Comments will not print unless you specifically choose them on the Print tab of the Options dialog box or in the Print What section of the Print dialog box.

The Reviewing toolbar appears whenever you work with comments.

Adding a Comment

For instructions on how to add a comment to a document see Figure 10.3.

To add another comment, move the insertion point to the next relevant place in the document and choose Insert | Comment again. The same window will open with a new comment started. The initial marker will show up again, with the number incremented by one to show that this is the second note. (If you add the second comment earlier in the text than the first one, then the one that appears first in the text will become comment 1.) Type the comment text and click Close again.

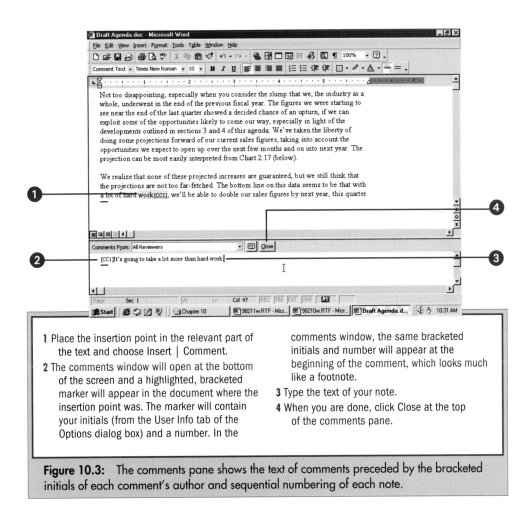

1 Place the insertion point in the relevant part of the text and choose Insert | Comment.

2 The comments window will open at the bottom of the screen and a highlighted, bracketed marker will appear in the document where the insertion point was. The marker will contain your initials (from the User Info tab of the Options dialog box) and a number. In the comments window, the same bracketed initials and number will appear at the beginning of the comment, which looks much like a footnote.

3 Type the text of your note.

4 When you are done, click Close at the top of the comments pane.

Figure 10.3:   The comments pane shows the text of comments preceded by the bracketed initials of each comment's author and sequential numbering of each note.

Reviewing Comments

To review the comments in a document, choose View | Comments. This will open the comments window at the bottom of the screen without inserting a new one.

- To see all the comments made by various people, choose All Reviewers in the Comments From drop-down list box at the top of the comments pane.
- To see just one person's comments, choose that person's name from the list.

Your comments will appear colored and underlined in the comments pane if you also happen to be showing tracked changes. However, you don't need to be tracking changes in order to use comments.

- If you want to incorporate suggested wording from a comment into the document, you can cut (or copy) and paste it (or drag and drop it) as you would normal text.

Routing a Document to a Series of Reviewers

SHORTCUT

If the Show/Hide ¶ button on the Standard toolbar is "pushed in," the initials for each comment will appear in the text. Double-clicking on the initials will open the comments window.

Although you can always put a document onto a disk and simply walk it over to someone (using the proverbial sneakernet), it's easier to just send it electronically. If you have a network connection with your coworkers (or if you can reach them via the Internet or an online service, such as CompuServe or AOL) and an e-mail program installed, you can route your document electronically to a list of people. The document can be automatically passed from person to person and finally back to you, or you can have each person get his or her own copy simultaneously and then send it back to you directly. Routing the document from person to person might take longer, but if you choose that method you will have the advantage of getting everyone's revisions in the same document.

To route a document to a list of people, choose File | Send To | Routing Recipient. In the dialog box that appears, choose a profile (such as Microsoft Outlook). This will bring up the Routing Slip dialog box.

See Chapter 11 for how to send documents by e-mail, in general.

Adding Names to the Routing Slip

Click Address to start adding names to your routing slip. This will bring up the Address Book dialog box, where you can choose names:

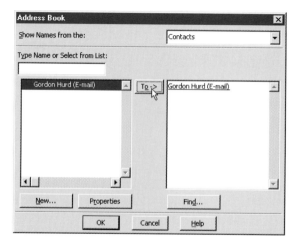

EXPERT ADVICE

If you have access to a Microsoft Office Server, you may want to try out Word's new Online Collaboration feature. Using Office Server extensions (see your network administrator or other technical wizard in your company) you can now set up discussion threads in or about your Word documents. You can access this new feature by choosing Tools | Online Collaboration | Web Discussions. Set up your server information and Word will connect you to it. From there you can participate or set up discussions with your colleagues. If you're familiar with Usenet newsgroups or message boards on the Internet, you'll be familiar with Online Collaborations.

If you have more than one address book available, choose the one you want in the Show Names From The drop-down list box at the top of the dialog box. Select the first person you want to route the document to, and click the To button. Repeat this process as many times as you need to.

If you need to use names in your Routing Slip that aren't in your Address Book, click the New button to add the name(s) to your contact list. When you're done, click OK.

Back in the Routing Slip dialog box, you can change the order of the names by highlighting the one you want to move and clicking the up or down Move arrow buttons.

You'll most likely want to use the Contacts option in the Show Names From The drop-down list.

Writing the Message to Accompany the Document

Word will suggest the first sentence of the document being routed as a subject line for the e-mail cover message that will accompany the document, but you can select it and change it if you like. Type a message in the Message Text box.

Deciding How the Document Will Be Routed

In the Route To Recipients area, choose whether you want the document to be sent to each person on the list successively or a separate copy sent to everyone at once.

EXPERT ADVICE

Of the Route To Recipients choices, I recommend One After Another unless you're on a tight schedule and are worried that the document will get bogged down along the way. Otherwise, you'll have to wade through one copy of the document for each person on the routing list (or use Word's sometimes frustrating Compare Documents command on the Tools | Track Changes submenu).

You should also consider making the following choices in the Routing Slip dialog box (see Figure 10.4) before you send the document on its way:

- If you leave Return When Done checked, the last person to get the document will be prompted to return it to you.
- If you keep Track Status checked, you can be notified by e-mail every time the document is sent along to the next person on the list.
- The Protect For list box at the bottom-right is equivalent to the Protect Document dialog box shown at the beginning of this chapter. The Tracked Changes choice is probably your best bet. This guarantees that changes made by the reviewers will be tracked and highlighted.

Sending the Document

If you later decide to make changes to the routing slip before sending the document, you can return to the Routing Slip dialog box by choosing File | Send To | Routing Recipient.

If the document is ready to go, click the Route button in the Routing Slip dialog box. If you intend to work on the document a little more before routing it, click the Add Slip button. Either way, the Routing Slip dialog box will disappear.

If you attached the routing slip without sending (for example, to edit the document further before sending), you can send the document on its way by choosing File | Send To | Routing Recipient. Word will ask you to confirm that you want to route the document with the routing slip and not just send a copy of it to a new person.

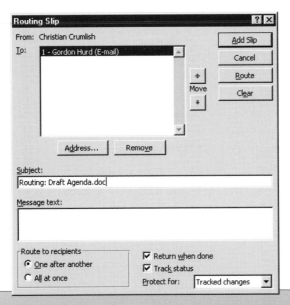

Figure 10.4: The Routing Slip dialog box

Reviewing a Document That Was Routed to You

If someone places your name on a routing slip for a document, the document will be sent to you as an attachment to an e-mail message. When you are notified that your mail has arrived, open the message as you normally would.

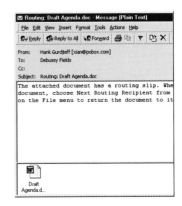

1. Double-click the embedded document icon to open and review the routed document.

2. Make your changes and/or add your comments.

3. Send the document along its merry way by choosing File | Send To | Next Routing Recipient. Word will ask you if you want the document sent to the next person on the routing list (or, if you were the last, to the original sender).

4. Click OK to route the document along.

There's More . . .

The features you've seen in this chapter make it possible to collaborate with others without generating huge piles of paper every time a change is made. More and more work is taking place on computer screens and never making it out to a printer (so much the better for the trees, eh?).

Chapter 11 will show you some other alternatives to printing, such as sending documents via e-mail (as was touched on in this chapter) or by fax. The rest of the book deals with specialized types of documents—plain or fancy reports, newsletters, huge documents, and Web pages.

Alternatives to Printing and Printing Alternatives

INCLUDES

- Sending documents via e-mail
- Faxing documents instead of printing them
- Printing page ranges
- Printing multiple pages
- Printing envelopes
- Printing mailing labels

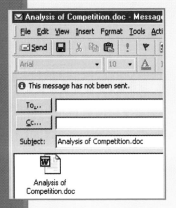

Send a Document via E-mail ➨ pp. 182–183

1. Open the document you want to send.
2. Choose File | Send To | Mail Recipient.
3. Type the recipient's address (or click on To and choose one from your address book) and press TAB.
4. Add names to the Cc list the same way, if you want, and press TAB.
5. Type a subject line and press TAB.
6. Type a message to accompany the document.
7. Click the Send button.

Fax a Document ➨ pp. 184–188

1. Open the document that you want to fax.
2. Choose File | Send To | Fax Recipient.
3. Follow the Fax Wizard, making sure that you've chosen the right document to fax and the right type of fax modem.
4. Type the name and fax number of the person to whom you're sending the fax.
5. Choose a style for the cover sheet (if you choose to use one, make sure that all your return information is filled in), and click Finish.
6. Fill out the cover sheet, and then click Send Fax Now to send the fax.

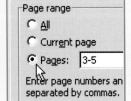

Print a Page Range ➨ pp. 188–189

1. Choose File | Print.
2. In the Pages box of the Page Range area, type the page numbers you want to print.
3. Click OK.

Print an Envelope ➥ pp. 190–191

1. Choose Tools | Envelopes and Labels.
2. If the Labels tab is in front, click the Envelopes tab.
3. Correct the addressee or return address, if necessary.
4. To print the envelope directly, click the Print button. To have the envelope attached to the beginning of the document, click the Add To Document button.

If you use Word and your computer as a typewriter, you'll probably want to print out your documents at some point. Nowadays, though, more and more work is being done from start to finish online, and other ways of distributing documents are becoming popular. One way to get your writing to others is to e-mail it to them. You'll save a lot of paper in your office if you and your coworkers are on a network. Yet another alternative to printing is faxing. Why print out a document and pay a courier to deliver it when you can fax it?

Still, these alternatives to printing do not completely obviate the need to print documents the traditional way. Furthermore, there *are* a couple of printing tricks you ought to know about as well, besides simply printing an entire document at the press of a button. We'll get to that at the end of this chapter.

E-mailing a Document

You can also make documents available to others by posting (or "publishing") them to Internet or intranet sites. See Chapter 14 for more on publishing Word documents electronically.

If your computer is on an intranet or other network or has dial-up access to a network, you can send copies of your document to others via e-mail. (The Word document will be attached to an e-mail message; it won't appear in the text contents of the message.) To do so, choose File | Send To | Mail Recipient. Word will drop you into a new message window for whatever e-mail application you use.

Adding Recipients

To route a copy of your document to several different recipients to elicit their comments and feedback, you should attach a routing slip, as explained in Chapter 10.

Type the address of the recipient in the To box or click the To button to open your address book. In the Address Book dialog box, choose a recipient and click the To button to add her to your list. You can send your document to more than one person by repeating this process. When you're done, press TAB.

EXPERT ADVICE

If your recipients have never before received a document via e-mail, you might want to tell them that they can double-click the Word document icon from their e-mail message to open the document you've sent.

If you want to send a courtesy copy to anyone besides the main recipient(s), click the Cc button. You'll see the Address Book dialog box again. Choose an additional recipient or recipients, and then press TAB again.

Press TAB to put the insertion point in the Subject box, and then type an informative subject line. This is all your recipient will see at first in her inbox.

Writing a Message to Accompany the Document

Press TAB again and type an explanatory message. You can format the message using the toolbar, and you can even add color for emphasis if you like (see Figure 11.1). When you're done, click the Send button.

Your e-mail program may differ in some details from what is presented here, but the general instructions should still be just about right.

CAUTION

As with printing, before sending your document, be sure to save it. You never know what might go wrong.

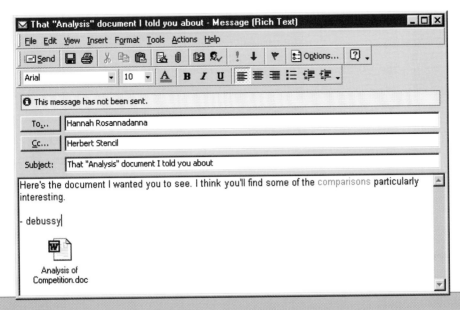

Figure 11.1: A completed message with attached document

EXPERT ADVICE

You won't be able to choose Microsoft Fax as your fax program unless you're still running Windows 95. With Windows 98, Microsoft no longer supports Microsoft Fax. Faxing capabilities are now supported through Outlook and its Symantec Fax Starter Edition program. For more information on using Outlook, see *Office 2000 for Busy People*.

Faxing a Document

You need a fax modem to fax a document directly from your computer. You might be able to do it over a network, but you'll need advice from your local computer guru to make sure it will work.

From Word's point of view, faxing a document is not much different from printing it, but the procedure is different for you. To begin, first make sure you have the correct document open and on your screen. See Figures 11.2 and 11.3 for instructions on how to send a fax.

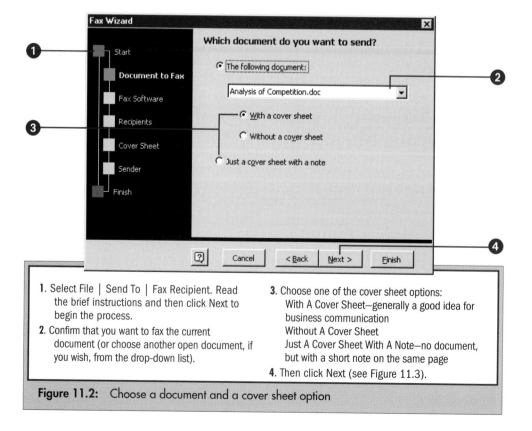

1. Select File | Send To | Fax Recipient. Read the brief instructions and then click Next to begin the process.
2. Confirm that you want to fax the current document (or choose another open document, if you wish, from the drop-down list).
3. Choose one of the cover sheet options:
   With A Cover Sheet—generally a good idea for business communication
   Without A Cover Sheet
   Just A Cover Sheet With A Note—no document, but with a short note on the same page
4. Then click Next (see Figure 11.3).

Figure 11.2: Choose a document and a cover sheet option

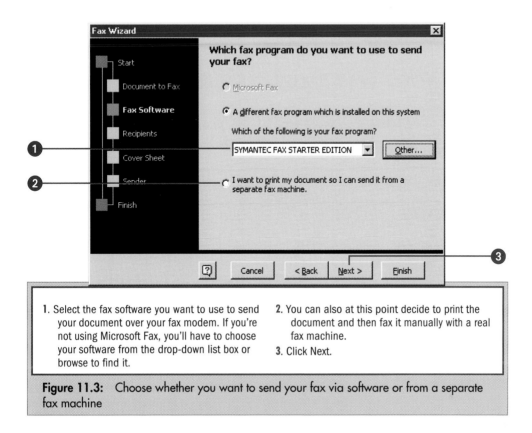

Figure 11.3:   Choose whether you want to send your fax via software or from a separate fax machine

After this initial process is completed, you can turn to addressing and actually sending the fax. In the past, Word sent faxes by treating the fax modem as an alternative printer. As you can see, it's now much easier to just use the Fax Wizard.

Adding Recipients

To add the name and fax number for each of your recipients, follow these steps:

1. Click the Address Book button.

2. Select a recipient.

3. Click OK.

4. Repeat steps 2 and 3 as often as necessary (as discussed earlier in this chapter).

5. Click Next.

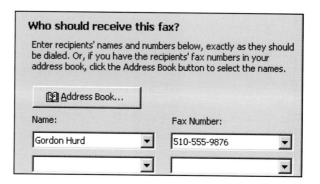

Choose one of the three fax cover sheet styles (if you're using a cover sheet) offered by Word (Contemporary, Elegant, or Professional—see Figure 11.4) and then click Next. Enter or confirm your own personal information, and then click Finish.

Finishing Up Your Cover Sheet

The Fax Wizard will disappear except for a floating toolbar with a single Send Fax Now button on it. The current document will be your

---

EXPERT ADVICE

If you find that you need to add names to your address book while going through the Fax Wizard, it's often easier to do it in your contact management program—Outlook, for example. The number of dialog boxes you need to go through can be a pain and rather unnecessary if you just add all the names before you try to send the fax.

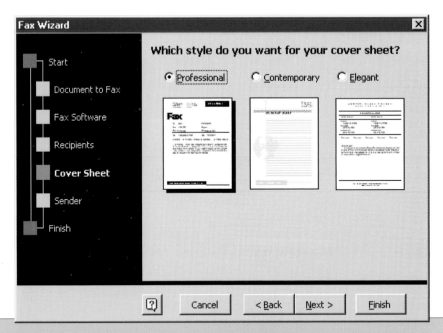

Figure 11.4: Choose a style for your fax cover sheet (they're all pretty classy looking)

new cover sheet (if you're sending one) or the document you're faxing. If you wish, you can make any changes you want or add any notes or additional comments to the cover sheet before sending (see Figure 11.5). When you're satisfied, click the Send Fax Now button.

Word may prompt you for the profile name of an information service by which to send the fax. Click OK.

When the Fax Wizard has finished sending your fax, it will tell you so:

If your fax modem is an external device (not a card inside your computer), make sure you've turned it on.

The profile name indicates the method for sending the electronic fax information over your network or modem connection.

Click OK again. Then close the cover sheet document (and save it if you like, but there's no real reason to).

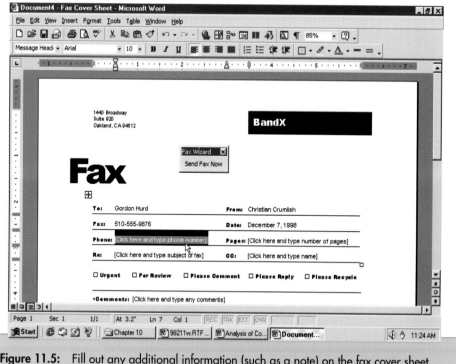

Figure 11.5: Fill out any additional information (such as a note) on the fax cover sheet

Special Printing Options

If you want to print your document the old-fashioned way, on a printer, but you don't want to print the whole thing or you want to print more than one copy, don't click the Print button on the Standard toolbar. Instead, choose File | Print. This will bring up the Print dialog box (see Figure 11.6).

If you need to print an irregular set of pages from your document, separate noncontiguous page numbers with commas. You can indicate a range of pages by typing the beginning and ending page numbers and putting a hyphen between them. You can also combine these two formats—for example, pages 2,5,7-9,15 (that is, pages 2 and 5, pages 7 through 9, and page 15).

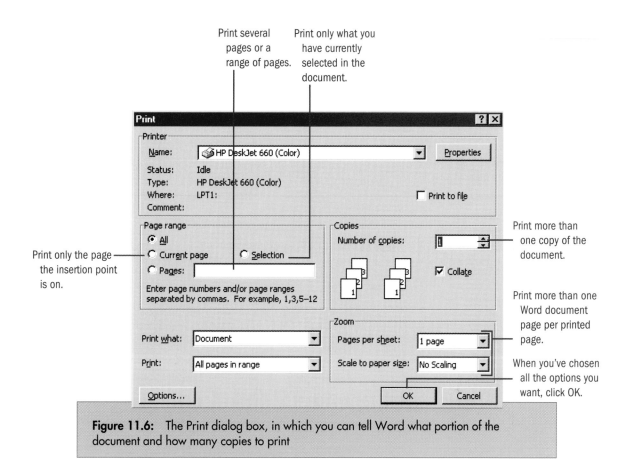

Print several pages or a range of pages.

Print only what you have currently selected in the document.

Print only the page the insertion point is on.

Print more than one copy of the document.

Print more than one Word document page per printed page.

When you've chosen all the options you want, click OK.

Figure 11.6: The Print dialog box, in which you can tell Word what portion of the document and how many copies to print

EXPERT ADVICE

If you're looking for ways to save time in printing jobs, try printing in reverse order. Then you won't need to reorder the pages once the job's done. Choose File | Print, click the Options button, and check the Reverse Print Order check box.

Printing Envelopes and Mailing Labels

After you have written a letter or composed some other form of correspondence, if you're not going to fax it or send it by e-mail or use smoke signals, you're going to need to put it in an envelope. To address said envelope, you can either print on it directly (assuming your printer can do that without chewing up the envelope), or you can print the recipient's address on a mailing label and stick it on the envelope.

Either way, Word has established a nicely automated procedure to take the pain out of positioning the text and fitting the address into the right space. First, let's do an envelope.

To print envelopes or labels for an entire mail merge run, see Chapter 9.

Printing an Envelope

Choose Tools | Envelopes And Labels. The Envelopes And Labels dialog box will appear. If the Labels tab is in front, click the Envelopes tab (see Figure 11.7). If it guesses wrong or nabs *your* address by

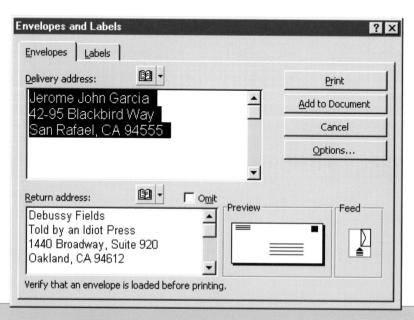

Figure 11.7: The Envelopes tab of the Envelopes And Labels dialog box

mistake, just type the address yourself (or copy it from the document and paste it into the window). Figure 11.7 also shows the return address, which Word gets from the User Information tab of the Options dialog box (Tools | Options).

To format the text on the envelope or choose a different envelope size, click the Options button. This brings up the Envelope Options dialog box (shown in Figure 11.8). The Envelope Options tab should be in front (click it if it isn't).

Back in the Envelopes And Labels dialog box, click the Print button to print the envelope immediately, or click the Add To Document button to have the envelope added (in its own section, with its own page size, and so on) at the beginning of the document.

SHORTCUT

To use an address from your address book, click the Insert Address button above either of the address boxes in the Envelopes And Labels dialog box.

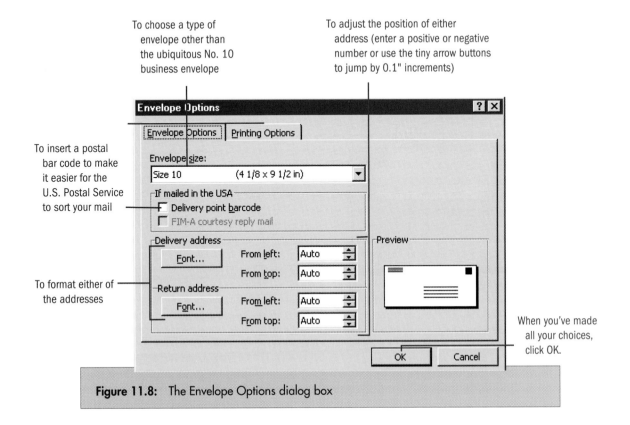

Figure 11.8: The Envelope Options dialog box

SHORTCUT

To use an address from your address book, click the Insert Address button above the Address box.

Printing a Label

Choose Tools | Envelopes And Labels. The Envelopes And Labels dialog box will appear. Click the Labels tab if it is not already in front (see Figure 11.9). If Word thinks the first few lines at the top of your letter look like an address, it will place those lines in the Address box as a suggestion. If it does not identify an address, the box will be blank. In this case, simply type the address yourself (or copy it from the document and paste it into the window).

The Label Options dialog box allows you to make specific selections with respect to the type of labels you are using (see Figure 11.10). Word can print to just about any type and size of label you're likely to run across.

If your label type is not listed, click the New Label button. This brings up the New Custom laser information dialog box. Type in the

To make labels of your own address, check Use Return Address. The Address box will then show your address from the User Info tab of the Options dialog box.

To print just a single label, click Single Label in the Print area. If you don't want to print on the label in the top-left corner, enter or click your way to another position in the Row and Column boxes in the Print area.

To choose a label type, click the Options button. This brings up the Label Options dialog box.

Envelopes and Labels

Envelopes | Labels

Address: ☐ Use return address

Jerome John Garcia
42-95 Blackbird Way
San Rafael, CA 94555

Print
New Document
Cancel
Options...

☐ Delivery point barcode

Print
◉ Full page of the same label
○ Single label
Row: 1   Column: 1

Label
Avery standard, 2160 Mini
Address

Before printing, insert labels in your printer's manual feeder.

Figure 11.9: The Labels tab of the Envelopes And Labels dialog box

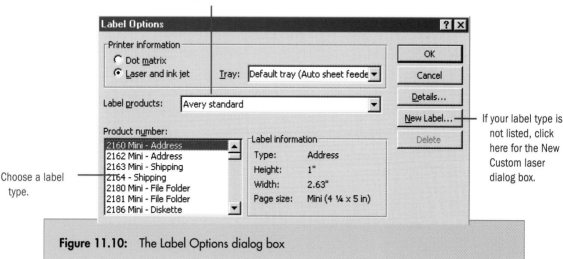

If your labels are not made by Avery, click here to look for your brand. If it's not there, leave Avery Standard selected.

Choose a label type.

If your label type is not listed, click here for the New Custom laser dialog box.

Figure 11.10: The Label Options dialog box

measurements of your labels. As you enter the new numbers, the preview illustration will adjust to reflect your changes. When you're done, click OK.

When you're finished with the Label Options dialog box, click OK. When you're finished with the Envelopes And Labels dialog box, click the Print button (and get ready to feed your labels into the printer). Word will print your label.

If the label packaging does not specify the dimensions, get out a ruler and measure each of the items specified in the Preview window.

There's More . . .

Ideally, some day in the future, we can stop printing out documents on paper completely and just beam images and text directly to each other's goggles. For now, though, you've got the essentials covered. The last four chapters in this book deal with special types of documents, from reports and newsletters to World Wide Web pages.

Deluxe Reports and Very Large Documents

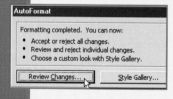

AutoFormat a Document ➡ pp. 201–204

1. Save the document (press CTRL+S).
2. Select the section to be formatted (if you don't want to AutoFormat the whole document).
3. Choose Format | AutoFormat. A small AutoFormat Dialog box appears.
4. Click AutoFormat And Review Each Change, or AutoFormat Now if you don't want to review the changes.
5. Click OK.
6. Click Reject All if you don't like any of the changes, or click Review Changes to sign off on the changes one by one.
7. Click the Find button with the right-pointing arrow (unless Word has already found the first change automatically).
8. To turn down a change, click Reject. To see the next change, click the Find button with the right-pointing arrow.
9. Repeat step 8 until you get to the end of the document.
10. Click Accept All to accept any unrejected changes.

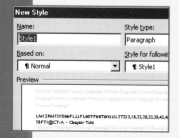

Define a New Style ➡ pp. 205–209

1. Choose Format | Style.
2. Click New.
3. Type a name in the Name box.
4. Choose Character or Paragraph in the Style Type box to indicate the kind of formatting you want to apply.
5. To base the new style on an existing style, click on the Based On drop-down list box and choose the existing style.
6. For paragraph styles, choose the style for the following paragraph.
7. Click Format and choose a type of formatting to apply.
8. Choose the formatting you want, and click OK.
9. Repeat steps 7 and 8 until you've completely formatted your style.
10. Check the Add To Template check box if you want your new style to be available to all new documents based on the current template.
11. Click OK.
12. To apply the style, click Apply; otherwise, click Close.

Draw a Table ➥ pp. 211–212

1. Click the Tables And Borders button on the Standard toolbar.
2. Click the place where the upper-left corner of the table should be, and drag to the lower-right to draw the rough outline of the table.
3. Drag the mouse within the outside borders of the table to sketch in row and column dividers.
4. Format the table with the Tables And Borders toolbar.

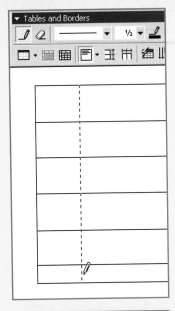

Link Data from Another Office Application ➥ pp. 215–216

1. Start the other Office program and Word, and open the Word document.
2. In the other program, select the section that you want to link to your Word document, and copy it (press CTRL+C).
3. Switch to Word.
4. Position the insertion point where you want to paste the link.
5. Choose Edit | Paste Special.
6. Choose a format for the link.
7. Click the Paste Link option button.
8. Click OK.

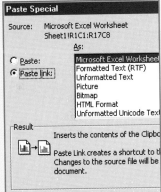

Look Up the Perfect Word in the Thesaurus ➥ pp. 217–218

1. Place the insertion point on a word you'd like to improve.
2. Press SHIFT+F7.
3. Choose a connotation of the word in the Meanings box.
4. In the Replace with Synonym box, select a word (or double-click a word to look up *its* synonyms).
5. Repeat step 4, if necessary, to zero in on the right word.
6. When you find the word you want, click Replace. (Click Cancel if you can't improve on the original word.)

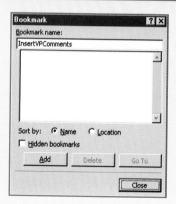

Find Your Way with a Bookmark → pp. 219–220

1. Place the insertion point or make a selection.
2. Choose Insert | Bookmark.
3. Type a name for your bookmark.
4. Click Add.

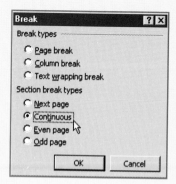

Insert a Section Break → pp. 223–224

1. Position the insertion point where you want the new section to begin.
2. Choose Insert | Break.
3. In the Break dialog box that appears, you can do one of several things:
   - To start the section after the break on a new page, choose Next Page.
   - To start the section where the insertion point is, choose Continuous.
   - To start the section on the next even or odd page, choose Even Page or Odd Page.
4. Click OK.

Edit an Outline → pp. 226–231

1. Choose View | Outline.
2. Use the Outlining toolbar to reorganize your outline:
   - Turn regular text into a heading with the Promote button.
   - Change the levels of individual heads or of entire selections with the Promote and Demote buttons.
   - Change the placement (not the heading level) of a selection with Move Up or Move Down.
   - Show or hide all the headings subordinate to a selection with Expand or Collapse.
   - Show all the headings at levels up to and including *n* with the Show Heading *n* buttons.
   - Instantly expand the entire outline with Show All Headings.

Create a Table of Contents ➡ pp. 235–236

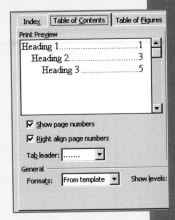

1. Place the insertion point at the beginning of the document.
2. Choose Insert | Index And Tables.
3. Click the Table Of Contents tab.
4. Choose a format from the Formats box.
5. Make sure the number in the Show Levels box reflects the number of heading levels you want.
6. Select a leader style from the Tab Leader drop-down list.
7. Click OK.

When you need to prepare a formal document, perhaps to hand out at a meeting or to fulfill a request from your boss, you have to pay some attention to the impression that the document will make. How is it formatted? How does it come across visually? Does it communicate as well as it should? Are there any stale word choices?

In an ideal world, it wouldn't matter how your document looks. Only the contents—your brilliant words—would matter. Like it or not, though, issues of appearance do matter. Getting the formatting right can take some time, so it's not worth bothering with in the early phases of the development of a report. As you get closer to the moment of truth, however, you will have to devote time to your document's appearance, no matter how busy you are. You can't skip getting dressed in the morning, can you?

EXPERT ADVICE

Before you start working with the appearance of a formal document, you should write a first draft and review it, making any necessary corrections and improvements. Only when the content is fairly stable are you ready to polish it.

Some arguments can be won with a picture, a clear diagram, a chart, or a persuasive table of numbers. The power to frame information is as valuable these days as it ever was. Although nobody likes gratuitous or confusing tables or charts, judicious use of such elements can help a report punch through the tedium of fat columns of gray focus-group results.

Big documents come with their own special problems: They take a long time to load up into your word processing program. You sometimes have to wait for other people to complete their work on one section before you can make changes to your section. A long document can be even harder to move around in, because it's no longer simply a matter of jumping to the top or bottom of the document and then hitting PAGEUP or PAGEDOWN a couple of times.

Long documents sometimes require specialized page numbers, chapter numbers, section numbers, and so on. A really long document can be difficult for readers to manage without a table of contents.

Don't just sit down and read this whole chapter from start to finish. Instead, jump ahead to the specific tricks you need to make your report shine or to manage that long document, and then move on. (In other words, treat this chapter as a reference.)

You can avoid some of the hassles involved with long documents by sharing and working on them online instead of printing them out millions of times. See Chapter 14 for more about online documents.

How To Look Your Best

By now you've probably played around a little with fonts, character formatting (such as boldface and italics), and formatting that affects entire paragraphs (such as indentation, spacing, and alignment). After a quick review of keyboard shortcuts for formatting tools, I'll show you how to let Word format your document for you, how to choose a predesigned template to establish the look of your document, and how to create your own styles from scratch.

Formatting with Keyboard Shortcuts

Perhaps the fastest way to apply formatting to individual words, paragraphs, or entire selections is by using shortcut keys on text that you have selected. Table 12.1 shows the most useful shortcut keys for formatting.

Font and paragraph formatting were introduced in Chapter 3.

Letting Word AutoFormat Your Report

In Chapter 3, you saw how Word offers to format your document automatically as you type (and how you can turn off this feature if you find it intrusive). That same interactive helping hand can be invoked more selectively when you're finished composing and you're ready to consider the format of your document.

To format a specific portion of a document, select that portion first. To format the entire document, do not make any selection. Begin the

CAUTION

Remember, always save your document first before you let the computer have a go at formatting it. Sure, you can reject the changes that Word makes—you can even undo them—but you never know what can happen. It's better to be safe and save.

Desired Result	Keyboard Shortcut
Change the current font (in the Formatting toolbar)	CTRL+SHIFT+F, UP ARROW or DOWN ARROW, ENTER
Change the current font size (in the Formatting toolbar)	CTRL+SHIFT+P, UP ARROW or DOWN ARROW, ENTER
Increase the font size by a preset increment	CTRL+SHIFT+>
Decrease the font size by a preset increment	CTRL+SHIFT+<
Increase the font size by a preset increment (one point size)	CTRL+]
Decrease the font size by a preset increment (one point size)	CTRL+[
Change the case of letters (all caps, all lowercase, initial caps)	SHIFT+F3
Change all letters to caps	CTRL+SHIFT+A
Format letters as small caps	CTRL+SHIFT+K
Apply or remove boldfacing	CTRL+B
Apply or remove italics	CTRL+I
Apply or remove underlining	CTRL+U
Apply or remove underlining for single words, not the spaces between them	CTRL+SHIFT+W
Apply or remove double underlining	CTRL+SHIFT+D
Apply or remove subscripting	CTRL+=
Apply or remove superscripting	CTRL+SHIFT+=
Apply or remove hidden text designation	CTRL+SHIFT+H
Remove formatting (restore plain text)	CTRL+SPACEBAR or CTRL+SHIFT+Z
Format text in single-spaced lines	CTRL+1
Format text in double-spaced lines	CTRL+2
Format text in 1.5 line spacing	CTRL+5
Add or remove one line of space preceding the paragraph	CTRL+0 (zero)
Center a paragraph	CTRL+E
Justify a paragraph	CTRL+J
Left-align a paragraph	CTRL+L
Right-align a paragraph	CTRL+R
Indent a paragraph from the left margin	CTRL+M
Remove a paragraph indent	CTRL+SHIFT+M
Create a hanging indent	CTRL+T
Remove a hanging indent	CTRL+SHIFT+T
Remove paragraph formatting	CTRL+Q

Table 12.1: Shortcut Keys for Applying Formatting

AutoFormatting process by choosing Format | AutoFormat. (To skip reviewing the changes, click AutoFormat Now.) Then click OK.

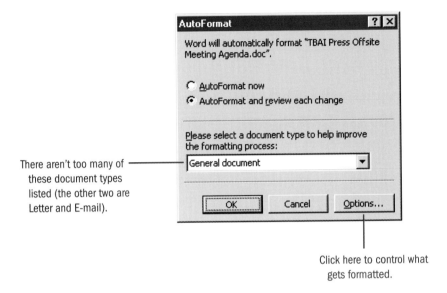

There aren't too many of these document types listed (the other two are Letter and E-mail).

Click here to control what gets formatted.

Reviewing Changes

When Word is done formatting your document, it pops up a dialog box giving you the options of accepting all changes, rejecting all changes, or reviewing the changes one by one. I recommend reviewing the changes. It's a good idea to see what Word has done to your report. Click the Review Changes button. The Review AutoFormat Changes dialog box will appear.

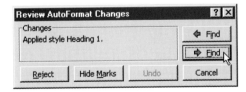

If Word does not automatically find the first change, click the Find button with the right-pointing arrow. A description of the change will appear in the Changes area. (You may sometimes have to move the

AutoFormat dialog box to see the change in your document.) At this point, you can do one of several things:

- Click the Reject button to veto a change.
- If you're happy with a change, click the Find button with the right-pointing arrow again to go to the next one.
- To unreject your most recent rejection of a change, click the Undo button.

If you've changed your mind about the AutoFormat or don't like the results, click the Reject All button.

Proceed through your document until you've reviewed all the changes. When you are done, click the Cancel button. To accept the rest of the changes (the ones you didn't reject), choose Accept All.

Rejecting All, After All

If you're not happy with any of the results of the AutoFormatting, click the Reject All button in the AutoFormat dialog box. You're under no obligation to actually like the way your computer wants to format the document. It's just following some rules that may or may not make good aesthetic sense in this particular case.

Establishing Consistent Styles

DEFINITION

Style:
In Word, a collection of character or paragraph formatting information that can be applied all at once to any selection. If a style is changed, all the text that has been formatted with that style will change automatically.

The only way to enforce consistency on your documents *and* make it possible to change the formatting of a single element throughout your document all at once, is to set up styles. The Blank Document template (Normal.dot) comes with a number of built-in styles, such as formatting for heading levels, but you can also create your own.

SHORTCUT

If you press SHIFT+F1, you can then click anywhere in your document to see the styles at that spot. Press SHIFT+F1 (or ESC) again to turn this feature off.

In Chapter 5 you learned how to create a style by using text you had already formatted. You can also create styles from scratch (or change the existing styles). When your boss finally agrees that his favorite sans-serif font is an eyesore in body text, you can choose the font you've always wanted to use by simply changing the style you used for the body text, *assuming that you did set up such a style.*

To create a style, bring up the Style dialog box by choosing Format | Style.

Defining a New Style

To create a new style, click the New button in the Style dialog box. This brings up the New Style dialog box. To create your new style, you need to give Word some information so that it can prepare and save your new style correctly. The steps shown in Figure 12.1 will get you started.

You can choose User-Defined Styles in the Style dialog box to filter out the styles that come with Word.

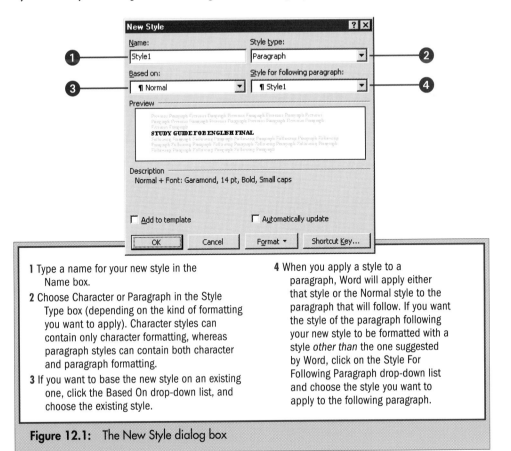

1 Type a name for your new style in the Name box.

2 Choose Character or Paragraph in the Style Type box (depending on the kind of formatting you want to apply). Character styles can contain only character formatting, whereas paragraph styles can contain both character and paragraph formatting.

3 If you want to base the new style on an existing one, click the Based On drop-down list, and choose the existing style.

4 When you apply a style to a paragraph, Word will apply either that style or the Normal style to the paragraph that will follow. If you want the style of the paragraph following your new style to be formatted with a style *other than* the one suggested by Word, click on the Style For Following Paragraph drop-down list and choose the style you want to apply to the following paragraph.

Figure 12.1: The New Style dialog box

EXPERT ADVICE

Many specialized types of document elements, such as headings and captions, should be followed by the base paragraph style (which is often the Normal style).

Now you're ready to do the dirty work. The next few sections will take you through all the procedures needed to actually create a new style.

Formatting the Style

Here's how you apply formatting to your style:

1. Click the Format button in the New Style dialog box, and a menu will appear.

2. From this menu, choose the type of formatting you want to apply, and then the appropriate dialog box will appear (Font, Paragraph, and so on).

3. Choose the formatting you want, and click OK.

4. Repeat this process as often as necessary to choose font and size, add enhancements such as bold or italics, change the line spacing, add borders or paragraph numbering, and so on. (I'll stop being so specific now. We all know what formatting is, right?)

Assigning a Shortcut Key to Your Style

If you want to assign a shortcut key combination to your style so that you can apply it easily in the future, click the Shortcut Key button in the New Style dialog box. This brings up the Customize Keyboard dialog (see Figure 12.2).

Press a likely key combination. The combination will appear in the Press New Shortcut Key box. If that particular combination has already been assigned to some other action, that action will appear in the Currently Assigned To area below the box. Good luck finding an unused key combination! My advice is to try CTRL+SHIFT+*something*.

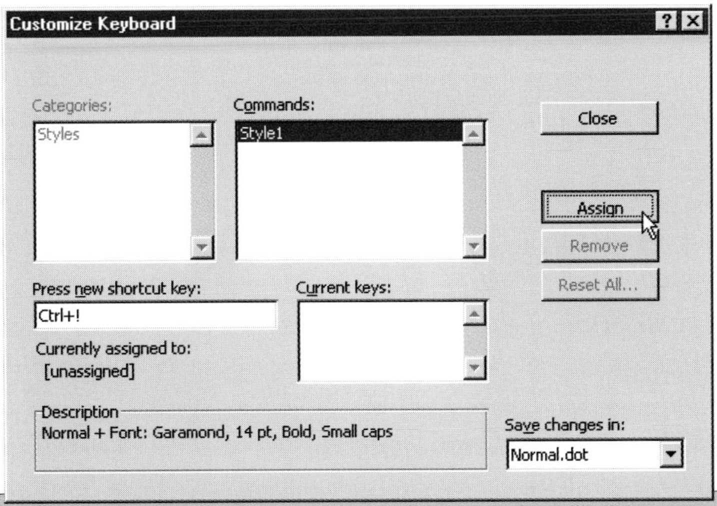

Figure 12.2: Assigning a keyboard shortcut in the Customize Keyboard dialog box

(You can override an underused shortcut if you want, but you'll disable that shortcut for whatever was using it before.) When you're happy with your choice, click Assign and then click Close.

Making Your New Style Available to Other Documents

To add your new style to the current template, check the Add To Template box in the bottom-left corner of the New Style dialog box. If you don't add your new style to the template, it will exist only in your current document and will be unavailable to future documents.

Let Word Update Your Style for You When You Change It

If you check the Automatically Update check box, Word will watch whenever you manually edit an example of the style and change the style's formatting for all instances. (If you leave it unchecked, you can still update a style after manually formatting an example of it by pressing CTRL+SHIFT+S, ENTER, and then clicking OK.

> **CAUTION**
>
> If you've changed some of the basic styles that come with Word (such as Heading 1), you probably don't want to add your edited styles to the Blank Document template, unless you really want to change those styles for all future documents.

Apply the Updated Style

When you are done creating your new style, you can apply it immediately to the text your insertion point is in by clicking the Apply button in the Style dialog box. If you don't want to apply the style right now, click the Close button.

Adding Any Style to Any Template

You can add a style you're creating or editing to the current template just by checking Add To Template in the New Style dialog box. To add a style that already exists to a template, click the Organizer button in the Style dialog box. This brings up the Organizer dialog box with the Styles tab in front (see Figure 12.3).

The styles in the currently attached template are listed on the left side of the dialog box. The styles in the Blank Document (Normal.dot) template are listed on the right. To add a style to a template other than the Blank Document template (or whichever

You can't change a paragraph style to a character style.

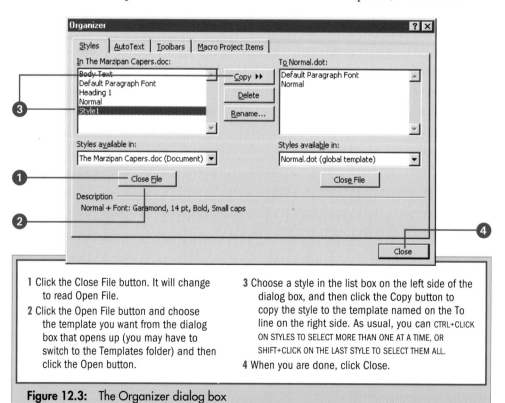

1 Click the Close File button. It will change to read Open File.

2 Click the Open File button and choose the template you want from the dialog box that opens up (you may have to switch to the Templates folder) and then click the Open button.

3 Choose a style in the list box on the left side of the dialog box, and then click the Copy button to copy the style to the template named on the To line on the right side. As usual, you can CTRL+CLICK ON STYLES TO SELECT MORE THAN ONE AT A TIME, OR SHIFT+CLICK ON THE LAST STYLE TO SELECT THEM ALL.

4 When you are done, click Close.

Figure 12.3: The Organizer dialog box

template is attached to the current document), follow the steps shown in Figure 12.3.

EXPERT ADVICE

You can copy styles in the Organizer either from left to right, or from right to left. The buttons change orientation depending on which side you click first.

Using Keyboard Shortcuts to Apply Styles

The following table shows some keyboard shortcuts for use with styles:

Desired Result	Keyboard Shortcut
Choose a style in the Formatting toolbar	CTRL+SHIFT+S, UP ARROW or DOWN ARROW, ENTER
Apply the Normal style	CTRL+SHIFT+N
Apply the Heading 1 style	ALT+CTRL+1
Apply the Heading n style	ALT+CTRL+n

Adding Tables to Documents

A table can often help you get right to the point, and they can be useful for clarifying numerical information. You already saw one use for tables (making a form) if you read Chapter 8. Think of tables whenever you have a tricky alignment problem. Table 12.2 shows the buttons on the Tables and Borders Toolbar.

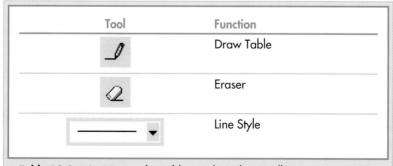

Tool	Function
	Draw Table
	Eraser
	Line Style

Table 12.2: Buttons on the Tables And Borders Toolbar

Tool	Function
½ ▼	Line Weight
	Border Color
	Outside Border (currently)
	Shading Color
	Insert Table
	Merge Cells
	Split Cells
	Align (Top, Center, Bottom)
	Distribute Rows Evenly
	Distribute Columns Evenly
	Table AutoFormat
	Change Text Direction
	Sort Ascending
	Sort Descending
Σ	AutoSum

Table 12.2:   Buttons on the Tables And Borders Toolbar *(continued)*

Drawing a Table

There are now three ways to insert a table into your document. The newest way may also be the easiest. (If you want to give it a whirl, start a new blank document first.) To get started, click the Tables and Borders button. This does three things:

- It puts the Tables And Borders toolbar on the screen.
- It selects the Draw Table button on the Tables And Borders toolbar (you can also do this by selecting Table | Draw Table).
- It switches the document to Print Layout view (the better to lay out your table, I guess).

Your toolbar may be floating above the page instead of anchored below the Formatting toolbar.

Then, click in the upper-left corner of the space where you'd like the table to appear, and drag to the lower-right corner to draw the rough outline of the table (see Figure 12.4). You can change anything about the table afterward, so don't be timid.

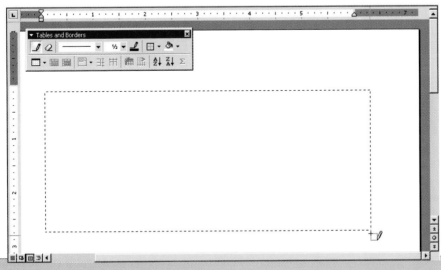

Figure 12.4: With Draw Table, you can sketch your table roughly, and then tighten it up afterward

Now you can start carving out rows and columns. Click on the left edge of the table, near the bottom of the first row you want to create, and drag the pencil pointer to the right. Word will quickly sketch in the row divider.

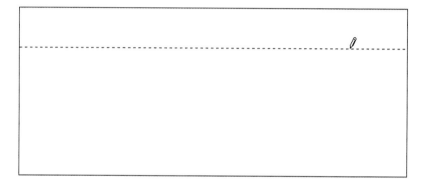

Draw the rest of the row dividers. Then, click on the top edge of the table and drag down to draw the column dividers. You can use trial and error. If you make a mistake, click the Eraser on the Tables And Borders toolbar, and then rub the pointer over the line you want to wipe out.

When the table is about right, you can click the Distribute Rows Evenly and Distribute Columns Evenly buttons on the Tables And Borders toolbar, if you want to even everything out. (Remember, you can always change things later.)

Inserting a Table (the Old Way)

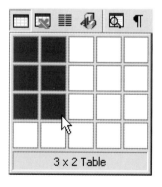

You can still insert a table by clicking the familiar Insert Table button on the Standard toolbar and dragging down and to the right to select the numbers of rows and columns. When the insertion point is in the table, the Insert Table button changes to Insert Rows or, if one or more columns is selected, to Insert Columns.

The original method for inserting tables—selecting Table | Insert Table, and then entering the numbers of rows and columns in a dialog box—still works as well, but it's definitely the most cumbersome. (You can mix and match any of these techniques, too.)

Converting Text to a Table

If you've got preexisting text, such as an aborted attempt to create a table using tabs, you can turn it into a table. Select the text, and then choose Table | Convert Text To Table. In the dialog box that pops up, indicate the character that should be treated as a cell divider (comma, tab, or paragraph mark, for example), and click OK.

You can also just select your text and then click the Insert Table button on the Standard toolbar. Most converted tables will come out a little screwy. If you can play with the table a bit to get it into shape, fine. If it looks too messed up, press CTRL+Z to undo the conversion and then try to straighten out the source text, perhaps by inserting or removing tabs or commas, before trying again.

Entering Text into an Empty Table

After you create a table, put the insertion point in the first cell (if it's not there already). Type the contents of the cell and then press TAB. The insertion point will jump to the next cell over in the same row. The following rules of movement apply to tables:

- You can press TAB to move across each row, and down to the next row if you are in the last cell of a row.
- You can also get around in a table by using the standard arrow keys or by clicking on the desired cell.
- If you press TAB when in the last cell of the last row of a table, a new row will be added automatically.

Doing Simple Sums in a Table

Probably the most common mathematical operation that's performed in tables is summing (totaling) the numbers in a column or row. To

To apply a predesigned format to your table, right-click anywhere in the table and choose Table | AutoFormat from the menu that appears. This brings up the Table AutoFormat dialog box.

 DEFINITION

Cell: A rectangle representing the intersection of a column and a row in a table. Each cell contains at least one paragraph and can be formatted separately. (Entire rows and columns can also be formatted at once.)

Try the AutoSum button in the Tables And Borders toolbar.

do this in a Word table, you will need to add a formula to it. First, place the insertion point in the cell where you want the total to appear. Then choose Table | Formula. This brings up the Formula dialog box.

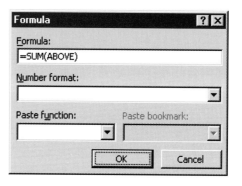

Word can usually make a pretty good guess about what you're trying to do, and it will probably suggest the formula =SUM(ABOVE) or =SUM(LEFT), depending on whether you're summing up a column or a row. If Word does not suggest either of these formulas, you can type the one you want. Then click OK.

If you want to do more complicated mathematics in tables, you might be better off using a real spreadsheet program and then linking the information into your document (as explained later in this chapter).

Formatting a Table

When you've finished entering the text into a table, you should think about how you want the table to look. (You can wait, of course, until you format the rest of the document.)

Start with general formatting, such as font and size. First select the entire table and apply whatever formats you want. Then select specific areas of the table, such as the top row or the rightmost column, to give any such areas distinctive formatting. Finally, format specific cells, if necessary.

Tables have some special selection shortcuts:

Don't confuse borders with gridlines. By default, a new table gets borders around each cell, but even if you take them off, the table will be indicated by shaded gridlines (unless you turn them off). These gridlines are there to make the table easier to work with, but they don't print out.

- To select the whole table, choose Table | Select Table.
- To select an entire row, click in the left margin next to the row.
- To select an entire column, hold down ALT and click on the column, or point to the top gridline and click when the pointer changes to a downward-pointing arrow.

To add lines and shading to your table, use the Border button on the Tables And Borders toolbar (or the identical button on the Formatting toolbar). On the Formatting toolbar, it's called the Outside Border button but that's only one of its eight variations.

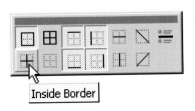

First, select entire rows or columns, groups of cells, or individual cells. Then click on the thin arrow button to the right of the Border button and choose one of the border options (they're pictorial, so it's hard to go wrong).

Whichever border option you choose will become the new default for the button. You can apply the current border option to any selection just by clicking the Border button.

Linking Data from Another Program to Your Document

If you want to add material created in another program to your document, including material that will continue to be updated in that other program, you can have that source material linked right into your Word document. You don't have to redo anything. For existing info, it's almost as simple as copying and pasting between the two programs. (Oops, I'm drawing your attention to the *programs* again.)

Linking with Copy and Paste

To copy data from another program into Word, do the following: Select the data in that other program, right-click, and choose Copy. Then switch back to Word, and place the insertion point where you want the copy to appear. You now have the following choices:

To have the pasted data become plain old Word data that no longer remembers the program it was created in, right-click and choose Paste.

To link or embed the data (so that the data will remember where it came from), choose Edit | Paste Special. The Paste Special dialog box will appear (see Figure 12.5). The dialog box will identify the source of the document (such as Microsoft Excel) and offer you several

CAUTION

Once you've linked data from another program (or from Word itself) into a Word document, don't delete, move, or rename the source, or your links will be broken. If you must delete, move, or rename the source, you'll have to recreate the links in the Word document.

DEFINITION

Link:
To insert data from one program (the source) into a document in another program, creating a connection that allows the insertion to be updated automatically when the source is updated.

Embed:
To insert data from one program (the source) into a document in another program without maintaining a connection to the source. When the source is updated, the data in the destination document will not be updated. This is different from pasting in that if you edit the embedded content, you do so using the features from the original program.

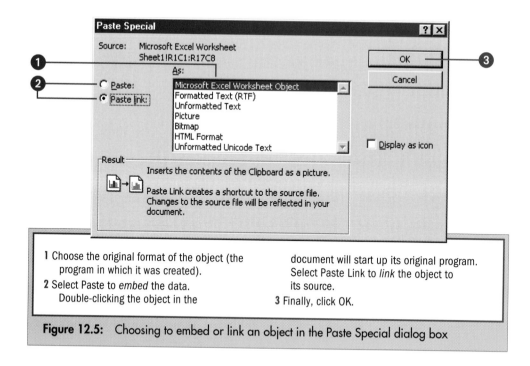

1 Choose the original format of the object (the program in which it was created).
2 Select Paste to *embed* the data. Double-clicking the object in the document will start up its original program. Select Paste Link to *link* the object to its source.
3 Finally, click OK.

Figure 12.5: Choosing to embed or link an object in the Paste Special dialog box

choices for the format of the data you're about to paste. (Word refers to the data from another program as an *object.*)

Linking by Inserting an Object

While in Word, you can insert an existing object that belongs to another program, as long as you also have that program installed on your computer. To do so, start by choosing Insert | Object. This brings up the Object dialog box. Make sure that the Create New tab is in front.

To insert an existing object, click the Create From File tab and choose the file from which you want to insert data.

Choose an object type in the Object Type list box, and then click OK. The object will appear in its native format. (If the object is, for example, an Excel worksheet, it will appear as a worksheet and have all the functionality of Excel.) When you move the insertion point back to the main Word document, the worksheet will look more like a simple table.

Double-click the object to bring back the controls of the program in which it was made. To delete an object, click it to select it, and then press DELETE.

Finding the Perfect Word in the Thesaurus

The last thing to do before presenting your work in a formal report is to proofread those pages carefully. Yes, this can involve printing the document out (double-spacing it first if it's not too long) and scanning it with your eyes. Word can help too, by checking your spelling, grammar, and suggesting alternatives to improve on repetitive or otherwise problematic word choices. You're probably familiar by now with Word's automatic spelling and grammar checking. Word also has features that can help if you notice that you are leaning on one word too often or when you have trouble coming up with just the right expression.

It's natural to sometimes get into a rut while writing and start using the same word over and over. Sometimes this is OK. If it's correct usage, you might as well just keep using it. It can be distracting when you realize that a writer is varying the vocabulary to avoid repeating a word. Then again, sometimes a word just gets stuck in your forebrain and comes out in many different contexts, robbing your ideas of their nuances.

Word comes with a built-in thesaurus that makes it easy to choose any word and look for words with similar meanings. Place the insertion point in the word you want to improve and choose Tools | Language | Thesaurus. This brings up the Thesaurus dialog box.

Press SHIFT+F7 to start the Thesaurus.

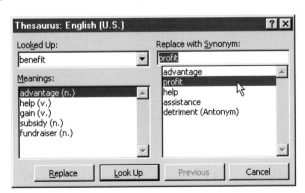

The Meanings box shows different possible senses of the word you're working on. Choose another meaning if the first one is not the one you were thinking of.

A list of possibilities will appear in the Replace With Synonym box on the right. You can double-click a word in the Replace With Synonym box (or select it and click the Look Up button) to look up further synonyms for that word. Continue this process for as long as you like. To review the words you've looked up so far, click the Looked Up list box (the one in the upper left). You can also retrace the history of your looked-up words, one by one, with the Previous button. When you have found the word you want, select it and click Replace to replace the original word with the suggestion. The dialog box will close. (You can click Cancel at any time to quit the thesaurus without replacing a word.)

 You can undo the replacement by pressing CTRL+Z.

EXPERT ADVICE

You can also type a new word in the Replace With Synonym box and click the Look Up button to have Word look up synonyms for the new word.

Getting Around in a Long Document

In Chapter 3, I showed you how to use Find, Go To, and Browse Objects. These methods become even more useful as the document gets longer. Go To, especially, can help you zero in on defined parts of documents very rapidly.

Word has also now added a feature, called Document Map, that lets you look at an overview of the document while still keeping the contents of the document on the screen (as opposed to Outline view, covered later in this chapter, which is great for reorganizing your outline but not especially good as a navigation tool).

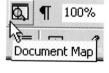

To view the Document Map of a long document, click the Document Map button on the Standard toolbar. This opens up a pane in the left margin showing the headings in your document (if you're using the standard Heading 1, Heading 2, etc., heading styles).

Try these tricks with the Document Map showing:

- Move the mouse pointer over any heading to see it in its entirety, even if it's hidden by the edge of the pane.
- Click a heading to select it and go straight to that part of the document (see Figure 12.6).

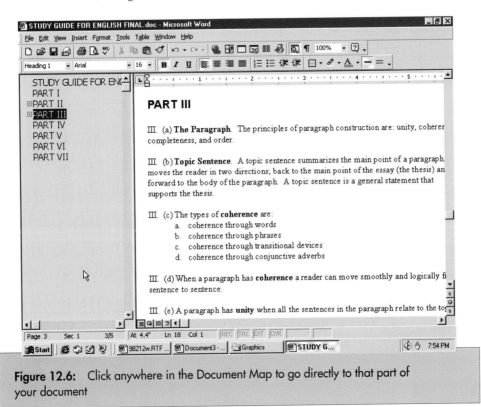

Figure 12.6: Click anywhere in the Document Map to go directly to that part of your document

Inserting and Going to Bookmarks

Besides being able to take you directly to a new page or section (see "Subdividing a Document into Sections," later in this chapter), Go To can also take you to locations you define with bookmarks.

It's easy to drop a bookmark into any part of your document. A bookmark can correspond to a specific place (the location of the insertion point when you created the bookmark) or to a selection.

DEFINITION

Bookmark: A code inserted into a document that marks an exact location so that the user can return to it at any time and from any point, much like a real bookmark placed in a book to mark a specific page.

After placing the insertion point or selecting the text you want to mark, choose Insert | Bookmark. The Bookmark dialog box appears.

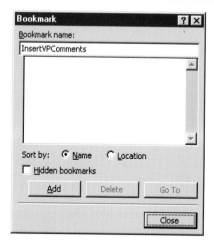

The box is empty at first, because no bookmarks have been defined. Type a name for your bookmark in the Bookmark Name box. Choose something that will help you remember what it refers to. (The length doesn't really matter, because you'll usually be picking the name from a list box; however, bookmark names cannot have any spaces in them.) Then click the Add button.

To see symbols representing the bookmarks that have been inserted in your document, choose Tools | Options, click the View tab, check Bookmarks, and click OK. To hide them again, repeat the steps.

To go to a bookmark, either double-click on the left part of the status bar or press F5. The Find and Replace dialog box will appear.

1. On the Go To tab, choose Bookmark.

2. Choose a bookmark from the Enter Bookmark Name drop-down list box.

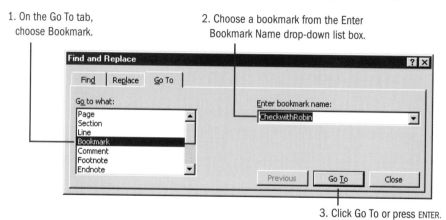

3. Click Go To or press ENTER.

Organizing Long Documents

One of the most difficult aspects of working with long documents is keeping the various subsections organized, numbered, and formatted properly. There are several different, equally valid approaches to doing this, each of which is more appropriate for some projects and less so for others.

The least complicated method (as long as the page numbering never changes) is to keep each separate section of a document in its own file and manually change the page numbering for each portion when they are merged together. If you don't expect to make too many changes, and if you'd rather do a little handwork than master some word processing geekery, this is the best way to go.

If you want to keep your whole document in one file but you want to apply different formatting or page characteristics (such as margins, headers and footers, orientation, and so on) to different portions of the document, you should create sections.

For more complicated documents, you should learn to work in Outline view. This enables you to look at overall structure down to the level of detail you need. It also makes rearranging portions of a document easy.

Combining Separate Documents into a Printed Whole

As I just mentioned, the tricky part about keeping portions of your document in separate files is making sure that the page numbering does not start over again at one in each portion. The solution to this is buried in dialog boxes, but it's really not too hard to do. Assuming that you've already inserted page numbers in each separate file, note the final page number of the first portion of the document. If you want the next section to start on an odd page, and the first document ends on an odd one, then you'll have to insert a blank page (by pressing CTRL+ENTER) at the end of the first document.

Don't worry about page numbering until you're almost done with a document—it's not worth it to keep renumbering the sections every time a change adds or takes away a page. Think of page numbering as one of the final steps before printing.

Now open the second document. Choose Insert | Page Numbers. The Page Numbers dialog box will appear. Click the Format button to get to a new dialog box, Page Number Format.

Here, click Start At in the Page Numbering area and enter the new page number (or increment the old number by clicking the tiny arrow buttons). Then click OK. Repeat for subsequent documents in the sequence.

DEFINITION

Section:
A portion of a Word document with its own page formatting (stored in the section break at its end). Each section can be set up differently from other sections in the document. Not to be confused with selection.

Subdividing a Document into Sections

Some formatting that applies to documents at the page level (such as formatting for margins; vertical alignment; headers and footers; columns; and paper size, type, and orientation) can just as easily be applied to separate sections within a document. Normally, the page formatting choices you make (or the defaults that are in effect) govern the entire document. But you can apply different page formatting to different parts of a document by dividing the document into sections. For example, a report with a title page, introductory text, and then text arranged in columns would require three sections. To create separate sections, you insert section breaks.

Inserting a Section Break

Position the insertion point where you want the new section to begin. Then choose Insert | Break. The Break dialog box will appear.

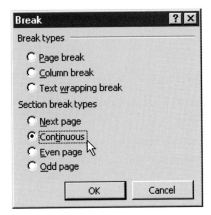

This dialog box offers you several choices:

- If you want the section after the break to start on a new page, choose Next Page. The break will force a new page to start.
- If you want the new section to start right where the insertion point is, choose Continuous. There'll be no page break.
- If you want the new section to start on the next even or odd page, choose Even Page or Odd Page.

Then click OK. A section break will appear in your document.

Section Break (Continuous)

Now you can format the two sections (the one before and the one after the break) separately. If you ever forget which section the insertion point is currently in, look in the status bar: the second item from the left shows the number of the current section.

Removing a Section Break

To remove a section break, simply select it and press DELETE. Or, if the insertion point is located just below it, press BACKSPACE. (Switch to Normal view if you can't see your section break.) Remember, all the formatting that applies at the section level (mostly page formatting) is stored in that break. Deleting a break, therefore, is a little like deleting a paragraph mark. The section before and the section after the break become a single section, which takes on the formatting of the latter.

CAUTION

When you delete a section break, the section before the break will take on the page formatting of the section that follows.

Going to a Section

To go directly to a section, click the Browse Object button and select Go To. In the Go To dialog box that appears, click Section in the Go To What box, and then either type a section number and press ENTER, or press the Next or Previous button as many times as necessary to get to the section you want. When you're there, click Close.

Formatting a Section

Most of the formatting that is applied to complete sections is page formatting. You'll notice that once you have established sections in your document, all your page formatting choices will include the option of applying the formatting to the current section only or to the entire document.

To format a section, choose File | Page Setup. This brings up the Page Setup dialog box, which is shown in Figure 12.7. Choose a tab. After making your choices, take a look at the Apply To drop-down list at the bottom of the dialog box. Each tab of this dialog box has a list like this, but the items in it vary depending on the state of the document (and on whether you made a selection before opening the dialog box). Click on the box if you want to choose a different option. When you are done with the first tab, choose the other tabs and make your choices in them, too. When you're done with this dialog box, click OK.

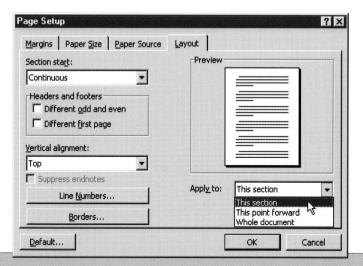

Figure 12.7: The Page Setup dialog box, showing the list box that gives you control over whether your changes will affect the current section or the entire document

Using Headers and Footers in Sections

Once you've got separate sections in your document, its headers and footers can be consistent from one section to the next, or they can change with any new section.

To create a header or footer that differs from the one in the previous section:

1. Place the insertion point in the section you want to change.

2. Choose View | Header and Footer. Word will switch into Page Layout view, highlight the header, and place the Header And Footer toolbar on the screen. By default, the Same As Previous button will appear pushed in, and the words Same As Previous will appear above the header itself.

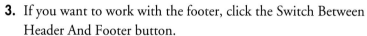

3. If you want to work with the footer, click the Switch Between Header And Footer button.

4. If you want headers (or footers) to change with each new section, click the Same As Previous button to deactivate it.

5. Type the text for your header or footer; then click the Close button on the Header And Footer toolbar.

EXPERT ADVICE

If you want page numbering to be continuous despite changing headers or footers, click in the second section, choose Insert | Page Numbers, click Format, click Continue From Previous Section, and then click OK. Repeat for each section.

Organizing Your Document by Outlining It

Mention the idea of making an outline, and just about everybody groans. It seems like extra work, doesn't it? Sure, it might help you get your thoughts sorted out and allow you to anticipate problems you might encounter further down the road, but there's still something onerous about having to make an outline. Word, however, has done a pretty good job of integrating outlines seamlessly into the document creation process.

In fact, although you might picture an outline as a document separate from your actual manuscript, Word's approach to outlines is to simply present a view of your original manuscript with only the outline showing. The Outline view is a way of focusing on the headings and subheadings of a document by hiding and allowing you to ignore the contents.

Word's outlining feature works only if you use the preset heading styles (Heading 1, Heading 2, and so on)—you'll be able to see a document using other headings in Outline view, of course, but you won't be able to promote and demote headings. You can edit these styles to make them look different, if that's what you're after.

> If you just want to browse the outline of your document without changing it, consider using the Document Map button, explained earlier in this chapter.

Outlining an Existing Document

Even if you haven't been using the preset heading styles, you can outline an existing document just by jumping into Outline view and then assigning levels to its headings. To do so, choose View | Outline, or click the Outline View button at the left end of the horizontal scroll bar.

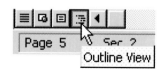

Your document will be presented as a series of indented headings, each of which is preceded by a plus sign if it contains subheadings or a minus sign if it does not (see Figure 12.8).

If your document does not use the preset heading styles, you can now select paragraphs (specifically, the short lines of text you want to use as headings) and assign heading levels to them. You can do this either by using any of the traditional methods of choosing styles (such as choosing one from the drop-down Style list box in the Formatting toolbar) or with the help of the Outlining toolbar, as explained in the following section. Be sure to use the preset styles called Heading 1, Heading 2, and so on.

Regular text paragraphs will appear preceded by hollow squares. If you have not yet created any headings, your entire document will appear this way.

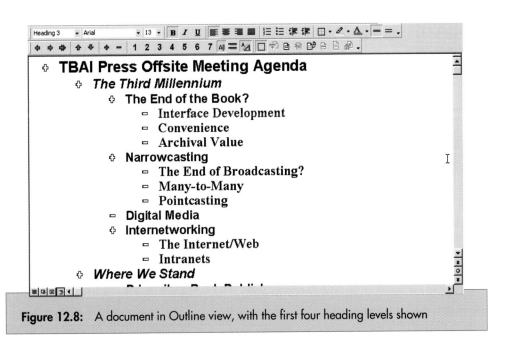

Figure 12.8: A document in Outline view, with the first four heading levels shown

Working in Outline View and Using the Outlining Toolbar

In Outline view, you can control the level of detail you'll see in your document. The main instrument you use to do this is the Outlining toolbar. Table 12.3 describes the action of each toolbar button.

Button	Name	Action
⬅	Promote	Promotes the level of an individual heading or an entire section by one; turns regular text into a heading
➡	Demote	Demotes the level of an individual heading or an entire selection by one
⇨	Demote To Body Text	Demotes the level of an individual heading or an entire selection to body text
⬆	Move Up	Changes the placement (not the heading level) of a selection
⬇	Move Down	Changes the placement (not the heading level) of a selection
➕	Expand	Shows all the headings subordinate to a selection
➖	Collapse	Hides all the headings subordinate to a selection
1 2 3 4 5 6 7	Show Heading *n*	Shows the headings that are at levels up to and including the number of the button you click
All	Show All	Instantly expands the entire outline
═	Show First Line Only	Hides everything after the first line of each paragraph of body text, creating a sort of mini-outline of each text section
ᴬ𝐴	Show Formatting	Hides or shows the formatting of the entire document
▢	Master Document View	Switches back and forth between Master Document view and Outline view

Table 12.3:   Buttons on the Outlining Toolbar

Creating an Outline from Scratch

To start typing an outline before you've created a document (good for you!), first switch into Outline view (as explained earlier). Then type the first heading. Word will automatically assign the Heading 1 style to this heading. When you press ENTER, Word will give the new line the same heading style as the previous line.

You can then click the Demote button (before or after typing the new heading, as long as the insertion point is still on that line) to make the line subordinate to the previous one. When you press ENTER again, the next line will get the same style as the previous line.

 Continue typing headings and promoting or demoting them as you go. You can enter regular text at any time by clicking the Demote To Body Text button.

Expanding or Collapsing an Outline

As you work on an outlined document, you'll want to see different levels of detail at different times. The primary benefit of outlining is this ability to choose between a view that shows only the first-level headings, a view that shows the entire structure, and views that show anything in between. At its most collapsed level, the Outline view shows just first-level headings. At its most expanded, it shows the entire document, though you can reduce each text paragraph to a single line.

To see an outline collapsed down to just a few headings, click the Show Heading button that corresponds to the number of the lowest level of heading you want to see (see Figure 12.9). The dotted gray lines that you might see under some headings represent collapsed headings and/or body text.

You can also select an individual heading and then expand or collapse the selection by clicking the Expand or Collapse buttons on the Outlining toolbar. Alternatively, you can double-click any plus sign to expand (or collapse) the entire outline family subordinate to it.

Although you can select text in the normal way in Outline view, clicking on the hollow plus sign to the left of a heading will select the heading and its entire family of subordinate headings. When the

EXPERT ADVICE

Whenever you need to enter large blocks of text, consider switching back to Normal view to do so, since it will seem more familiar and, well, normal. Then switch again to Outline view to continue working on the organization of the document. Or consider using the Document Map.

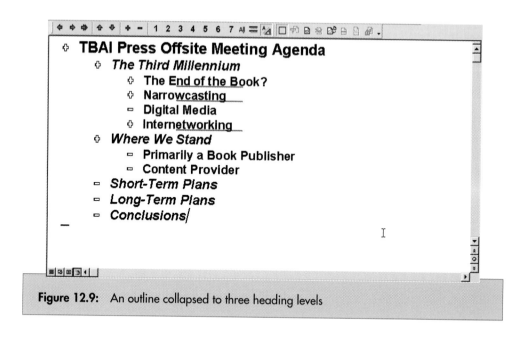

Figure 12.9: An outline collapsed to three heading levels

cursor is positioned over the plus sign, it will appear as a quadruple-headed arrow.

Rearranging an Outline

Another convenience of outlining is the ease with which you can rearrange the items in the outline, changing their order and altering the structure until you arrive at the best possible organization.

MOVING HEADINGS   To move a heading or heading family from one place to another in an outline (in other words, to reorder the headings), first make your selection. Then either click the Move Up or the Move Down button in the Outlining toolbar, or click the plus or the minus sign icon for the selection and drag it up or down. When you click Move Up or Move Down, the selected head will move up or down one position in your outline. When you use the drag-and-drop method, the pointer will change to a four-headed arrow. A dotted horizontal line with an arrowhead on it will move up and down as you move the mouse, showing the potential destinations for the selection as you drag. When you release the mouse button, the headings will move.

You don't have to select a heading first if you plan to drag it by its plus (or minus) sign.

PROMOTING AND DEMOTING HEADINGS   To promote or demote a heading or heading family, first make your selection. Then either click the Promote or Demote button in the Outlining toolbar, or click the plus or minus sign icon for the selection and drag it left or right. If you use the drag-and-drop method, a dotted vertical line with a box hanging off it to the left will move left or right as you move the mouse, showing the levels you're dragging to. When you release the mouse button, the headings will move.

SHORTCUT
You can also demote a heading by pressing TAB or promote a heading by pressing SHIFT+TAB when the insertion point is in the line.

Using Master Documents

If you are working with a very large document, perhaps one that has been created by several different authors in collaboration, and you're willing and able to invest a little extra time in structuring it, you can set up what's called a *master document*.

Once you have done this, each of the subdocuments in the master document can be worked on separately and then reintegrated into the master document at any point. Any numbered elements, including page numbers, headings, captions, and tables, will increment correctly from subdocument to subdocument, saving you the hassle of micromanaging the sort of details that computers keep better track of anyway.

You can turn an existing document into a master document, designating portions of the original document as subdocuments. You can also create a new master document from existing subdocuments. To create or work on a master document, choose View | Outline.

Master Document view is a close variation of Outline view. The document appears with outlining marks and the Outlining toolbar appears, along with the Master Document toolbar, shown here:

DEFINITION
Master document:
A document that contains several subdocuments, each of which can be treated as a separate document.

Subdocument:
One of the component documents of a master document.

CAUTION
Master documents can be tricky and frustrating to work with. For example, it's a little too easy to delete the contents of a subdocument (without realizing it) from within the master document.

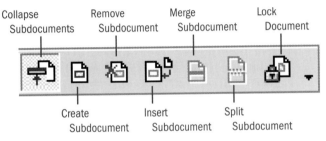

Collapse Subdocuments   Remove Subdocument   Merge Subdocument   Lock Document

Create Subdocument   Insert Subdocument   Split Subdocument

The outline will automatically be set to show all levels, regardless of the level you were viewing previously, but you can just click on a Show Heading button again to return to the overview you want.

Creating Subdocuments from an Existing Outline

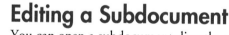

I n Normal view, subdocuments are separated by section breaks.

After entering Master Document view, create an outline of your document (if one does not already exist) or work on the existing outline. To designate a portion of the outline as a subdocument, select the heading (or headings) involved and click the Create Subdocument button. The part you've turned into a subdocument will appear surrounded by a rectangle with a subdocument icon in the top-left corner.

Repeat the process to create as many subdocuments as you want in the master document. When you're done, choose File | Save As, type a name for the master document, and click the Save button. Word will save the master document under the name you typed, and it will save each of the subdocuments under a name based on the first words in the heading.

Editing a Subdocument

CAUTION

If you want to change the name of a subdocument, open it from within the master document, or the master won't recognize the new document. Also, keep all the components of a master document together in the same folder.

You can open a subdocument directly, as you would a normal document, or you can open a subdocument from within a master document. To do the latter, just double-click the subdocument icon in the top-left corner of the subdocument area. Word will open the subdocument in Normal view. (The master document will still be open.)

Inserting Existing Documents into a Master Document

You can also build a master document from existing documents. To do so, start a new document and enter Outline view. On the Master Document toolbar, click the Insert Subdocument button. An Insert Subdocument dialog box (a clone of the Open dialog box) will appear. Choose the document you want to insert, and click the Open button. Repeat this process as often as you need to.

EXPERT ADVICE

Elements such as a title page or introductory text can be part of the master document because the master is itself a normal document, separate from the inserted subdocuments. Headers and footers, tables of contents, and indexes must all be part of the master document (not a subdocument) to apply consistently to the whole.

Once you've inserted a subdocument, it's linked into the master document. When you make changes to it in one place, it changes in the other as well. If you want to delete some of the text of the subdocument from the master document without actually cutting from the original subdocument, you *must* first put the insertion point in the subdocument portion of the master document and click the Remove Subdocument button.

The Remove Subdocument button does not actually remove any text from your document; it just disassociates the text of the subdocument within the master document from the external subdocument file. In making this change it also removes the subdocument rectangle and subdocument icon from the master document, leaving the text that was within the rectangle. After this, you can change the text without affecting the original subdocument.

Tricks for Long Documents

Some Word features are really only useful for long documents. In this section I'll show you how to create cross-references and tables of contents, and how to count the words in a document.

For very long documents, cross-references are essential tools that help you organize the information. How many of the projects you work on can be adequately explained in a simple, linear fashion? If you had to explain complex information to someone in conversation, you'd probably jump forward and back, make asides, and occasionally say "Don't worry, I'll get to that." In a long document, you similarly want to be able to point a reader ahead or back to pertinent information or to acknowledge a link between separate parts of the overall work. Cross-references serve that very purpose.

A table of contents is a more straightforward tool and is also valuable for a long document. It allows readers to go directly to the section of the work that they need. It also helps, much as an outline does, to convey a sense of the overall structure of a document.

Finally, you'll sometimes need to adhere to a maximum word count, or stay close to a specific range, or simply know the number of words in the document so you can note it on the title page. Naturally, Word can count the words in your document automatically.

Cross-References

Cross references work like hyperlinks in that, if you click a cross-reference, you'll be taken to the text it refers to. (See Chapter 13 for more on hyperlinks.)

Word can maintain automated cross-references to many different types of document elements. The cross-references are automated in the sense that if they specify the page number of the referenced text, for example, and if the page number changes, the reference will change as well. A cross-reference can also cite the exact wording of a heading or caption and will reflect changes to the text automatically.

To insert a cross-reference, place the insertion point where you want the reference to go. Type the regular portion of the reference, such as **For more about Antilles mule-frogs, see . . .** or **See page . . . .** Then choose Insert | Cross-reference. The Cross-reference dialog box appears:

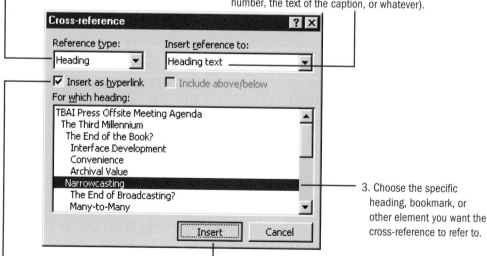

1. Choose the type of document element to which you want to refer.

2. Choose the aspect of the element you want to refer to (the number of the page it's on, the heading or paragraph number, the text of the caption, or whatever).

3. Choose the specific heading, bookmark, or other element you want the cross-reference to refer to.

4. Check Insert As Hyperlink if you want the cross-reference to be linked to the referred text.

5. Finally, click the Insert button, and then click Close. The cross-reference will appear in your document. Finish the sentence or edit the spaces around the inserted reference to make everything fit smoothly.

Tables of Contents

If you have an existing outline (based on the preset heading levels) or even a consistent set of headings of your own, creating a table of contents (also known as a TOC) from the headings is no problem.

To create a table of contents, place the insertion point at the very beginning of the document and choose Insert | Index And Tables. Click the Table Of Contents tab in the Index And Tables dialog box that appears (see Figure 12.10).

Using Different Styles for the TOC

To base your table of contents on a different hierarchy of headings, click the Options button in the Index and Tables dialog box. This brings up the Table Of Contents Options dialog box.

- Check all the styles that you want to correspond to a level in the table of contents.
- Enter a number in the TOC Level box across from it. Scroll through the list to see all the available styles.

When you're done, click OK.

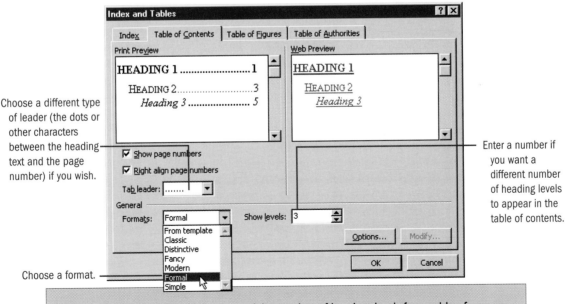

Choose a different type of leader (the dots or other characters between the heading text and the page number) if you wish.

Enter a number if you want a different number of heading levels to appear in the table of contents.

Choose a format.

Figure 12.10: Choosing a format and the number of heading levels for a table of contents

Inserting the TOC

When you're done in the Index And Tables dialog box, click OK. Word will insert your table of contents at the beginning of the document (assuming that you put the cursor there, as directed). You may want to insert a hard page break at the end of the table of contents to separate it from the rest of the document.

Updating a TOC

Word will automatically update a TOC just before printing a document.

If you end up revising a document after making a TOC (and believe me, you will), you can update the TOC by clicking anywhere in it and pressing F9. (Pressing F9 updates fields, and the TOC is made up of fields.) Alternatively, you can right-click in the table of contents and then choose the Update Field command from the shortcut menu, as shown in Figure 12.11.

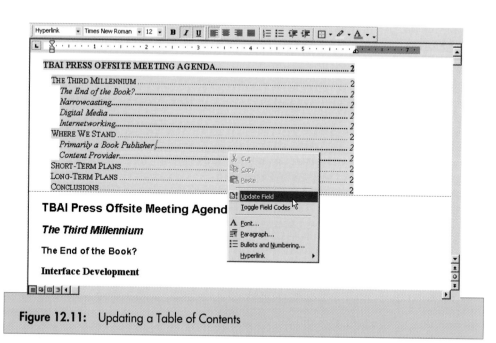

Figure 12.11: Updating a Table of Contents

Counting the Words

Word considers any character or characters before a space, period, comma, or other punctuation to be a word. To count the words in your document, choose Tools | Word Count. It will take a moment or two for Word to complete the count, and then grayed out numbers will be replaced with solid numbers reflecting the current totals. Copy down any numbers you may need to refer to. (There's no way to copy and paste them directly!) Then click Close.

There's More . . .

Now that you know all the tricks for formatting splendid-looking documents, you've really mastered Word, perhaps more than you realize. The only frontiers left to you are the kinds of documents that require such a high degree of organization, design, and creativity that they are called *publications.*

Chapter 13 will show you how to design Web documents, and Chapter 14 will show you how to publish documents (or make them downloadable) on the Web as well as on intranets.

Designing Web Documents

INCLUDES

- **Converting existing documents to Web documents**
- **Creating Web documents from scratch**
- **Formatting Web documents**
- **Adding hyperlinks to Web documents**
- **Creating forms for Web browsers**
- **Working with frames**
- **Previewing Web documents**

Convert an Existing Document to a Web Document ➡ pp. 243–246

1. Open the source document.
2. Choose File | Save as Web Page.
3. Click the Change Title button, type a page title, and click OK.
4. Type a one-word filename.
5. Click the Save button.

Create a Blank Web Document ➡ pp. 246–247

1. Choose File | New.
2. Select the General tab.
3. Choose the Web Page template.
4. Click OK.

Start with a Predesigned Web Document ➡ pp. 248–249

1. Choose File | New.
2. Choose the Web Pages tab.
3. Select one of the dummy page layouts or choose the Web Page Wizard.
4. Click OK.

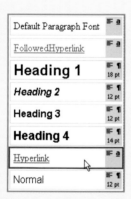

Format a Web Document ➡ pp. 249–251

Using buttons on the Formatting toolbar, you can

- Select styles (such as headings) from the Style box
- Change font sizes
- Apply boldface, italics, and underlining
- Change alignment
- Create numbered and bulleted lists
- Insert horizontal lines
- Choose a background color

Add a Hyperlink to a Web Document ➥ pp. 257–259

1. Select the text for the active link.
2. Click the Insert Hyperlink button on the Standard toolbar.
3. Indicate the type of link you're inserting in the Link To bar.
4. Enter a Web address (for a remote resource) or type or browse for a path and filename (for a local file).
5. Click OK.

Preview Your Document in a Web Browser ➥ p. 263

1. Save the document as a Web document.
2. Select File | Web Page Preview.

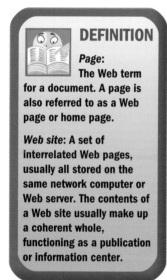

DEFINITION

Page:
The Web term for a document. A page is also referred to as a Web page or home page.

Web site: A set of interrelated Web pages, usually all stored on the same network computer or Web server. The contents of a Web site usually make up a coherent whole, functioning as a publication or information center.

The fastest growing part of the Internet today is the World Wide Web, an international network of interconnected documents and Internet sites containing archived information. The next thing you know, your company will establish a presence on the Web (if it hasn't already), and your department will need to start putting information out there for the benefit of customers, colleagues, or clients.

The Web model has also been imported to local networks that are run along Internet lines, called *intranets*. It's very likely that your company or department will soon be putting information up on a company intranet, or sharing information or collaborating over such connections.

Until recently, creating Web documents (also called Web pages) was a matter of learning how to insert HTML (HyperText Markup Language) codes, called *tags*, into plain-text documents. With Word, though, you can now convert existing files directly into HTML format, and you can create Web documents using familiar Word commands and similar toolbars and dialog boxes.

Planning a Web Site

Before you start plunging in and converting existing documents to Web pages or creating a set of interlinked Web documents from scratch, take some time to think through the organization of your proposed Web site. You'll want to create a home page to serve as the front door and central hub of all related documents. You'll also want to organize your documents into a logical system of folders so that you or others can easily fix errors and make changes to the site. Setting up the documents for the first time is only half the job. The other half of the job is maintaining the potentially complex set of Web pages as the information within them evolves.

Preparing to Use Word's Web Tools

When you start following along with the instructions in the rest of this chapter, you may discover something's amiss. It's possible that your copy of Word 2000 was installed without the Web Page Authoring (HTML) tools that make all this Web-tomfoolery possible. If so, no harm done; just rerun the Setup program, choose Custom installation, and be sure to choose "Run From This Computer" for Web Page Authoring this time around. See the Appendix if you have any other questions about installing Word.

Converting Word Documents to Web Documents

Often, when a company or academic department decides that it is time to make information available via the World Wide Web (or an intranet), it proceeds to do so by converting reams of existing documents into Web documents (also called HTML documents). In the early days of the Web, this could be tricky, but with Word it is fairly straightforward.

Once the documents have been converted and made available on the Web, your documents will no longer look exactly as they do in Word. Each Web browser out there (and there are hundreds) displays the various HTML elements slightly differently, and many browsers have custom display options that can be set by users. The important thing is to make sure that the relationships between the levels of the headings and the parts of the document make sense so that any reader with any browser will get a sensibly organized document.

DEFINITION

Web browser: A handy program used to magically connect to Web sites, display Web pages, and jump from link to link.

Some Things That Don't Convert

Not all of Word's features have Web equivalents, so some formatting and other embellishments will disappear when you convert a document. Word features that will disappear include:

- Columns
- Comments
- Embossing, engraving, small caps, double-strikethroughs, and outline formatting
- Headers and footers
- Margins
- Page numbering (there are no page breaks in Web documents)
- Revision marks

Things that won't convert completely include:

- Footnotes and endnotes (they get moved to the end of the page)
- Fields (their results will appear in the document, but they can't be updated)
- Tabs
- Graphics (they get converted to the GIF format)
- Some aspects of tables
- Most styles

Saving a Document as HTML

To convert a Word document to Web format, first open it. Then select File | Save As and choose Web Page in the Save As Type drop-down list box at the bottom of the dialog box (see Figure 13.1). If you want to save yourself a couple of steps, choose File | Save as Web Page (you are a busy person after all).

Then, click Change Title to give your document a title. Type a title and click OK.

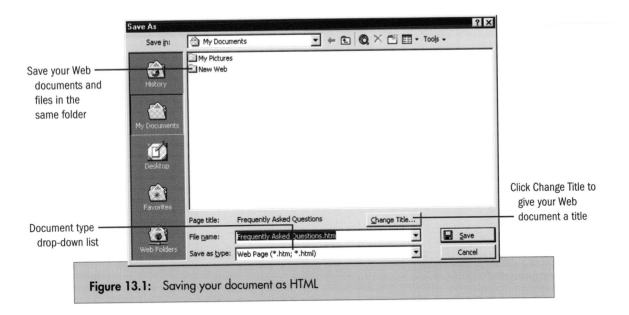

Figure 13.1: Saving your document as HTML

Callouts on figure:
- Save your Web documents and files in the same folder
- Click Change Title to give your Web document a title
- Document type drop-down list

Choose a folder as you normally would (all the documents for your Web site should be stored in the same folder or in subfolders of a main folder), type a one-word filename (with no spaces in it so that it will be compatible with all computer systems), and then click the Save button.

EXPERT ADVICE

Each Web document needs a title that is distinct from the filename and from the first heading, although it can be identical to either in content. The title is what is displayed in the title bar of the browser window when you view the Web page. Web pages without plain-language titles constitute a classic newbie mistake.

Turning an HTML Document into a Web Template

If you're designing an involved Web site with more than one or two pages, you'll soon realize that you want to avoid having to format each page individually if they're all going to have the same basic formatting (we'll get to formatting Web documents in a moment). To conserve time and effort, you can save a copy of your prototype Web document as a template, and then base the rest of the documents on that template.

It's easy enough to do. Just design and format the document (as explained in the upcoming sections), save it normally, and then select File | Save As. Then select Document Template in the Save As Type drop-down list box at the bottom of the Save As dialog box. The view in the dialog box will switch to show your Templates folder. Then type a filename for the template, and click Save.

Creating a Web Document from Scratch

In addition to converting existing documents to HTML format, you'll also want to create new Web documents from scratch. Wow your boss and colleagues with your mastery of this esoteric science without letting them know that all you did was format a document almost exactly as you normally would have in Word.

In general, you have three starting points for creating a new Web document: a blank Web document (you create all the design and formatting), a predesigned Web page (work from a template's design and formatting), or use Word's Web Page Wizard to interactively specify the type of design and formatting you wish to use.

Starting with a Clean Slate

To create a blank Web document, start by choosing File | New, and then click on the General tab in the New dialog box, if it isn't already visible. Select the Web Page template and click OK. You will then be presented with a blank Web document—a clean slate from which to begin your Web page project (see Figure 13.2).

Web Page Templates

If starting from scratch isn't exactly to your liking, creating a Web document from one of Word's more evolved templates can offer you more choices in layout and presentation. To access these templates, see the instructions in Figure 13.3.

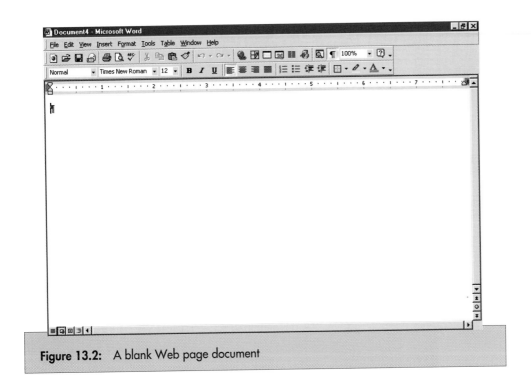

Figure 13.2: A blank Web page document

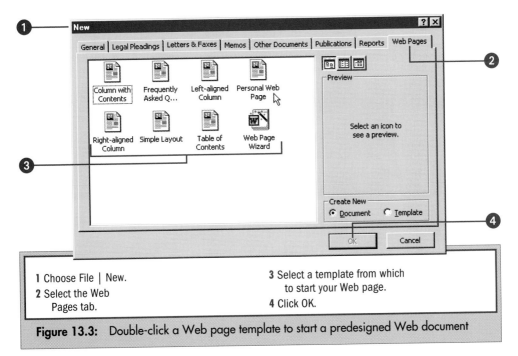

1 Choose File | New.
2 Select the Web Pages tab.

3 Select a template from which to start your Web page.
4 Click OK.

Figure 13.3: Double-click a Web page template to start a predesigned Web document

Web Page Wizardry

If you choose to start with the Web Page Wizard, you can have more control over how your Web document or documents will appear, and how they are organized. If you need to utilize an elaborate design or wish to have multiple pages in your Web document, the Web Page Wizard is the way to go. Once you begin the Web Page Wizard, you can specify a number of aspects of your Web documents, including page titles, page organization and navigation, the location for saving the documents, and the visual theme of the project. To start the Web Page Wizard, choose File | New and select the Web Pages tab. Select Web Page Wizard and click OK.

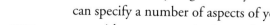

Web Page Wizard

One of the more welcome additions to this new version of the Web Page Wizard is the ability to make frames in your documents. Frames can help make navigation within your Web site efficient and easy for the viewer, because you can have links to your various pages available no matter how deeply the viewer ventures into your Web site. To create frames, click on the Navigation section of the Web Page Wizard and choose either a horizontal or vertical design (see Figure 13.4). When

For more on editing frames, see "You've Been Framed," later in this chapter.

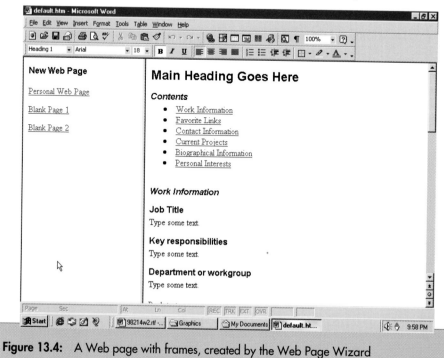

Figure 13.4: A Web page with frames, created by the Web Page Wizard

you finish going through the rest of the Wizard steps, you will have a set of Web pages based on a frames-oriented design—something that used to be quite a hassle when coding HTML by hand.

Using the Wizard is fairly simple; just follow the instructions in each section and, before you know it, you'll have a set of Web documents ready for you to plug your content into (text, graphics, video, and hyperlinks). However, you may want to start out by arranging the elements and getting your pages formatted just the way you like.

Formatting Your Web Document

Once you have the content in your Web page, you can apply Web formatting, which usually amounts to nothing more than headings, horizontal lines, and hyperlinks (you can look through the style list to see what's available).

See Chapters 5 and 12 for more on styles.

Headings and Styles and Lists, Oh My!

Web documents generally start with an H1 heading, so select the title of your document and assign the H1 style. Make subordinate headings H2, and so on. The easiest way to apply styles to selections is to choose the styles from the Style drop-down list box in the Formatting toolbar.

To indicate that text is an address, a block quote (block quotation), a comment (not to appear on the screen), preformatted text, or any of a number of other HTML formatting choices, just select text and then choose the format in the Style list box. Use the Bold, Italics, and Underlining, alignment, and list buttons to format your text, much as you would in any Word document.

Fun with Horizontal Lines

Web documents can't have borders all over the place the way Word documents can. The only standard type of line in a Web document is the horizontal rule (which Word calls a *horizontal line*). To insert one, click the Horizontal Line button found in the Borders drop-down menu.

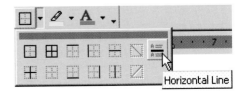

A shadowed, engraved-looking line will appear at the level of the insertion point. Text below the insertion point will move down below the line.

To move the line, click and drag it. To change its length, click it once to select it, and then click and drag the right end of the line to a different position.

Color Choices

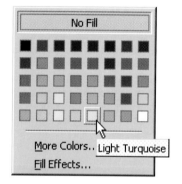

Word provides several ways of adding a splash of color or texture to your Web documents. You can have a background color, or even a background image, tiled (repeating) behind the text. To select a color, click the Choose Format | Background and then select a color from the palette that drops down.

If you don't like any of the suggested colors, click the More Colors button near the bottom of the palette, select a color from one of the two tabs of the Colors dialog box, and then click OK.

Word comes with a starter set of background images (though you can use any suitable image you can dig up, create, or cause to be made). To find one, choose Format | Background | Fill Effects. This brings up the Fill Effects dialog box, from which you can choose a Texture or a picture to use as a tiled background image.

Click the Textures tab and scroll though the Texture swatches, choose one you like, and click OK (see Figure 13.5). If you have more textures in another folder somewhere, click the Other Texture button, browse through your storehouse of textures, and select one from there.

CAUTION

Maybe you've figured this out, but remember to choose background colors or images that contrast with your text color selections, or your pages will be unreadable.

EXPERT ADVICE

If you choose to add a texture to your Web document, Word will save the texture as a GIF file in your default Web document folder.

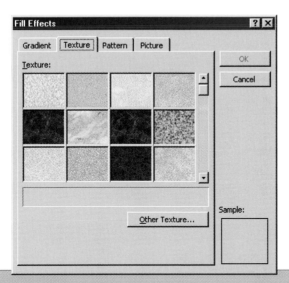

Figure 13.5:   Choose a texture and then click OK to make your document beautiful (or unreadable)

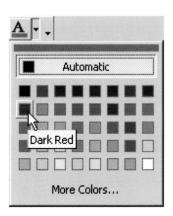

You can also color any text selection, regardless of what the default text or link colors are. To do so, select the text, click the Font Color button, and then choose a color from the palette that drops down. To make the selected text match its default color, select Automatic. For more elaborate text tricks, such as scrolling text, see "Pictures and Multimedia," coming up.

Word also provides a variety of themes from which to choose. Themes offer preset collections of color, background, and hyperlink styles, all based around—you guessed it—themes! To apply a theme to an existing document, choose Format | Theme, select the theme you want, and click OK.

To create a new Web document with a theme, use the Web Page Wizard, discussed in the "Web Page Wizardry" section, earlier in this chapter.

EXPERT ADVICE

Given the state of most browsers today and most users' preferences, you're better off using tables instead of frames to align the design and navigation elements in your Web documents.

Web Tables

Most sophisticated Web pages are designed with tables. Figure 13.6 shows a sample Web document that uses a table to break the page into two columns: one with a picture and caption, and another with text and headings.

Make tables just as you would for a normal Word document. Web documents display gridlines differently (as beveled borders) and under different circumstances (based on their set width and whether there's any text in a given cell), but you can create and edit tables using the techniques you learned in Chapter 12.

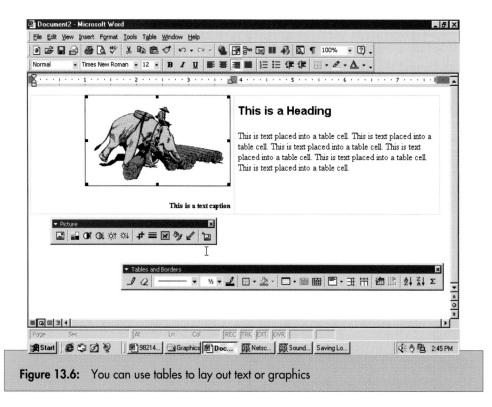

Figure 13.6: You can use tables to lay out text or graphics

Pictures and Multimedia

Web pages are popular not just for having text and formatting, like normal word processing documents, but also for having pictures and sometimes even other media formats (such as video, animation, or sound) embedded into them. The Web doesn't just lie there, it also gets up and dances every now and then!

Word Converts Pictures to a Web Format

The tricky part of dealing with pictures on the Web is that only certain picture formats are viewable by most browsers. Word converts any pictures you insert into your document to GIF format. If you want to display a photograph, you may want to convert it to the JPEG format instead, with picture or photo-editing software. Most other graphic images will look fine as GIFs.

To insert a picture, choose Insert | Picture, and select either Clip Art or From File. If you choose ClipArt, this brings up the Insert ClipArt dialog box (see Figure 13.7). Browse to and select your image,

CAUTION

Just because you find artwork somewhere on the Web and can save it to your own computer doesn't necessarily give you the right to insert it into a Web document and publish it on the World Wide Web. Be as considerate towards other people's copyrights as you would have them be towards your own intellectual property.

See Chapter 12 for more on inserting pictures.

Figure 13.7: The Insert ClipArt dialog box

and then click OK. If you choose to insert a picture From File, the Insert Picture dialog box appears. Find the location of your picture in the Look In drop-down list, choose your insert option (Insert, Link To File, or Insert And Link), and press ENTER.

Word inserts the image into the document (at the insertion point) and the Picture toolbar appears. (If the Picture toolbar does not appear automatically, you can right-click any toolbar and select Picture from the shortcut menu.)

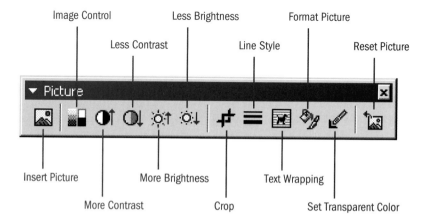

The toolbar is useful for setting how (or whether) you want text to wrap around the image, as well as for controlling the image's contrast, brightness, and size. You can also determine whether you want one color in the image to be transparent, which is helpful if you want the object in the image to appear to "float" on the page background, instead of having a rectangular edge.

Some people on the Web use nongraphical Web browsers and won't be able to see your pictures. You can insert a text description of your images (where appropriate) that will be displayed as an alternative on nongraphical browsers. To do so, select a picture and click the Format Picture button on the Picture toolbar (or right-click a picture and select Format Picture). This brings up the Format Picture dialog box. Click the Web tab and then type your description in the Alternative Text area of the tab.

To fine-tune the horizontal and vertical distances between the edges of the picture and the surrounding text, click the Layout tab and then click the Advanced button at the bottom. Click the Text Wrapping tab and enter values (in inches) in the Vertical and Horizontal boxes in the Distance From Text area of the tab.

When you're done formatting your picture, click OK.

To resize the picture, just click it once to select it, and then drag it by the square handles at the corners and on the middles of the sides.

If you have your view options set to display hidden text, you may see some strange field codes here and there in your Web documents, but you can safely ignore them.

Inserting Movie Clips

You can insert video clips into your page (what Word now calls *movie clips*), but this feature may be more effective on a corporate intranet, which can carry video at a tolerable, Ethernet-based speed, than on the Web, where your viewers might rebel against video even at 56,000 bits per second (or on an older computer with a slow video system). Still, if you want to do it, Word can help.

The simplest way to get a video file onto your Web page is to display the Web Tools toolbar (you can do so by right-clicking any toolbar and selecting Web Tools from the shortcut menu). The rest of the steps are shown in Figure 13.8.

EXPERT ADVICE

It's also an easy affair to insert a sound file into your Web document. Just click the Sound button on the Web Tools toolbar.

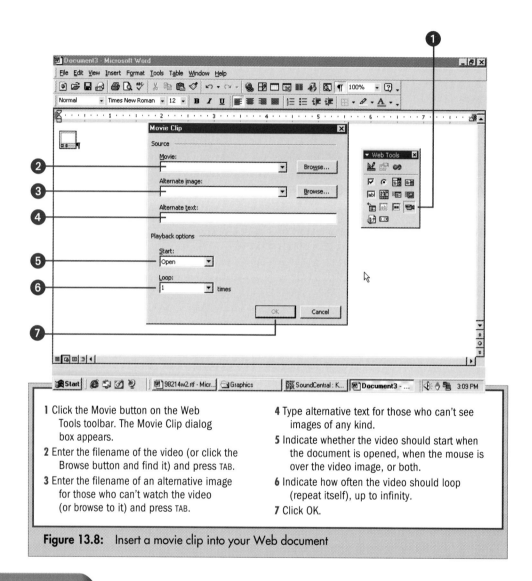

Figure 13.8:   Insert a movie clip into your Web document

1 Click the Movie button on the Web Tools toolbar. The Movie Clip dialog box appears.

2 Enter the filename of the video (or click the Browse button and find it) and press TAB.

3 Enter the filename of an alternative image for those who can't watch the video (or browse to it) and press TAB.

4 Type alternative text for those who can't see images of any kind.

5 Indicate whether the video should start when the document is opened, when the mouse is over the video image, or both.

6 Indicate how often the video should loop (repeat itself), up to infinity.

7 Click OK.

CAUTION

This scrolling-text trick is supported only by Microsoft's Internet Explorer browser (and not by Netscape Navigator).

Wahoo! Scrolling Text

I admit it: I'm being a little sarcastic. Microsoft introduced the concept of a marquee (scrolling text, as on a ticker tape) to the Web and has been proudly supporting it ever since. Scrolling text has its uses, to be sure, but usually in a news context where some software is at work updating the text regularly. The "welcome to our company" shtick gets old fast scrolling past the page, but that's just my opinion.

To animate your text in this sense, just click the Scrolling Text button on the Web Tools toolbar, and follow the instructions in Figure 13.9.

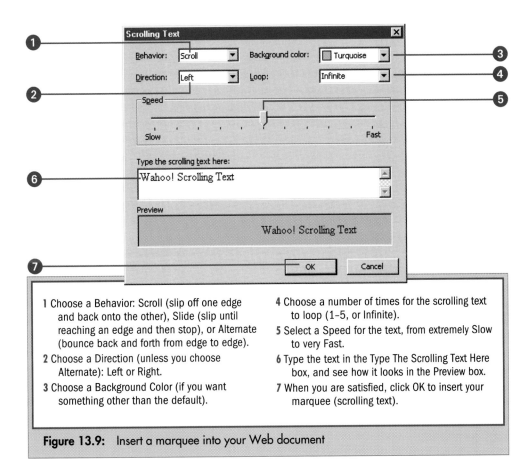

1 Choose a Behavior: Scroll (slip off one edge and back onto the other), Slide (slip until reaching an edge and then stop), or Alternate (bounce back and forth from edge to edge).

2 Choose a Direction (unless you choose Alternate): Left or Right.

3 Choose a Background Color (if you want something other than the default).

4 Choose a number of times for the scrolling text to loop (1–5, or Infinite).

5 Select a Speed for the text, from extremely Slow to very Fast.

6 Type the text in the Type The Scrolling Text Here box, and see how it looks in the Preview box.

7 When you are satisfied, click OK to insert your marquee (scrolling text).

Figure 13.9:   Insert a marquee into your Web document

Adding Hyperlinks

Web documents can stand alone, but a prominent feature of the World Wide Web is that so many of the documents on it are interlinked, with embedded hypertext links pointing to other documents.

DEFINITION

Hyperlink:
Also known as a link, or hypertext link, this is a highlighted portion of a document that, when clicked or otherwise activated, connects the reader to another document, another portion of the document, or another site on the Internet.
URL: **Web address. It stands for uniform resource locator.**

Adding hyperlinks to documents is a simple operation with Word, yet the Insert Hyperlink dialog box is still a very powerful tool. With it, you can insert links to documents, Web pages, or e-mail addresses. You don't need to make much effort to keep track of things that you want to link to because the dialog box keeps track of all your recently accessed files, Web pages, and addresses for you.

To create a hyperlink, select the text (or graphic) you want to use as the launching point to the link destination. Click the Insert Hyperlink button on the Standard toolbar (or choose Insert | Hyperlink). The Insert Hyperlink dialog box appears (see Figure 13.10).

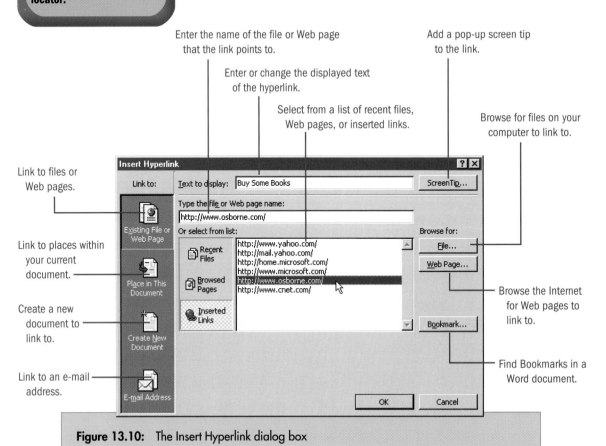

Figure 13.10: The Insert Hyperlink dialog box

After you have set up your hyperlink the way you want it, click
OK. The text that activates the link will appear underlined and in blue
type (as is typical of links when they are displayed in Web browsers).
You can move the mouse pointer over the hyperlink to see its
destination. You can also change the text the same way you would edit
normal text.

There are shortcuts for inserting links, as well. If you copy a Web
address (or document from a folder window), you can select Edit |
Paste as Hyperlink to insert a link in the current document (and then
change the anchor text from the filename or URL to something in
plain English). You can also right-click a link to edit it, copy it, or
even browse to it (browsing with Word is covered in Chapter 14).

Survey Says . . . (Forms)

In Chapter 8, I showed you how to design forms (including onscreen
forms) with Word. One way to make Web sites more interactive and
to encourage audience input is to incorporate forms (such as survey,
registration, or order forms) in your site. Web forms have many
elements in common with Word forms, but they are not exactly the
same, so Word has special Web form design tools available. To access
theses tools, right-click on or near any toolbar, and select the Web
Tools toolbar.

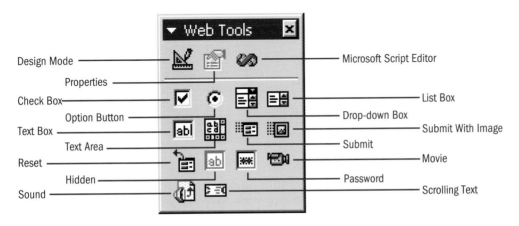

To insert any of the standard Web form elements (such as a check
box or drop-down box), click the button on the Web Tools toolbar.

For elements that need default text or a list of options, select the inserted control and click the Properties button. Then, in either tab of the Properties dialog box, enter the text in the Value box (for multiple entries, such as in a list box, separate each entry with a semicolon and no spaces). Don't forget to include a Submit button on your form!

You've Been Framed

CAUTION

When you select Format | Frames | New Frames Page, Word opens whatever document you have active as a new frames page in a new window. You haven't lost your work, it's just been given a brand new face.

Frames within Web documents can often be clumsy and complicated, but Word does offer a number of ways to easily create and edit frames. One way is to have the Web Page Wizard create them for you. Another way is to create a new document, or open a document you've already worked on, and choose Format | Frames | New Frames Page. In either case, you'll be presented with a document ready to be framed.

Each frame is actually a separate document. You can click and drag the frames border in the middle of the page to resize the frames. Add text, links, graphics, or other content to the frames as you would with any document (see Figure 13.11).

If you don't see it already, right-click any toolbar and select Frames in order to see the Frames toolbar. With this toolbar you can add or remove frames, change their properties, and keep control of their contents.

Delete
Frame

Table Of Contents
In Frame

Frame
Properties

If you want to change the borders or edit the content of a particular frame, select it by clicking anywhere inside it, and click the Properties button of the Frames toolbar. Click the Borders tab to turn borders

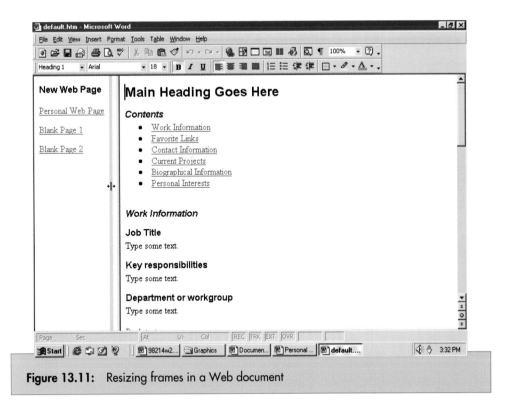

Figure 13.11: Resizing frames in a Web document

on or off, to change the size and color of text in the frame, or to
determine how the frame will appear if the browser window is resized
(add scrollbars or allow it to be resized by the viewer). Click the Frame
tab for more options dealing with what appears inside the frame or
how it appears. You can link the frame to a file, change the name of
the frame, or set the height and width of the frame (do this if you
don't want the frame to resize).

EXPERT ADVICE

If you want to create a table of contents within a frame, there's a button to do so on the Frames
toolbar, but the easiest way to do this is to use the Web Page Wizard. The Wizard will
automatically create a table of contents frame for you. For more on tables of contents, see Chapter 12.

Web Stuff Word Can't Do

DEFINITION

Image maps are hyperlinked pictures that send you to different destinations depending on where you click on them.

Word is still not the ultimate Web-design program. Microsoft deserves credit for the Web-design tools it's already built into Word, but the Web evolves quickly, and you have to get up with the chickens to keep up. (In Chapter 14, I'll show you how to download upgrades to your Web-authoring tools as they become available at the Word Web site.) For example, Word still can't make image maps.

If you want to explore more sophisticated Web design elements, consider getting Microsoft FrontPage (or other full-fledged Web-design and Web-site management software). I mention FrontPage specifically, because it shares a lot of features with Word and other Office programs (and it's included in the most complete Office package).

Different Views of Your Web Document

Once you start working with documents that are intended to be viewed onscreen instead of being printed out, some of the basic concepts of document creation start to change. Not all of the metaphors of the typewriter world make sense when you're talking about online documents, and some terms have evolved new meanings already (witness the word *page* when used in the Web sense). One effect of this is that there are now several more views, or ways of looking at your documents in Word, that are related to onscreen reading of Web documents.

See Chapter 14 for how to use Word as a Web browser.

Web Layout View vs. Normal View

As soon as you started working on a Web document (whether you started by converting an existing document or by creating a new one based on a Web-page template), Word switched to Web layout view. (You can verify this by clicking the View menu and seeing what's selected.) This is mainly so that you can see some of the elements that appear only in this mode. This mostly has to do with background colors and patterns, multimedia objects, and scrolling text.

Also, Word's Web layout view is not geared solely toward the creation of Web documents. If you are working in an environment in which Word, or Office more generally, is standard issue, you can actually set up an intranet site with Word documents in addition to or instead of HTML documents. If you do so, you'll be risking incompatibility with Web browsers (though some of them can, with plug-ins, view Word documents), but this may not matter in a closed system.

Previewing Your Document in a Real Web Browser

Word does a fairly good job in its Online view of showing how your Web page might appear in a typical Web browser, but there's no substitute for really previewing a page in an actual browser (such as Netscape Navigator or Microsoft Internet Explorer), especially if you have some idea of which Web browser most of the people in your audience are likely to use.

To get a look at your document in a real Web browser, choose File | Web Page Preview. Word will then launch your default Web browser and display the Web document you've been working on in the browser.

There's More . . .

Sometimes, Word reminds me of a Swiss army knife: many gadgets and widgets screwed into its body, some of which you never end up using or ever seeing, much less figuring out. Kind of handy to have around when it happens to have just the right tool. Add to all the page and document creation tools the new templates, wizards, and customized commands for Web-authoring, and you've got a pretty decent platform for turning out Web sites and intranet environments.

Once you've built up your pages and linked them all together into a coherent site, you'll then need to make that site available to its intended audience, whether it be the members of a small local network or the global community of Internet users. Either way, you can place your pages exactly where you need them with Word. You can also open up documents directly off the Web (or your intranet) when the time comes to correct or change them. Chapter 14 will tell you all about publishing and browsing online with Word.

Web and Intranet Publishing

INCLUDES

- Web browsing with Word
- Opening remote documents
- Publishing documents with Save As
- Working with Web Folders
- Telling Word about FTP sites
- Maintaining a Web site

Browse the Web from Within Word ➡ pp. 268–270

Right click on any toolbar and choose Web to bring up the Web toolbar with which you can do the following:

- Follow hyperlinks
- Retrace your path by clicking the Back, Forward, or Go buttons
- Visit your favorite Web sites by clicking Favorites
- Add Web documents to your hot list by clicking Favorites | Add to Favorites
- Drop by the Word Web site for the latest tools and templates

http://www.syx.com/

Open a Document from the Internet ➡ pp. 271–273

Either enter a Web address directly in the Address box, or:

1. Select File | Open.
2. Type an Internet address, or click the Web Folders button and choose a Web folder.
3. Browse through folders, if necessary.
4. Click the Open button.
5. Type a password and press ENTER, if prompted.

Connect to an FTP Site with Word ➡ p. 274

1. Select File | Open.
2. Click the drop-down list box and choose Add/Modify FTP Locations under FTP Locations.
3. Type the Internet address of the FTP site, choose Anonymous or User, enter a username and password if need be, and then click Add.
4. Click OK to return to the Open dialog box.
5. Double-click the FTP site's name in the Open dialog box.
6. Browse the site and open a document.

Publish a Document on the Web
or an Intranet ➡ pp. 276–278

1. Select File | Save As.
2. Click the Web Folders button and choose a Web folder, or click the Look In drop-down list box and select an FTP site from under FTP Locations, or look under Network Neighborhood for file servers connected on your intranet.
3. Browse to the folder your document is destined for.
4. Make sure the filename is correct, and click the Save button.

In this last chapter I'll show you how to use Word as a Web browser so you can visit sites, view pages, download documents, and work on your remote files. I'll also show you how to connect to Internet or intranet sites and both view remote files and publish your own Web documents with Word's familiar Open and Save As dialog boxes. The distinction between Internet sites and intranet sites is the size of the potential audience. An Internet site is truly available to the public and can generally be seen by anyone who knows the address (although it's true that some Web sites are protected by passwords). An intranet site is generally based on a private network and can only be seen by authorized people, usually employees of the same company, members of the same workgroup, or some other assortment of colleagues. If you work in an office or other environment where everyone has Word and other Office programs installed, then you can place ordinary Office documents directly on the intranet site and everyone will be able to view them without even having to load up a separate Web browser.

Word as a Web Browser

Most programs that help users create a Web document require users to open the document within a separate program—a Web browser—in order to test it. Word has now turned itself into, among other things, a decent Web browser. This means you can test the Web pages and links you create (or find and connect to any resources on the Web or your intranet) using Word. You do, however, need direct Internet access to use Word to browse the Web.

To browse the Web from within Word, right-click on or near any toolbar and select Web. The Web toolbar appears (see Figure 14.1).

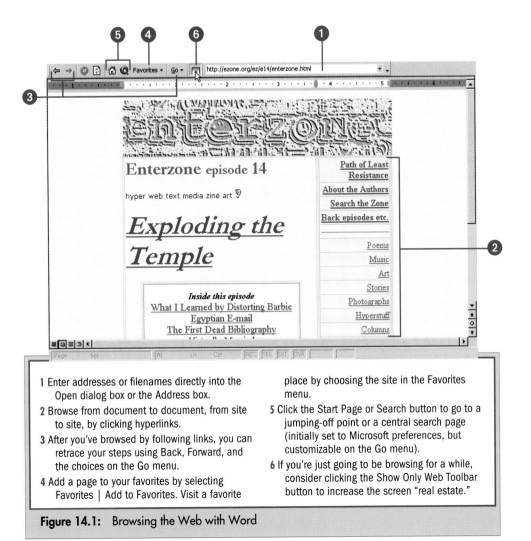

Figure 14.1: Browsing the Web with Word

1 Enter addresses or filenames directly into the Open dialog box or the Address box.

2 Browse from document to document, from site to site, by clicking hyperlinks.

3 After you've browsed by following links, you can retrace your steps using Back, Forward, and the choices on the Go menu.

4 Add a page to your favorites by selecting Favorites | Add to Favorites. Visit a favorite place by choosing the site in the Favorites menu.

5 Click the Start Page or Search button to go to a jumping-off point or a central search page (initially set to Microsoft preferences, but customizable on the Go menu).

6 If you're just going to be browsing for a while, consider clicking the Show Only Web Toolbar button to increase the screen "real estate."

EXPERT ADVICE

You can make a page of links to your favorite documents (both locally and on the Net), using the Insert Hyperlink button on the Standard toolbar, as explained in Chapter 13.

Browsing to Web Documents (to Edit Them)

You can use Word as a Web browser, but frankly, you'll probably prefer Netscape or Internet Explorer. The best thing about Word's ability to open and show Web documents is that you can use it to edit your pages (or to borrow other people's pages and rework them—be careful not to steal anyone's text or art, though, or their specific design!).

EXPERT ADVICE

If you think you're seeing too many boxes on the pages that you're browsing in Word, try choosing Table | Hide Gridlines. While this default display may be helpful in understanding how others design their Web pages, it can be a bit of an eyesore after a while.

You should be able to go to any document on the Web by typing its URL in the Address box, but, depending on how your system is configured, this may result instead in your Web browser (some program other than Word) starting up to open the file. Give it a try now: simply click in the Address box and type the URL *carefully,* letter for letter. When you're done, press ENTER.

EXPERT ADVICE

That Address box, like the File Name box in the Open dialog box, remembers filenames and addresses you've typed there in the past. Just click the drop-down button to save typing an address you've visited recently.

Downloading Documents with Open

If the Address box won't open documents for you directly in Word, you may have an easier time with the Open dialog box (yes, the same old Open dialog box you've been using all along).

Opening a Document from a Web Site

You can open any document available on the Web (or on an intranet you have access to) in the Open dialog box, by selecting File | Open:

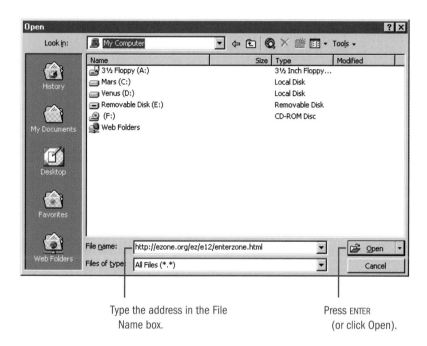

Type the address in the File
Name box.

Press ENTER
(or click Open).

Word will show you its progress as it transfers the file from the Web server and opens it. (If you type an incorrect address, Word will display an error dialog box. Click OK and try again.)

Word includes HTML documents among those it considers Word documents, so you don't have to change the Files Of Type entry when you're opening a document from the Web.

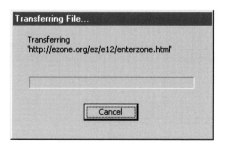

Opening a Document from a Web Folder

Depending on the type of Web server hosting a site, you may be able to open documents directly from within Word using the new Web Folders feature. To do so, press CTRL+O to get to the Open dialog box, and then click the Web Folders button in the bottom-left corner of the dialog box. To open a Web folder, click it and click the Open button (see Figure 14.2). The dialog box will then list the contents of the site as it would the contents of an ordinary folder on your computer. If the Web site you want to access is not yet listed, you can add a Web folder for it.

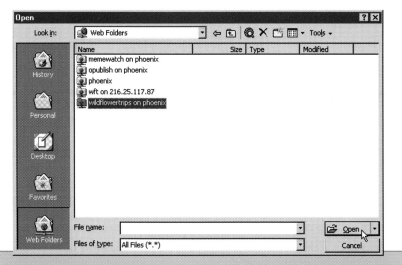

Figure 14.2:   You can open documents from some Web sites with the new Web Folders feature. For others, you'll need to use FTP, as explained a little later in this chapter

Adding a Web Folder

To add a Web folder, first press CTRL+O to get to the Open dialog box and click the Web Folders button in the bottom of the left-hand pane.

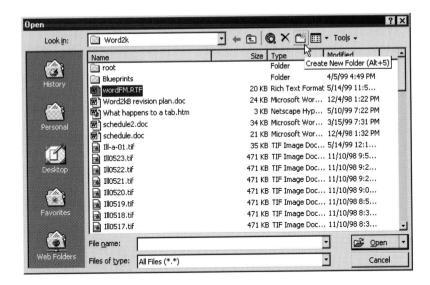

Then click the Create New Folder button (the manila envelope with a gleaming asterisk) or press ALT+F5. This opens the Add Web Folder dialog box. Type the URL of the site for which you want to create a Web Folder and click Next >.

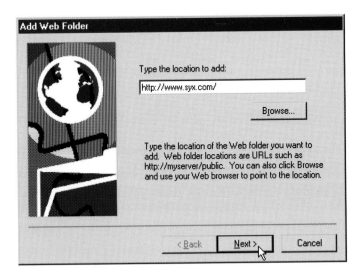

Word will verify the legitimacy of the address you entered (and ask you to try again if the verification fails). Then click Finish.

Opening a Document from an FTP Site

Once you start working with published Web documents, you'll need to do more than browse to pages available on the Web. You'll either want to add your site as a Web folder, as explained in the previous section, or you'll need to log in directly to the FTP (File Transfer Protocol, the Internet file-server standard) site associated with your Web site. With FTP, you can enter the back door of a public site, look in directories that are not visible at the Web site, and, most importantly, save your own documents (publish them) onto the server, which is something you can't do with a normal Web address.

To open a document from an FTP site, see the instructions in Figure 14.3.

If this is the first time you've connected to this site during this session, you'll be prompted for a username and password. If you're connecting to a public FTP site, click Anonymous and then click OK. Browse through the folders and select the document you want. If you're connecting to a private site (more likely if you're doing Web publishing), click User, type (or select from the list, if you've done this before) your username in the list box, press TAB, type a password, and click OK.

As you burrow deeper into an FTP site, Word keeps track of the local folder structure for you, but this only lasts while you're connected. Word will remember this FTP site for you from now on (but not your password).

EXPERT ADVICE

If you're working on an intranet, the process will be much the same. Your local file server will most likely appear as one of the options in your Network Neighborhood, or you can take advantage of Web Folders, which are shortcuts to Web servers in Windows 98. See your system administrator or consult your Windows documentation for more information.

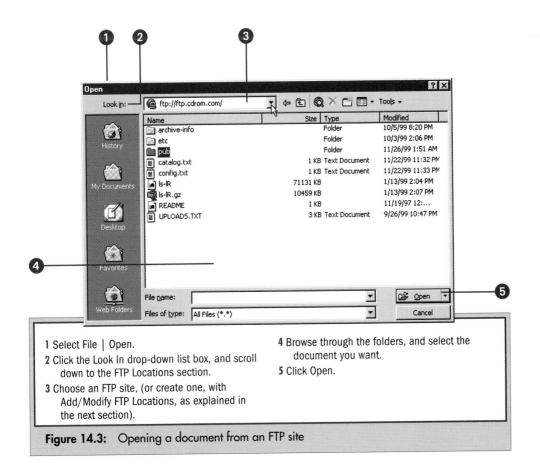

1 Select File | Open.
2 Click the Look In drop-down list box, and scroll down to the FTP Locations section.
3 Choose an FTP site, (or create one, with Add/Modify FTP Locations, as explained in the next section).

4 Browse through the folders, and select the document you want.
5 Click Open.

Figure 14.3: Opening a document from an FTP site

Adding an FTP Location

You can add a new FTP location to the list in your Open dialog box at any time. To do so, Select File | Open and click the Look In drop-down list box. Select Add/Modify FTP Locations under FTP Locations. This brings up the Add/Modify FTP Locations dialog box. Figure 14.4 lists the steps for using this dialog box.

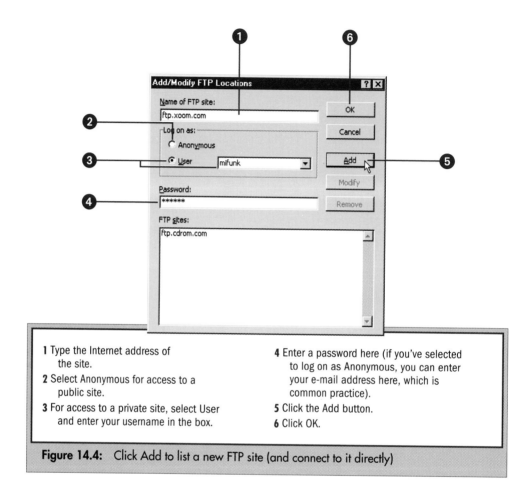

1 Type the Internet address of the site.

2 Select Anonymous for access to a public site.

3 For access to a private site, select User and enter your username in the box.

4 Enter a password here (if you've selected to log on as Anonymous, you can enter your e-mail address here, which is common practice).

5 Click the Add button.

6 Click OK.

Figure 14.4: Click Add to list a new FTP site (and connect to it directly)

Publishing on the Web

To make a Web site visible and available to the Internet at large (as opposed to keeping it within the confines of a local network), you'll need access to a *Web server*, a computer running software that serves Web pages when requested by Web browsers. Your employer or Internet service provider may offer access to a server. You'll have to ask technical support about this.

If you're planning to publish your Web pages on a local intranet, then you still need access to a file server. The name or location of the server may differ, but the process is the same.

Publishing to a Web Folder

If your Web site's host server permits direct HTTP publishing, then you can add the site as a Web folder (as explained earlier in this chapter), and then publish pages to the site directly by choosing its Web folder in the Save As dialog box. To do so, just click the Web Folders button in the bottom of the left-hand pane, double-click the Web folder to which you wish to publish, as shown in Figure 14.5 (the Open button will change to Save once you choose a folder). Browse to a specific folder at the Web site (if need be), and then click the Save button.

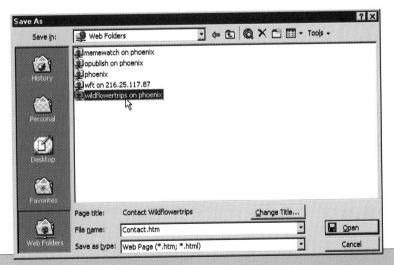

Figure 14.5: Publishing to a Web folder is as easy as saving to an ordinary folder

If you don't have any FTP locations set up yet, you'll need to enter the address directly into the File Name box or set up an FTP location (as explained earlier in this chapter).

Publishing to an FTP Location

Word makes it easier than it's ever been before to publish documents on the Web (or on an intranet). It's hardly more complicated than saving a document into a new folder. To do so, follow the steps in Figure 14.6:

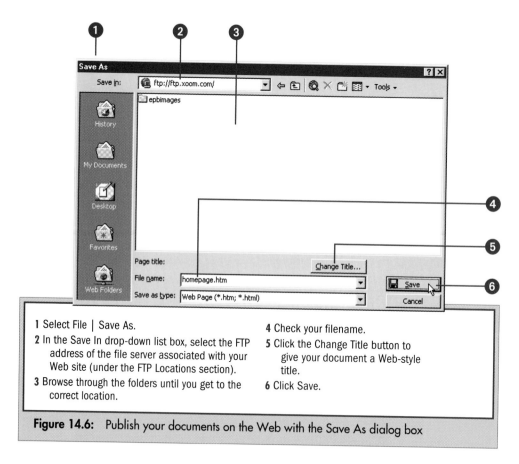

1 Select File | Save As.
2 In the Save In drop-down list box, select the FTP address of the file server associated with your Web site (under the FTP Locations section).
3 Browse through the folders until you get to the correct location.

4 Check your filename.
5 Click the Change Title button to give your document a Web-style title.
6 Click Save.

Figure 14.6: Publish your documents on the Web with the Save As dialog box

Maintaining Your Site

Once you've got all your pages out there for public consumption, you'll discover that online publishing means a long-term commitment to keeping the content fresh and up-to-date. If your site is geared toward the public, you'll have to start working on promoting it (and

listing it in various search engines). Even if it's just for your
department, you'll still have to make sure it's accurate and timely.

Changing and Correcting Pages on the Fly

With Word, updating a Web site is easy. If you know a page needs
changing, open it directly from the file server or Web site as explained
earlier in this chapter. Edit and format the document in Word, as
explained in Chapter 13 and the earlier chapters of this book. When
the page is corrected, save it directly back to the Web server with Save
As. What could be easier?

Using FrontPage with Office

If you get heavily involved with Web publishing, you may start
yearning for a product that is designed to help you maintain and
oversee an entire Web site *and* that is also compatible with the
Web-authoring tools you've already learned about in Word. If and
when that time comes, you might want to consider picking up
Microsoft FrontPage. FrontPage is a Web site design and maintenance
program. FrontPage is fine-tuned to work with Microsoft
applications, servers, and operating systems.

FrontPage also offers automated WebBots—routines that enable
you to develop dynamic content and interactive pages, and that help
keep your hyperlinks accurate.

Getting Help

The scope of this book doesn't allow me to do much more than give
you the quick overview of Web publishing that you have just read.
The Internet and the World Wide Web constitute entire universes of
information that we've only just begun to explore. If at any point you
run into terminology you don't understand, or strange behavior from
any of the special Web-authoring or Web-browsing toolbars or
commands, you might want to check out some of Microsoft's help on
the Web.

See my book, *Internet for Busy People*, (Osborne/McGraw-Hill, 1999), for more about the Web and the Internet, in general. If you would like more details about Web publishing using FrontPage, see my book, *FrontPage for Busy People*, (Osborne/McGraw-Hill, 1999).

To do so, choose Help | Office on the Web. Word's regular Help and Office Assistant question-and-answer tool can also explain or demonstrate all the key Web-authoring tricks packed into Word 2000.

The World of Microsoft Word

Now that you've learned how to convert Word documents to make them available on the Web (and on intranets), you've reached a pinnacle of sorts. Your mastery of Word (in a very short time, I might add) enables you to share information not just with the people down the hall, but with people all over the world.

If you've been paying attention, you've probably jumped around in this book, picking the plums you need right now and saving time by skipping extraneous information. Now it's time to put this book on the shelf and use it as a reference. The next time something doesn't work the way it should, or the next time you need to try something new, take this book down again and head directly for the answer you need. Now get back to work!

Installing Word

INCLUDES

- Upgrading from an earlier version of Word
- Installing Office or installing only Word
- Upgrading Internet Explorer
- Registering Word

It's easy to install Word (or Office) yourself, but it's easier still to have someone else do it for you! If you're the one who gets stuck with the job, this appendix will help you past any bumps you might encounter. For the most part, you click OK until the process is done.

Before You Begin

How you proceed with an installation depends on several factors, specifically:

- Whether you're installing Word for the first time or upgrading from a previous version
- Whether you're installing Word as part of an edition of Microsoft Office 2000 or as a separate application

In the first instance, the difference may be merely a couple of clicks. In the second, there are some elements in the Office 2000 package that you will want to add to your installation, if you are installing from that package. This appendix assumes that you'll install from the Office 2000 package.

If You Are Upgrading

If you are upgrading, you must also decide whether you want to overwrite your previous version of the program. By default it will be overwritten, but you can change that during the setup procedure.

If You Are Installing with Office 2000

If you are installing with Office 2000, and you have never installed Office 2000 before, you should install whatever components of the Office suite you expect to use. As long as you have enough room on your hard drive, it's easier to install all the components you will use at once, so that you don't have to dig up the CD every time you want to use a new feature. This appendix will simply tell you what components of Word 2000 to install.

Performing the Installation

To begin the installation, place the installation CD in your CD-ROM drive. From the Start menu, choose Run. Use the Browse button to go to your CD-ROM drive (in most cases, this is drive D). Double-click the file called Setup.exe, and click OK.

The Setup window will appear as the program searches for previous installations and examines your system. A sidebar in the window lists the steps to be taken, and highlights each one as it becomes current.

If you're installing from a CD, just inserting the disc in your CD-ROM drive may get you started.

Setup.exe

Entering Personal Information

Enter your personal information in the first three fields. In the boxes along the bottom, enter the CD Key, which you will find on your CD case. Click Next or press ENTER. You will be taken to the license screen. You must accept the license agreement in order to proceed. Click I Accept The Terms Of The License Agreement, and click Next or press ENTER. Then click Customize.

Choosing a Location

The first screen displayed after you click the Customize button allows you to choose a drive and path where you want to install Microsoft Office 2000, of which Word is a component. Under most circumstances, you can accept the default. If there's not enough room on drive C, and you have another drive with more room, it's perfectly acceptable to install on another drive. You can even change the name of the folder to which you install, although it's not recommended. When you've entered an acceptable installation path, click Next or press ENTER. If you chose a path to a folder containing a previous version of Office (or Word), you will be warned that your old program will be overwritten. If you don't want that to happen—if you want to preserve a previous version of one or more of the programs, click the Back button, and enter a new path. Click Next when you're done.

Choosing Whether to Remove Previous Versions

At the next screen, the Setup program offers to remove all components of your previous versions of any Office programs you have. If you have a previous version of Office, and a separate version of Word, Word will be included in the list. If you're just installing or upgrading Word, you should check the box labeled Keep These Programs.

Upgrading Internet Explorer

You will then be asked to upgrade to Internet Explorer 5, if you haven't already. You are given the choice of a Standard upgrade, which includes the Web browser, Outlook Express, the Media Player, other multimedia enhancements, and some components used by other programs in Office 2000, or a Minimal upgrade, which installs only the first two components. You can also choose not to upgrade. The Standard upgrade is the default. Accept it.

Choosing Components to Install

On the next screen, you'll see a tree diagram. This is where you choose the components to install, and how they should be installed. You have the option of running various components from your hard drive or from the CD.

There are at least two advantages to running from your hard drive. First, the computer reads information more quickly from a hard drive than it does from a CD. Second, you don't have to locate the CD every time you start a process that you haven't used before.

- Run From My Computer means that the component will be installed on your hard drive.
- Run All From My Computer means that the component, and everything nested under it in the tree will be installed on your hard drive. (If there are subcomponents, there will be a plus sign to the left of the drive icon.)
- Run From CD places a shortcut on your system to the program on the CD, as well as placing a few files in your Windows and System folders.

- Run All From CD sets up the program so that the component and all its subcomponents run directly from the CD, via a shortcut on your hard drive.
- Install On First Use (not found on all the menus) means that the item will appear on a menu or in a dialog box, but will not be installed on your hard drive. The first time you choose the item, you will be asked for the CD, so that it can be installed.
- Not Available means "Do not install this component."

Click on any drive icon to change the way the attached item will be installed.

EXPERT ADVICE

As a rule, it's easier to install things once and be done with it. For this reason, you're better off installing to your hard drive any components you expect to use.

To install Word 2000, click the drive icon next to Microsoft Word For Windows, and choose Run All From My Computer.

Next, click the plus sign next to Office Tools. You'll see an expanded tree. You'll need to install several components from this list, as well. Scroll down the list and make sure that Office Web Components and, still further down the tree, Web Discussions and Web Publishing, are to be installed on your computer. They should be installed by default.

EXPERT ADVICE

You have the option of turning off the Office Assistant—the little animation that pops up when it thinks you're going to do something it can help with—from this list. If you don't want it, click it and choose Not Available.

When you're done, click Install Now or Upgrade Now, depending on whether you're doing a first installation or an upgrade. Setup checks over what you've done and begins the installation. At this point you can go clean the bathrooms, read your mail, or go out to lunch. The process probably won't be complete when you return.

When it's finished, Setup will close all open programs and wait for you to click OK to restart the computer. When you have done so, Windows shuts down and restarts. Don't take the CD out of the drive yet, because it will be needed. When the desktop appears, a progress bar indicates that Setup is continuing to install the product. When it's finished, you should see your normal desktop.

Registering the Product

To start Word, click the Start button, and then choose Programs | Microsoft Word. You will be asked to register the product. Fill in your name in the registration form. Click Next or press ENTER, and fill out your personal information. Click Next or press ENTER, and you will see this screen. Here you can opt out of being included on Microsoft or other mailing (probably e-mailing) lists.

Click Next or press ENTER to finish the registration process. Your default Dial-Up Connection window appears, to connect you to the Internet. If you prefer, you can click Cancel, and choose from the following methods of registering:

- E-mail
- Internal Fax
- External Fax or Postal Mail (that is, printing out a form and sending it)
- Telephone

If you prefer, you can click Register Later.

If Something Goes Wrong

If something goes wrong or if you interrupt the installation, Setup will display a warning dialog box. Click OK, and then try to install the program again.

If the installation is stopped while Setup is copying files, it will display a different dialog box, asking if you want to quit. Click No to continue with Setup as usual, or click Yes to end the installation (for now). If you choose to halt the installation at this point, you'll have to repeat parts of the installation next time you install Word.

Uninstalling Word

If at some point you want to take Word off your computer, close all programs, choose Start | Settings | Control Panel, and double-click the Add/Remove Programs icon. Then, choose Microsoft Word in the lower half of the dialog box that appears, and click the Add/Remove button.

Click the Remove All button in the installation dialog box that appears. Setup asks if you're sure you want to do this. Click Yes.

Setup mysteriously tells you that it is once again checking for necessary disk space. (It needs disk space to remove files?) A dialog box reports on Setup's progress as it removes files. Setup then tells you that it is updating your system, and finally announces that Word was successfully uninstalled.

You can remove Word and keep other Office components, if you wish.

Index